ISBN 978-88-6242-372-4

First English edition November 2019

Third Italian edition May 2019
Second Italian edition June 2004 – Alinea Editrice
First Italian edition December 1995 – Alinea Editrice

© LetteraVentidue Edizioni
© Emilio Faroldi, Maria Pilar Vettori

The reproduction, also partial, by any means, electronic or mechanical, including photocopying, even for in-house or educational use, is forbidden. Under Italian law, photocopying is permitted only for personal use, as long as it does not harm the author(s) in any way. Therefore any photocopying that prevents the purchase of a book is illegal and represents a threat to the survival of a way of communicating knowledge. Those who make photocopies of a book, provide the means for doing so, or encourage this practice, take part in a theft and a practice that is harmful to culture.

Translation: Stephen Piccolo
Book design: Raffaello Buccheri

LetteraVentidue Edizioni Srl
Via Luigi Spagna 50 P
96100 Siracusa, Italia

www.letteraventidue.com

Emilio Faroldi
Maria Pilar Vettori

DIALOGUES ON
ARCHITECTURE

Franco Albini
BBPR
Lodovico B. di Belgiojoso
Guido Canella
Aurelio Cortesi
Gabetti e Isola
Ignazio Gardella
Vittorio Gregotti
Vico Magistretti
Enrico Mantero
Paolo Portoghesi
Aldo Rossi
Giuseppe Terragni
Vittoriano Viganò

LetteraVentidue

Acknowledgments

The preparation and publication of this text involved the cooperation of many people. We are very grateful to the persons interviewed, and as the editors of this volume we would like to thank all those who for professional courtesy or friendship have contributed – in different ways and roles – to make the initial idea become a reality. In this sense, an initial thought turns to Fabrizio Schiaffonati and Antonio Scoccimarro.

We would also like to thank the various counterparts who in the individual studios played a fundamental role, stimulating and establishing relationships with the protagonists of the *Dialogues*. In alphabetical order: Elisabetta Annovi and Andrea Leonardi of Studio Aldo Rossi; Antonella Bergamin of Gregotti Associati; Maria Canella and Luca Monica of Studio Canella; Ezi Cicerone and Marcello Lanzillotti, Studio Gardella; Tiziana Di Gioia, Studio Viganò; Rosanna Guella, Studio Albini-Helg-Piva; Katia Guglielmi, Studio Cortesi; the geometer Franco Montella, Studio Magistretti; Susanna Michellini, Studio Portoghesi; Cristina Molinari and Vittoria Spinelli, Studio BBPR.

Thanks also to Matilde Baffa, Jacopo Gardella, Michael Graves, Paolo Zermani, for their contributions.

Finally, thanks to Barbara Corradi and Roberto Venturini for their patient editorial work; to Ugo Iorio and Maria Paola Gambara; Nanda and Nadir, Donata and Stefano. And a special thought for Ferdinando, always a presence in our work.

In the life span of 23 years the book *Dialogues on architecture* some of the protagonists of Italian modern architecture have passed away. Our thoughts turn to them, in particular, to express our gratitude for the works of architecture they have given to the community and to the Italian territory, and for the teachings they have transmitted to successive generations, indelible signs of continuity and indispensable tools for those approaching the architectural profession.

We fondly remember Lodovico B. Belgiojoso (1909-2004), Roberto Gabetti (1925-2000), Ignazio Gardella (1905-1999), Enrico Mantero (1934-2001), Aldo Rossi (1931-1997), Vittoriano Viganò (1919-1996), Vico Magistretti (1920-2006), Guido Canella (1931-2009), to whom we will be forever grateful for the commitment, dedication and collaboration during the preparation of *Dialogues on architecture*, and for the friendship they offered us through their empathy and signals of approval regarding the results of the work.

Perhaps it has been precisely the idea of summing up in a single volume the theoretical contributions of such a highly qualified group of master architects, brought together in the attempt to interpret their thinking regarding the role of architectural design in contemporary culture, that has become the qualitative factor leading to the success of this operation, prompting the publication of a new, updated edition that in any case keeps faith with the first version, dating back to 1995, and the second edition in 2004.

The same reasons, combined with the force and depth of the debate conducted by "active criticism" regarding Italian postwar architecture and its main protagonists, like behind the publication, two years after the book's release, of the volume in Portuguese edited by Emilio Faroldi, Maria Pilar Vettori, *Dialogos de Arquitetura*, Editora Siciliano, São Paulo 1997, with an introduction by Oscar Niemeyer. The work was presented at the *Faculdade de Arquitetura e Urbanismo da Universidade de São Paulo* on 9 April 1997 within the seminar "As relações Brasil-Italiana Globalizaçao da Arquitetura" organized by the Italian Cultural Institute in São Paulo, Brazil.

The third edition is based on the spirit of not interfering with the temporal location of the individual contributions, encouraging diachronic reading: a spirit that translates into the attempt to leave intact the logical and methodological structure of the work, implemented by an introductory text that sets out to translate and emphasize the contemporary character and intact timeliness of the theoretical message contained in the essays, flanked by bibliographic research that in line with this assumption is kept separate, for taxonomic clarity, and not integrated with the original version. In this regard, we thank Lorenza Campodonico for the collaboration on the finding of the texts and the principle publications on these topics, in the period from 1995 to 2004. For this third edition, thanks to Giulia Faruffini and Erika Siverio for their help in the preparation of the material, and to Cecilia Rostagni for her work on the capillary implementation of the bibliography, covering the time span of 2004-2018.

The success of the book, together with the growing dynamic of internationalization of the cognitive and formative processes of architecture, have encouraged the production of the volume in English, to be completed in 2019.

Always and once again, we would like to dedicate the results of our work to Luca and Lorenzo.

	Lodovico B. di Belgiojoso
57	Pluralist Architecture. BBPR
	Ignazio Gardella
71	Choral architecture
	Roberto Gabetti and Aimaro Isola
91	Conversational Architecture
	Paolo Portoghesi
111	Material Architecture
	Aldo Rossi
129	Architecture of the idea
	Guido Canella
141	Architecture of dissent
	Vittoriano Viganò
157	Architecture of experience
	Vico Magistretti
171	Architecture of reality
	Vittorio Gregotti
185	Gradual architecture
	Enrico Mantero
201	Architecture of the essential. Giuseppe Terragni

ILLUSTRATIONS
219 Selections of sketches, drawings and images

COMMENTARIES
295 Designing in differences

PORTRAITS
313 The studio on Via Panizza
315 The table of BBPR
317 Ignazio Gardella: self-portrait
319 Open letter to Roberto Gabetti and Aimaro Isola
321 Rome, an architecture studio
323 The "museum" of Aldo Rossi
325 Portrait of Guido Canella
327 Studio Viganò: a home for architecture
329 Vico Magistretti and the "non-existent" studio
331 The workshop on Via Bandello
333 The everyday life and studio of Giuseppe Terragni

APPENDICES
335 Selected bibliography
339 Sources of illustrations / Photography credits
340 Index of names

"The soul, when thinking, is simply carrying on a dialogue; it asks itself questions and answers them itself, affirms and denies."

Plato

"How many billion blows of the chisel
has Architecture cost
since the beginning
of the world?
Gigantic efforts for the joy of but a few.
Houses, palaces, fortresses and cathedrals.
And the extraordinary
history of art and human progress
drowned in the sea of sweat
of myriads of ignorant makers
who physically, with pickaxes and hammers
emptied hills and mountains
to translate stone into geometry
and nature into silent harmonies.
What it worth it?
Perhaps only for the Parthenon."

Lodovico B. Belgiojoso
Milan, January 1989

Dialogues on architecture

An open book for theoretical and applied research in contemporary design

The logic of the "open book" conveys reflections regarding contemporary architectural design, updating of its paradigms, and the transformation of its role and organization.

In the age of communication and image, the contemporary architectural discipline fosters individualism and isolation of its manifestations: a paradox that translates into a rejection of recognized theory as opposed to practice marked by explicit freedom of expression and the staking out of individual zones of autonomy. In this progressive passage from unity to isolation, the distinctive trait of modernity, *differences* shift from being moments of dialogue and discussion to act as elements of divisiveness, limits to communication. Personalization counters standardization, differentiation is promoted without critique at the expense of uniformity, personal quirks persist in the face of a technical and cultural scenario that expresses, in a mirror image, the need for complementary and comparability of contents of a qualitative, not merely quantitative character.

Such logic seems in appearance to decidedly compress any form of reflection and sedimentation of design activity, of its nature and the principles that set it apart, in favor of actions that do not pertain to the capacities and formation of the architect in historical terms. The concept of the *school*, understood not as a signal of linguistic homogeneity but as the sharing of an ethical and cultural lineage, also seems to be headed towards depletion, faced by a reform of pedagogical methods and structures oriented towards superficial factual knowledge, reinforced by the increasing fragmentation of roles.

The splitting up of knowledge, the complexity of the operative tools and the critical need to identify reliable methods of design encourage an interpretation of architecture and its related grammar that is at once comprehensive and synthetic, calling on architecture to manifest itself as a discipline of a general character, as an interdisciplinary science capable of combining various sectors of expertise in a transversal way. The contribution offered by different cultural and educational spheres, the expression of different methods of interpretation and decision making, the increasingly compartmentalized organization of the phases of the project, the multiplication of tools of control, the demand for identification of architecture, point to the systematic management and organic coordination of procedures and forms of expertise as fundamental requirements for the functional, morphological and technical definition of the work of architecture.

Based on these assumptions, the reinterpretation of cultural models that can be traced back to the personalities, both professional and intellectual, of the protagonists of Italian architectural culture is oriented towards revision of the boundaries of new methodological stimuli in the management of processes of invention and production of the project: architecture becomes a moment of synergy that identifies the figure of the architect as an element capable of conceiving and interpreting processes of innovation, facilitating its application. Therefore the reinterpretation of the architectural phenomenon and its codes constitutes "an open book for theoretical and applied research in contemporary design" with the character of an open, flexible and never rigidly closed structure. The processes of reconfiguration of the identity of the architect as a professional, and the related educational contexts, reveal a transformation of the traditional designer into a figure whose expertise allows him to interpret "modification," confirming the need for debate on the meaning of architecture and its specific techniques, in the relationship between different languages and relative apparatus of implementation.

The *Dialogues on architecture* have attempted to get beyond the mere narration of reality, through the reconstruction of theoretical and methodological projects, even with their occasionally radical differences. The *architecture of differences* takes on a strategic role in this situation, both in teaching and in the learning process, interpreting the needs of contemporary design that impose an interdisciplinary approach, a method of cultural clarification, a "technical rationality" capable of restoring centrality to the specificity of construction through a redefinition of roles and responsibilities of the protagonists of the act of building.

The critical reinterpretation of the masters is therefore able to provide the project with a "total" character, rescuing it from the danger of excessive specialization, and at the same time leading it back to actions that encourage a "return to the profession" by setting the boundaries of the craft, accompanied by formative processes aimed not at the overlapping of types of knowledge, but at their synthesis.

Analyzed from this standpoint, the wide range of figures of the Italian panorama of modern architecture can represent a significant overview of paradigmatic models and roles that can be updated in the methodological project-construction relationship, expressed both through the action of theorizing and critical investigation, and through "constructed books" metaphorically represented by manifesto works. Architecture and the tools utilized for its configuration constitute the main factors of transmission of continuity, placing the "how" in the point of passage between past and future, as a variable that is not independent of historical evolution, but instead indicates the pertinence to an epoch, its techniques, its materials, its organizational tools. Hence the role of models and their influence: the analogy, by assent or dissent, with existing paradigms, to be conveyed not so much through figurative matrices as with respect to the phenomenological and process variables, constitutes a method through which to raise awareness of design behavior useful to consciously approach the complexity of the post-industrial and post-modern era, updating contents, expressions and rules.

The architectural scholar or enthusiast, through the *Dialogues,* is stimulated to come to terms with the various contributions, the values of uniqueness and of possible transmission and adaptation of the themes addressed. The interpretation and review of the model as a methodological and not formal practice leads with greater ease to the *reading of architecture* as the result of a path of design and a cultural attitude regarding the process of invention, design, construction and management, translating and summing up, without shortcuts, the detailed series of interactions that exist between factors internal and external to the mental process of the designer.

A form of knowledge based on experience, on the already lived, aware of the necessity to *describe* architecture in order to *know* it, through a procedure of analogy with respect to buildings, figures and texts, antique and modern, takes on strategic importance in a historical period lacking in forms of transmission of disciplines. Teaching, as a concrete form of knowledge transfer, becomes a stimulus for *imitation:* not passive emulation of languages and poetics, but critical and diachronic awareness of making architecture.

The circular and almost never linear process of the evolution of architectural culture reveals a value of historical *continuity* that is also expressed in technological terms: the reading of the relationships existing between the constituent elements of the artifact can be expressed in a concept of *technological proportion* understood not as a mechanical method or formula, but as a logical system between the parts and the whole, as coherence of the rules that govern the relationships between the individual constructive elements, independent of the constructive alchemy applied or the technological philosophy of reference.

The protagonists of the *Dialogues,* as an example of knowledge of technological and constructive resources in relation to the nature of the intervention, suggest in different forms the recovery of the "technical dimension" of the project itself, as a factor that triggers the essence of the implementation of a work, permitting the passage from an abstract idea to a concrete idea. The assertion of a "creative dimension" of technology, as procedural organization and a material tool for experimentation, cannot exist without the contemporary and complementary existence of "cultures of form" and "cultures of technological know-how."

The critical reading of the *Dialogues* permits identification of that attitudes that have led to the educational premises of the contemporary architect, a social figure that cannot abstain today from absorbing knowledge related to innovation, of both process and product, to the evolution of regulations, the scales of the project in trans-scalar terms, detecting the delicate relationships that exist between territory, city, architecture and technology. The scenarios of competitive advantage and professional collaboration, the adequacy of infrastructural networks, the level of environmental and settlement quality, represent the fundamental requirements for cultural growth and the appeal of operating within the European context. The control of the relationship of timing, costs and quality, carried out through integrated and multi-scalar design of environmental compatibility, suggests a radical adaptation of forms of expertise, of methodologies and tools for the management of complex interventions of strategic importance, through the definition of new figures connected to experiences of construction.

Recent architectural research has wisely challenged the marginalization of the constructive aspect within the design praxis, investigating the relationship the architectural project establishes with the place and its identity, reinforcing a position that interprets the constructed object as something directly involved in the process of transformation of the environment and the territory, by means of a dynamic utilization of resources.

The themes that set the character of the contemporary world, if they are translated and traced between the lines of the volume, can be seen to have been already there in the practice of a number of figures of the postwar era in Italy: getting beyond a simplistic interpretation connected with terminologies correlated with the various historical periods, themes like eco-compatible architecture, the conception of the continuum formed by internal spaces, spaces of transition and external spaces, the need for an urban regeneration delegated to new building types connected to logics bordering on sustainable renewal, the integration of technological-energy systems in processes of design synthesis, can be observed in the work of the protagonists of the school of *Rogers* or, backdating the thought, in the loftiest rationalist and functionalist gestures of the Italian Modern Movement.

The *Dialogues* confirm how the concept of sustainability emerges from the pursuit of a point of balance between history and experimentation, between local values and global phenomena, with respect for the history of architecture and its consolidated syntax. In a context in which it seems clear that the new technologies are destined to play increasingly central roles in the sustainable use of environmental resources, the Italian approach to architecture and the identity of places represents an element of innovation, as a variable moving against the current of obligatory internationalization, which consequently inhibits the productive values of the context, which constitute one of the main foundations of architectural culture.

The recovery of the landscape as a paradigm of architecture and, in parallel, the interpretation of construction as a new form of naturalness, partially sum up the issue. The architectural project seen as interpretation of the landscape expresses structural forms and norms that put man into relation with the environment, making it possible to understand how the physical-natural phenomena of the territory, the economic resources together with the culture of dwelling and the branching network of social relations, have represented in history the generating motivations of location, formation and spirit of human settlement.

The consolidation of environmental culture inside a panorama marked by the demise of the major ideological references requires the use of new behavioral scores, updated regulatory vocabulary, a malleable discipline of the system of planning of territorial organization, and therefore of procedures for design.

The opportunity arises to think of architectural design no longer as a science aimed at an envisioned solution to a problem, but as a proposal of dialogue to represent the requirements of human beings, a tool with which to interpret a contextualized reality, a technical event recognized by collective perception, as well as an act of great ethical and scientific responsibility inside a scenario of shared environmental policies channeled by dynamics of participation.

In the society of complexity and the rule of information, the universalizing determinism of classical science has been overtaken by a panorama in which the dimension of difference and otherness, contingent and local, random and unrepeatable prevails, values that assert themselves today, bringing upheavals on a philosophical, scientific, humanistic, technological and, as a result, design level.

The problem intrinsic to the productive reorganization of the project has to do with the "process of socialization" that impacts professional activity, immersed in a reality marked by progressively variable, ramified demand. The need to control the claims and positions pertaining to the design process and specific disciplinary spheres has meant that over the last 30 years the field of education has undergone a widening of the disciplinary horizon, while nevertheless leaving the *technical and technological culture* of the project without coverage. From a didactic standpoint, the protagonists of the *Dialogues* offer an effective contribution on the themes of civil significance of the craft, and therefore of the resulting cultural and social responsibilities, besides supplying a synthetic vision of the roles and processes capable of knowing, controlling and orienting behaviors and results in a framework of intensive interaction.

Positioned in epochs in which "quantity" was constructed at the expense of "quality," using construction procedures and criteria consolidated by a long tradition, the protagonists of Italian architecture represent the synthesis of the "reasons of construction" and the "reasons of design." What emerges from the overall picture is the need to adjust educational profiles, with the aim of having an impact on the capacity for introspection and reflection, in instruments of renewal and explanation of the contemporary world.

In the contemporary era, the assumption of originality and autonomy of Italian architectural culture, with its areas of light and shadow, intrinsic to the production sector, has its foundations in the modes of interpretation, by negation or agreement, of the phenomena of genetic mutation, that involve the architectural project, its statutes, its organization in terms of processes, players and tools, stimulating research and thinking on the founding aspects of design practice, on the levels of concept and method, on the operative scales internal to building processes, connected to strategies of urban transformation within a dynamic European scenario.

In the past the Italian context has played a leading role in the area of innovation, understood as a tool of response to the changes of cultural and productive models. In the light of the modifications introduced by the present regulatory structure and the renewed modes of public-private co-participation at the basis of processes of urban renewal, transformation of the territory and the construction of works, the paradigm of Italian architecture, for its history, complexity and social value, stimulates meaningful critical reflections on the transformation of the scientific paradigms of the technological project.

Faced with the consolidation of what has been defined as the *crisis of the state and the dispersion of power*, and by a clientele no longer capable of clearly playing a decisive and positive role in the configuration of the city and the environment, the timeliness of the *Dialogues* can be found in the fact that the work is simultaneously research and investigation that set out to explore, in advance of the formulation of models, the main coordination of the architectural project. Italy, though it represents a context marked by structural, infrastructural and productive problems, is indicated as a model in various ambits: the singular character of Italian culture is also reflected in the approach to the themes of the project and construction, where we can observe particular modes of participation in the processes of ideation, development and implementation of products and structures destined to be distributed. Today, these potentialities are underutilized.

The present marginal status of Italian architecture cannot be remedied through hybridization, but by laying claim to its autonomy and identity, stimulating openness to and active interaction with the international context, absorbing the processes of transformation that involve architecture on a super-national scale, translating them into conceptual and substantial terms, but also terms of *globalization* and *digitalization,* the importance of networking systems and forms of communication and transmission of information.

To seek a way out of the crisis that has impacted the debate on architecture and the city, it may be useful to reinterpret and reread the theoretical positions expressed by Italian culture in relation to design: the biographies and works of certain architects today at the margins of the critical discourse, through their contribution can represent significant approaches with respect to the construction of a theory of architectural design.

The obsessive representation of "complexities and contradictions" of the contemporary landscape, and the interdisciplinary thrust that has emerged in recent years, have to some extent overshadowed the role of architectural language as a critical tool of interpretation and transformation of reality through poetic techniques capable of promoting design at the level of problem solving. Such approaches constitute the constants for a renewed interest regarding history, seen not as a reservoir of references on which to draw, but as a process in which to identify forms of continuity. The heightened focus on the new, perceptible in the spheres of teaching and publishing, is weakening this continuity, causing a superficial reading of history. To reclaim the autonomy of Italian architectural culture today therefore means recovering reflection on the theories, tools and techniques of design, not paying tribute to its rhetorical detachment.

The construction of architecture seen as professional experience prompts the identification of references, principles, stimuli. To have a dialogue – live or at a distance – with figures like Giuseppe Terragni, Franco Albini, Ignazio Gardella, BBPR, Vico Magistretti, Vittoriano Viganò, Gabetti & Isola, Aldo Rossi, Paolo Portoghesi, Vittorio Gregotti, Guido Canella, does not mean approaching the theme from an exclusively historical standpoint, but proposing the construction of an interpretation of the present in a state of becoming, on the line of continuity of the historical evolution that has impacted the architectural discipline, seen not as a sequence of events dominated by a complexity that is hard to control by definition, but as an element of constant reflection on the reasons behind the architectural project.

To recognize and re-examine the main episodes of outstanding construction of Italian architecture does not mean encouraging a self-referential approach, but instead implies reinforcing the conception of the project as research, to emphasize its inner and discrete autonomy within the construction of the environment.

Reading the past and analyzing it in its essence, with particular reference to the "scientific biographies" of figures that in spite of different positions have expressly or indirectly come to terms with the relationship that exists between a theory of design and a never pre-set vision of architecture, means taking the opportunity to insert the project itself in a narrative and operative dimension, in the attempt to make architecture and comprehension of urban phenomena interact in a synergic, non-oppositional way. The modification of the environment, in fact, requires continual reflection on its meaning: to design means to activate a critical attitude regarding the context, respecting the resources of architecture and its spatial, functional, technological and not just figurative values.

An aware construction truly exists as such when it establishes a relationship of dialogue with existing features, whether they are natural or artificial, produced by man. It refers to the experience of places, to knowledge acquired over time by means of observation and practice; it is a directly experienced circumstance, and is thus difficult to transmit. Its meaning in architecture should be seen in continuity with the concepts of *initial determination* and *improvisation*, of *will* and *ability*, expressed by E.H. Gombrich, when reflecting on the *Topics of Our Time* he assigns the correct values to the actions that lead from invention to execution, indirectly outlining a method.

The question of technique, a central point in the debate on modern architecture, has brought out the impossibility of understanding the meaning of techniques of implementation without seeing them in relation to the formal and functional determinants that contribute to the definition of the work of architecture. The progressive separation between ideation and execution has caused the technological component of the project to control the complex set of operations aimed at governing the interrelations between design and implementation.

The present moment of disorientation that involves architecture also reflects the phenomena of fragmentation that across the 20th century have had an impact on all human knowledge, making it increasingly difficult to regroup the design discipline within stable, definitive forms of codification.

The response to this situation can be sought not in renunciation of any systematic or theoretical effort, placing the project in the sphere of unrepeatable, personal and unique creative experience, but in the attempt to identify tools and logics capable of governing the *making of architecture,* in a relationship not of opposition but of complementarity between theory and practice. A concept that is even more meaningful in the field of education, where the reasoning on the project cannot be separated from the study of constructed works in all their concrete specificities.

The architectural project is not the exclusive territory of chosen disciplinary elites, but the place of confrontation and synthesis of recognized forms of scientific knowledge. To design does not mean to compose, and – even more so – the composition, if isolated, does not determine the design.

To use the words of Carlos Martì Arìs, we believe that "architectural knowledge is inscribed and deposited more powerfully than any treatise or exegesis, precisely in the works and projects of architecture, where it infiltrates and remains shrouded, safe from reductive interpretations and vulgar applications. This knowledge is hidden but not lost; it is enciphered by not indecipherable. To recover it and make it operative, it is necessary to dig into the work, to manipulate it and dismantle it, trying to understand how it is made."

The *Dialogues on architecture* constitute an opportunity for reflection on the latest formalized theories of design developed by Italian architectural culture: a reflection that does not necessarily move through the commemoration of the work of the masters, but stimulates the construction of a wide overview of positions on design theory that can be translated into recognizable and transmissible forms and procedures. Steering clear of nostalgic gazes at the recent past and unproductive praise of individual poetics, coming to grips with these figures means reactivating a relationship with the past, and (where required) redefining an interpretation of experience that acts as a critical device in the contemporary cultural context: a reality that has not been capable, to date, of dynamically settling the score with that heritage.

In recent years we can observe – in the applied expressions and formulas – an accentuation of the short circuit created inside the paradigm that connects the theoretical and experiential spheres. The compartmentalization of the areas of expertise of the architect and the teaching of architecture creates the enforcing conditions for a separate and distant trajectory of the two worlds.

This contradicts the principal assumption at the basis of the art of designing and building, which has its seed precisely in the transmission of experiential value through a circular type of process that points to teaching and learning as noble, irreplaceable action.

The need emerges for a concrete critical review and update of the forms of transmission of the principles of architecture, which unlike the pioneering epoch in which the protagonists of the *Dialogues* operated see international challenge and discussion as the primary motors of the debate.

The training of the architect of our time as a social as well as technical agent calls for deeper reflections on the foundations of paths, instruments, models of teaching and learning. The dichotomy between *theory* and *practice*, *notion* and *application*, *knowledge* and *technical expertise*, is what defines the specificity of the role of the architect.

To educate young people in the disciplines of architecture is a tiring, difficult task: to make and transmit architecture, furthermore, requires aptitudes that are not widespread. This is true above all in our digital age, in which rapid, easy access to major platforms of information, bearers of a large quantity of knowledge, tends to weaken the *teacher-student* relationship.

Nearly all the protagonists of the *Dialogues on architecture* have been simultaneously architects and teachers: for them, teaching architecture was not just a matter of "giving," but also of "receiving," in a reciprocal relationship of exchange and collaboration. Ernesto Nathan Rogers, in a lecture delivered at the Politecnico di Milano in 1963, stated: "this way of considering the Chair as a kind of pulpit from which the Word is given forth is extraneous to me, because in fact I see that my task is ennobled by being able to take part with increased responsibility in the life of the school, mingling with my assistants and all the students in a continuous, reciprocal dialogue. [...] This enables me to renew myself, namely to always learn. And there is no better nourishment that what comes from young people."

The architect has to return to playing the role of an intellectual figure, capable of governing material processes of a higher social significance. Alberto Campo Baeza, in a conversation we had last year, published in the scientific magazine *Techne_Journal of Technology for Architecture and Environment*, emphasized the "necessity of coherence between thought and action," a phenomenon that has always been representative of architecture. The clearly visible fragmentation and autonomous specialization of knowledge and expertise should be opposed, in order to foster a heightened critical capacity, of dialogic and choral comprehension of phenomena.

A professional figure properly trained in a wider approach will be more easily able to come to terms with the "unknown," the "surprising," and to solve complex problems never come across before.

The dynamics of modification of professional positioning and the labor market, also involving an extension of the boundaries of reference between the national context, must base their premises on to goal of providing high levels of critical capacity and comprehension of phenomena, granting value to the ethical aspects of responsibility that are more necessary than ever today in order to approach the challenge of the complexity of social, technological and environmental change.

This logic leads to the desire to encourage the spread of theoretical thought of a school – the Italian school – that can base its own cultural re-establishment, after years of forced intellectual and constructive torpor, precisely on the action of updating its message for the contemporary situation. Starting from the concept of bringing value to its identity and its history, where the latter is seen in the dual guise of a burdensome legacy and an enormous opportunity. History, then, as a barometer of the contemporary: memory as the key of perspective for its innovative reinterpretation.

These are the premises behind the critical rereading of the *Dialogues* as a legacy to pass down to new generations, along with their translation and publication in an updated English-language edition.

Milano-Siracusa, October 2019

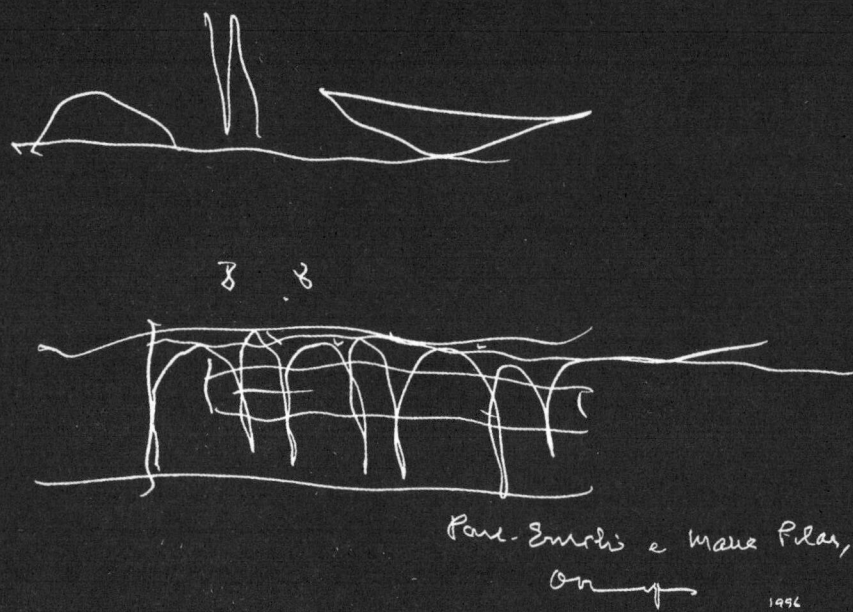

Oscar Niemeyer
Rio de Janeiro, 24 October 1996

I have enjoyed this book. The formulation of the texts. The problems addressed by the architects. The way they think and design. The remarks gathered herein demonstrate that architecture can be different and varied, and as such it can bring emotions to architects in the unfolding of their work.
Some architects have concentrated on pursuit of the beauty that should identify architecture; others approach the social and functional issues, making works of architecture at the service of human beings; others still look to the past that moves them, which they are not able to forget. The most curious are looking for new forms; the successful ones, instead, move in freedom towards surprise and the architectural spectacle.
All this is due to the genetic legacy, which influences all of them, for better or worse.
And so we move in architecture, subject to hopes and inevitable disappointments.
It is obvious that the most active, the oldest, or those who have spent a lifetime bent over a drafting table, have an idea of architecture that will be hard to disrupt. Architectural ideas and forms express new principles that spring from the way of working and are gradually inserted within it, granting it greater force. Principles that become increasingly recognizable.
Very often this brings the designer to a position of deplorable rigidity, as if his work were the only bearer of truth.
But when the architect grasps the fragility of things, understanding that in the end architecture is not really so crucial, and that what is important is life, the family, friends – in a world we have to improve – then he begins to understand his profession more completely, the natural scale of architecture and the human solidarity that ought to be part of its character. This is the most important message offered to us by this work.

Gostei deste livro. Dos textos elaborados. Dos arquitetos a revelarem seus problemas. O que pensam e como fazem a arquitetura.
As vozes aqui reunidas mostram como a arquitetura pode ser diferente e variada e como se empolgam com ela os arquitetos.
Uns preocupados com a beleza que deve identificá-las; outros, com os problemas sociais, a economia – a arquitetura servindo ao homem; outros, ainda, voltados para o passado que os comove e não podem esquecer. E os mais inquietos procurando a forma nova, os grandes vãos livres, a surpresa e o espetáculo arquitetural.
E tudo isso comandado pelo nosso sósia genético, que em todos influi, no bom e no mau sentido.
E assim vamos caminhando pela arquitetura, sujeitos às esperanças e decepções inevitáveis.
É claro que os mais ativos, os idosos, ou os que passaram a vida inteira debruçados na prancheta, assumem uma arquitetura difícil de repensar. São idéias e formas arquitetônicas, novos princípios que o trabalho criou e nela foram se inserindo pouco a pouco, dando-lhe mais unidade. Mais fáceis de reconhecer.
E isso leva, muitas vezes, o arquiteto a uma posição de intransigência lamentável, como se a sua obra fosse a única e verdadeira.
Mas quando ele sente a fragilidade das coisas, que no fundo a arquitetura não é fundamental, que o importante é a vida, a família, os amigos – este o mundo que devemos melhorar –, aí ele passa a compreender melhor a sua profissão, a escala natural da arquitetura e a solidariedade humana que a deve caracterizar. Essa é a mensagem mais importante que esta obra nos oferece.

The identification of figures representative of *making* and *narrating* architecture involves inevitable selections and the setting of boundaries for the field of investigation. The scientific depth of their theoretical and design research justifies the choice: the architects involved, in spite of their specificities, in this context constitute a paradigmatic sample for an operation that sets out to reconnect the threads of a history to be protected and passed on. The order of the dialogues proposed represents a subtle key of interpretation that outlines – without any claim of classification – a possible sequence of the positions of method that have emerged.

Aurelio Cortesi

Architecture of Connections.
Franco Albini

Franco Albini, architect *against the current*

Let's observe the pathways of Albini's architecture, to investigate the cultural references of the beginnings, and to narrate the sudden, troubled allegiance to the world of the European avant-garde, in the light of the partly serious, partly facetious statements he made on more than one occasion. In his account, this was an illumination; a "cathartic influence" caused by a harsh reprimand on the part of Persico, which had cured him of the "Deco virus" that assailed him: an inoculation injected into a young apprentice in the studio of Ponti and Lancia.[1]

Thus far we have the myth of the outset, offering a glimpse of an elite influence, against the current, expressed in the adherence to the Modern Movement or at least to what could be gleaned in its regard by a young Milanese intellectual in the early 1930s, together with persistent observation of himself, of his role as an intellectual, though within the rigid path set out by the most radical trend o the architectural avant-garde.

The compliance with European avant-garde developments could only be manifested through fideistic positions based on a minority share and struggle in the movement's progress. The fact that he belonged to the group of Milanese "functionalists" in the early 1930s made him aware of being in this minority that was soon to become the opposing faction, but fought to carve out spaces of operation to the extent that it offered advanced definitions of the approach to social housing. Albini moved inside an already watered-down rationalism, aware of feeding on the strong political motivations of a corporate state, negotiating proposals of evolution (the Fabio Filzi area[2], for example) with the possibility of access to an introspective attitude, in tune with the still traditional idea of the artist, as he deemed himself. This dual character pervades his cultural action: on the one hand, the acceptance of the political program that was advancing in Europe through the avant-gardes, and on the other a reflection that translates into facts the autobiographical references for which the factors induced by the Modern Movement are simply part of a whole.

An interpretation of Albini's early work cannot help but linger over his powerfully inventive impulses, tellingly in opposition to his everyday existence, of a profession defended and cultivated with thrift. At a certain point one begins to have doubts about whether his refined stylistic output corresponds to the sober, stolid reasoning on which it is based. His specifically caption-like assertion, expressed in a coherent way, seems rather to correspond to an erratic advance, continuously concealed from itself, in which the substance of the poetic factor that crosses the materic or linguistic experimentation of its premises becomes tangible, reaching the point of a redemption of fantasy. An irregular and occasional though conscious victory, suffered and enjoyed by a moralist who discovers in himself the dichotomy between his declarations of intent and his work as an artist.

Franco Albini has the particular characteristic – almost merit – of having presented himself as the most inflexible exponent of the architecture of the Modern Movement, without ever stating the dual intentions of his poetics, practicing an interpretation of his world, his position, in his identity as a designer. This helps to clarify his successive *conduct* in relation to a series of works, which starting from Cervinia in 1949-50[3] triggered a true cultural revolution, recouping what was also a political perspective in design, and allowing him to develop recognizable lines of an architecture of reality as a whole that would set the tone, from the postwar period, of his own invoked personal notation: to get beyond the moralism of a merely wishful anti-Fascism.

An attitude, therefore, that was in line with the traditional assertion of the *work of art;* the attempt, that is, to certify oneself in terms of the model with which, until then, the architect had always operated. Franco Albini represents the expectations of the Modern Movement without openly revealing this more inner attitude, and in fact making his "rationalist" or "movement" intention occasional and detached, to convey in facts an observation of himself that recovers a creativity associated with a craftsmanlike way of doing things and of organizing the work. This aspect of an Albini far from ideological enticements is seldom analyzed. His figure is generally given an interpretation in which the personality emerges in line with the forceful ethical references of an architecture governed by trends considered as belonging to a group.

In this reality, Albini was always an architect *against the current.* In this sense, the choice of having conceded nothing to the standardizing apparatus of consensus should be seen precisely in terms of participation in international artistic movements and his contemporary creative reflections. Dissent as taking one's distance, rather than an architecture of opposition, follows from those reflections, expressed, however – starting from the lodge in Cervinia – in keeping with a character of "aristocratic" isolation. An architecture that implements diverging cultural positions: on the one hand, an exploration of traditional techniques – descriptive visions of the work of art – as opposed to propositions of a memory of the avant-garde, by then residual in nature.

To name some architects *not against the current,* close to him in terms of age and cultural background, as well as of expressive force and quality, the figures of Gardella and Michelucci come to mind, restless architects but ones who interpret the system in which the operate, more than does Albini; figures who express themselves by accepting the traditional role of the architect, which continues to exist in Albini, but is laden with an ulterior suspension, the result of the certainty of doubt. An identified otherness of that path of architecture already glimpsed, perceived and interpreted in the 1950s.

With respect to the architects of consensus, Albini displayed a sort of oppositional isolation. In the linguistic-methodological results of his work, we can immediately grasp the meaning of this unstated, hidden *antinomy.*

Albini writes about and narrates his architecture only when he senses the need to take a distance from the standardized, prevailing cultural attitudes and behaviors: i.e. when he recognizes the sensation of his isolation. The writings and statements within the debate on architecture and the national tradition[4] reveal a "defensive" position of his "revisionism" that can be interpreted as opposition to the world of the avant-garde from which he had silently freed himself.

Examining Albini's design logic in relation to both the worlds in which he operated, it should be stated that the formalization of the "rationalist" idea of the moment does not stray from the norm, or from the indications of a typological-technological character promoted by the Modern Movement, with the exception – we can glimpse it – of the furnishings, where a metaphorical idea pulls towards the sort of *magic* Albini seeks, probably only in those years. This happens in the sector of his architectural specificity, and not in the wider context of the culture of the time, where the idea of the abstract and the immaterial was postulated through a magical realism, in pursuit of a new idea of space.

Therefore the matter at hand is to underline how Albini, inside this prompted enchantment and abstraction, is able to achieve results of immateriality, introducing – perhaps in spite of himself – elements of an irony barely hinted at inside the Modern Movement. We can consider his surprising contributions at the 6th Triennale (the memorable "Room for a Man"[5]) where the indications already surface – later detected by the world of modern art criticism – that put his primary characteristics in the spotlight; indications of unique imagination obtained through the overlaying of glassy and realistic, even fable-like elements: something that was definitely his.

In the description of this *design intentionality,* his creativity – observed along the path of the process of taking form – asserted the completeness of the initial programmatic moment, of a rationalist type, through achievement of a suspension that becomes the distinctive feature of his way of making architecture.

Where the postwar works are concerned, on the other hand, we can indubitably see constant, in-depth research on the characteristics, above all, of the use and weight of materials, which in keeping with his statements have to obey the rules of the materials themselves. From the *Museum of the Treasure of San Lorenzo*[6] onward, in his works this close bond between the physical-semantic properties of the material and the way it is used is always legible, underscored by the pleasure and display of those geometric references that were deployed in the designs, case by case.

Getting back to the programmatic themes he forcefully defended, and I am referring in particular to the debate on the national tradition, it should be said that Albini felt almost obliged to intervene, above all because he had moved in this direction – as had Rogers, Michelucci, Gardella, and BBPR – prior to the others, though without having set out its theoretical principles. Albini was deeply engaged with these themes on an emotional level, also because he followed the aura of the time, as well as the "substance of things hoped" by the Modern Movement in those years. Crisis, indeed, but as Rogers said of great growth, making the architecture of the 1950s – which I was able to witness, at the time – capable of winning that critical acclaim which in this moment, I believe, still resists today, which all things considered has continued, since those years, to preserve hegemonic elements through cyclical extemporaneous rediscoveries of an "Italian architecture" whose renown has spread all over the world through its most colorful names and variegated solutions[7].

The language of criticism

Much has been written by Albini and on Albini. For many years now, however, there has been silence in his regard.

Franco Albini had the good fortune to have his works illustrated in the magazine *Zodiac* from various viewpoints, and across a long span of time: the article written about him by Giuseppe Samonà – a minor monograph – formulates the dialogue with Albini through a languages that links back to the analysis proposed by Argan in the 1950s. His narrative clarifies the identification of a *pre-war* Albini as opposed to a *post-war* Albini: a discourse (to simplify its content) that indicates greater magic and imagination in the architect's early works – which Samonà had seen published in architecture magazines – than in the later works – which he was able to directly experience in the postwar period[9]. What emerged from this analysis was the image of an Albini who had lost that design enchantment that was his initial distinction: an idea that was questioned and later challenged by Francesco Tentori.

Samonà's observation was influenced by the language with which the images of Albini's early works reached him, on the wide, glossy pages of *Casabella,* "whitened" pages that had suggested that "storybook" narrative whose traces he was unable to find in the later works, seen in terms of physical presence, of the 1950s and 1960s.

The language with which he expressed the existence of a "before" and an "after" has stimulated deep reflections in the field of architectural criticism, regarding what we might define as "the language of criticism." Samonà's interpretation, derived from Argan, is one that favors a hermetic approach, where the sound of the words, their sequence, their overall phrasing, tend to place the figure of Albini in a hermetic aura, in which the intentionally repetitive terms also attempt to sympathetically interpret the architectural material. I remember a complete discussion on Albini's frameworks, their transparency, their sequences[10]. The rhythm of the description takes on an extraordinary impact: the phrases in their *rhetorical* depth penetrate the material and the architectural approach of a Franco Albini who is considered the epitome of the *anti-rhetorical.*

The examination and critique of Albini's work supplied instead by Francesco Tentori[11] emphasize a language that sets out to frame the material it is investigating, in keeping with a perspective of mending aimed at filling the gaps caused by the "abstract" interpretation of Samonà. The goal is to better root Albini the *teacher,* Albini the *designer,* Albini the *architect* in a discourse that uses a language belonging to the cultural debate of the time of realism[12].

Tentori performs a major operation of clarification of the work of Albini as a designer, delving deeply into themes of research he introduced in works like the Sampo-Olivetti store in Paris in 1958, or in all those works in which the focus is on the structural element under tension, and the use of bracing in a sort of web assigned the task of connecting the constituent parts[13]. A production system, a way of making architecture that Tentori compares to a curious mechanical character in a story by Kafka, Odradek, which laughs but without lungs, and thus cannot be heard[14]: this is the identification, on the critic's part, of an Albini linked to the most significant cultural references of the century, characterizing links from that point on in architectural criticism.

Later other contributions have attempted to position Albini's work by identifying – along the lines suggested by Samonà – a sense of the immaterial, leaning towards a "magical abstraction." The essay by Marcello Fagiolo published in *Ottagono*[15] represents a meaningful episode to understand the approach of criticism to Albini, and as a result that of Albini with regard to criticism. The article was written as part of the publication on his output produced in honor of his winning of the Premio Olivetti, as happened one year earlier in the case of Ignazio Gardella. Giulio Carlo Argan had edited the monograph on Gardella[16]; one year later, in Albini's year, Argan delegated the job to his young student.

The book was never published, because as Franca Helg told me, Albini took offense: "Gardella gets Argan, but not Albini?" The book was not released.

Minor animosities or misunderstandings were part of his character, and of an accurate grasp of his personality.

Another telling episode of the critical reception of the work of Albini is the exhibition catalogue published in 1979, where the contribution of Cesare De Seta[17] stands out, on the culture-architecture relationship in the 1930s and 1940s. This piece too reflects what we have seen as a widespread trend towards a focus on the early career of Albini. The spotlight is on Albini the designer – the Albini of greater freedom – without taking the importance of his subsequent research into sufficient account.

Portoghesi conveys a historically reasoned viewpoint on the Rinascente building at Piazza Fiume in Rome. The article published in *L'Architettura. Cronache e storia* sheds light on the environmental formulation, as well as the rigorous way of establishing a dialogue with the image of the existing city, and the capacity to get beyond the contradiction of method that only apparently separates modern and historic architecture[18].

Meeting Franco Albini

The first job for which I was hired in 1956 in Albini's studio at Via Panizza 4 was a project on an urban scale for Batista's Cuba: it was called *Habana del Este*[19] and was for a zone beyond the tunnel passing under the canal of the port.

Based on this hypothesis of circulation, a certain Mr. Gaston – I think he was from North America – asked Albini to design a new city: in practice, it was an allotment plan. There was already a project for the area prepared by the firm Skidmore, Owings and Merrill; this project organized residences around a planimetric system like an *Archimedean spiral* with a square base; the scheme would be repeated along the beach, in keeping with well-known models of the Modern Movement. But even Gaston thought it was not possible to move forward with this initial hypothesis: he assigned the commission to Franco Albini as the standard bearer of a new architecture that was gaining credibility and authority all over the world in those years[20].

Albini, then, was seen as a representative of Italian style halfway through the 1950s. The project, in the wishes of the client, had to embody all those "Italian" traits that appeared in illustrated magazines at the time: Rossellini, Ingrid Bergman... (I have always wondered, and still do, who this Mr. Gaston might have been, and what mysterious channels had led him, in the 1950s, to turn to an Italian architect, moreover one known for his moralistic inflexibility).

I remember developing a project that with unwitting irony translated the themes of a renewed architecture, between knowledge and awareness of history. The project sought the consolidated figures of architecture in the outstanding features of the layout. The cathedral, for example, was stylistically based on that of Orvieto; the internal routes of the new city retraced the passages of the city of Venice, with footbridges as the outstanding and characteristic features; other elevated passages offered consolidated commercial characteristics, in the manner of Por Santa Maria or the Frezzeria. The citations constituted the main urban-architectural features, aptly inserted in a framework with a Roman layout, which Albini suggested testing "with footsteps on the real" in the orthogonal grid around Via Montenapoleone. The streets I measured were reintroduced as the scheme of circulation and organization of the new city of Havana.

So I did my first project with Albini, with his way of working, his methodological reality of design.

I "returned" to Cuba a few years ago and had a chance to see the site of my first "Albinian" work and to "revisit" the city of Havana; I say "revisit" because I had first known its historical center only through words, discussions, images and photographs brought back by Albini: he taught me to love that city in the form of an almond – but, as he said, a *bitter* one – from a distance.

Havana is a colonial city that repeats the quadrant through a series of connected, silent and sheltered squares, all the way to the sea's edge and the canal of the port, with rising towers and the chain of Spanish forts. This *architectural narrative* of the old city was extended in Albini's project for the new city: the first overall view was gradually configured in excerpts and developed through careful study of the sections of the beach that sloped slowly towards the sea. The centuriation was overlaid on a scheme that made reference to two extremities, emerging poles of intervention: one of them was the cathedral.

The peripheral circulation layout of the city was remarkable, forming a traffic ring of double avenues inside which the parking areas were placed; this rotary circulation layout constituted – and still does today – a source of great pride for me: I invented those features, back then, working for him. And precisely through that particular solution, Albini evaluated my way of understanding things and – this was important for him – measured my capacity to transform them.

The parking area, the strong point of the whole layout, connected two parallel streets: the middle part was organized in a herringbone arrangement, with entrances and exits channeled without stoplights. A fantastic drawing emerged: it was taken personally by Albini to Havana. When he returned, the only thing he said – echoing an observation made by the clients – was that the urban planning layout, in graphic terms, did not correspond to the type of landscape insertion, definitively remaining on a more abstract level. I spent hours drawing very tall *real* palm trees over my drawings, with their beautiful nude trunks, which I later saw again on the access roads of the 19th and 20th century sugar factories, still conserved and functioning today.

Among the habitual collaborators of Albini for his Cuban work, I remember

Enea Manfredini who had designed items for the streets, and on the beach, some of which were built.

After the *castrista* revolution the hypothesis was confirmed of the development of Habana del Este, through a project in the Soviet style based on heavy prefabrication, with a very different, extremely weak urban organization. The failure of Fidel Castro in architecture can probably be attributed to lack of comprehension of the innovative proposals that came from Europe, and from Italy in particular, in the 1950s. The lack of implementation of Albini's project was later matched by the abandonment of the *Foro dell'Arte* of Vittorino Garatti, an architect of the Milanese school, designed with Gottardi and Porro (respectively a Venetian and a Cuban at the school of the CIAM in Venice).

Designing *on pencil point*

Albini had the characteristic of drawing architecture with sharp lines, *on pencil point,* as if carrying out an operation of polished finishing even as he was engaged in a procedure of progressive information on the conditions of the project, making the proposal taking form always tirelessly start over from the beginning.

In Gardella's drawing, for example, we can instead perceive a way of materializing the design idea in a rapid, immediate form: a "straw-like" sign, recognizable in the web of intersecting lines. The spaces themselves, in their geometric representation, are retraced in a circular movement of the pencil, through the undulating smoothing of the technical-circulatory regularity of the initially proposed program. "His" rule was then recovered in a second phase by the collaborator/draftsman, assigned the task of taking the architectural object back to the correct dimensional and proportional reality. In Gardella's case, this was research conducted essentially through the study of the plan. I mention Ignazio Gardella because when I was still a student – after having completed the course of Elements of Composition at the Politecnico di Milano – I worked in his studio on Piazza Aquileia, a small workplace of two rooms inside his home, like my father's studio, as was customary at the time.

In Albini the reasoning of the composition took on a different aspect: in his design the indications of a technological character were prevalent, even constituting the pretext for the identification of a recognizable and logical process inside the project. *Connection* of finished parts and their assembly was the rule.

Even in his works that were never built – just consider the drawings for a villa for Roberto Olivetti[21] – the process of connection stands out, with at the same time a separation of the construction elements, seen in a complete way but also with a margin of abstraction. The connections to the surroundings always represented traumatic moments for Albini: the ground seam, for example.

The geometric arrangement prevails, providing indications of a technological character, making the drawing *on pencil point* become proposal and control over the degree of definition of the structures and the constituent parts of the project. Instead, in Gardella the drawing is linked to a simultaneous, complex comprehension of the spaces, expressed through stronger, more impulsive types of graphic-formal representation. In Albini that was never the case: his drawing was always technical, aimed at achieving a program, which precisely in the moment of the choices established its uniqueness, in a concrete case.

Albini never posed the problem of being or not being a good draftsman: his drawings were excellent, and that was all. Through a sequence of small, complete signs his drawing set out the entire "story" of the project, the result of his obstinacy, of his way of being pithy and conceptual. Regarding those drawings, I remember the particular care that went into the cutaways of the buildings, which showed the sequences of successive transformations. For him a lack of simultaneous reading of all the three-dimensional aspects of the project was inconceivable, and that reading took place through the traditional orthogonal geometric drawing.

Having had the good fortune to work by his side, I noticed that my possibilities to design were linked to an elementary process in which given conditions could be achieved exclusively in a single solution. Albini, arriving at the studio, often from far away and therefore tired after a long trip, would sit at the table and after having received the indications that had led to the choice of that single designed proposal, invented through dialogue an entire series of ranges of possibility that came into being in a thousand different projects, all of them exceptional. The paths to follow were not to be taken as mere diverging or converging indications, but were true complete projects in their own right: each time, they contained the confirmations of their formal plausibility.

Faced with the quantitative, layout-based or technological aspects and references submitted for his scrutiny, Albini continuously varied the possibilities of interlocking of the variables in play. His exceptional virtuosity emerged in precisely these moments: an extensive and intense ability. A sort of *design miracle* he was able to enact, in real time, whenever he was presented with new themes and new design queries. Quite the opposite of our laborious exercises with inexperienced staff, which more often than not left fringes of the surrounding context untouched, which remained blurrier, as in a camera's lens. In Albini the project margins were very tightly controlled and above all aimed at a connection of assembly.

So Albini had an extremely skillful way of drawing, expressed on very light sketching paper: he "improvised" on it, depending on the information he received from his counterparts, either clients or collaborators. He had a remarkable ability to immediately translate the facts, even of a quantitative nature, since he was capable of simultaneously varying dimensions and structures, depending on the evolution of the discussion and the reasoning.

He was able to change the direction taken and to follow others, in response to indications of a quantitative character: with respect to the information her received – *on pencil point* – he continued to develop, to shape the result, altering the structures, raising or lowering levels, removing or adding construction parts. All this was done without observations of a formal nature, because the forms had already been selected in his mind: he reinvented the organism spontaneously, in keeping with the variation of conditions and functions, keeping the elements of the composition fixed, and to himself: such as the structures of elevation, for example, which were conceived and interpreted as rigid elements that in a *magical* instant would be assembled.

His outstanding ability to reconsider forms and volumes with which he had already experimented emerges in the comparison between two elements like the connection slab of the Terme Luigi Zoja at Salsomaggiore Terme and the dining hall of the office building of SNAM at San Donato Milanese, both designed at the end of the 1960s[22]. We can observe the roof, stepped in both cases. At Salsomaggiore the configuration of the roof is an indispensable part of the overall image of the spa[23]; while in the case of San Donato[24] it refers to a building that constitutes an incongruous completion of the system of growth of the large Lombard cloisters – from Filarete to Piermarini – initially designed and later abandoned by the client. A coherent object: its "configuration" already experienced at Salsomaggiore, which contributes to block the large blades of San Donato. Through the design insertion of one of his single architectural objects – the dining hall - Albini concludes the by-then failed hypothesis of virtual and ideal expansion of San Donato, with an artifact whose form was inside him, to the point of allowing him to simultaneously propose it – reinterpreted – in two different contexts.

Getting back to his relationship with the physical aspect of the artifact, we can understand how in the works with a structure in reinforced concrete there is no perception of a focus on the sculptural qualities and flow of concrete, while we can see his tendency towards an analytical breakdown of the structural elements.

In order to operate, Albini always needed elements that could be traced back to the priority of the initial idea, broken down and reassembled according to modules and frameworks, continuous iterations with slight shifts of the same element in different forms, obeying those specific functions that gradually attempted to take on form, in the wider or more limited context of the information perceived. While the works in reinforced concrete bear the impact of this layered passage, the gradual character of the connections of those in iron reflects coherent demonstrative didactics; almost a narrative approach that emerges through geometric expression to establish its own theorem through the strategy of coherent formulation.

The project was changed and shaped along the way with speed and immediacy: a continuous invention of forms that already existed, an articulation of the theme that led to easy, productive alterations.

Furthermore, Albini assembled details: the design was composed of many separate, apparently independent parts, which converged in a final unification. This attitude can be traced back to the original sin of Milanese design, a logical-mental process organized around the principle of assembly, where the technological references of prefabrication are thus congruous with the compositional principles. This mechanism of composition-breakdown into single elements, applied on all scales, was already inside Albini: from the works of greater complexity to the individual episodes, the furnishings (like the *Veliero* bookcase, the *Fiorenza* armchair, the *Luisa* chair, repeatedly revised, or the glass radio[25]).

The project was never finished: with its end, the most all-encompassing dramas began.

Especially the passage from drawing to implementation – though the design left little margin for error, since all its variables had already been controlled in advance – caused veritable micro-dramas in the studio. The famous phrase "you can't trust Giuseppe" (referring to one of the staff), resulting from the lack of verification of the definitive drawings for the reinforced concrete of the municipal offices in Genoa[26], involving the failure to vary the angle of the pillars in the sequence of the levels, remained emblematic for years – not only inside the studio – reflecting the atmosphere of trepidation and the tension towards perfectionism experienced at Via Panizza.

The studio monitored all the phases of project development: the definitive drawings, once the final version had been decided on, were developed by the best draftsmen, undoubtedly achieving a very high level of quality. These were usually drawings on a very detailed scale – 1:10, 1:5 – to study the play of attachments of stones, panels, materials. Extensive use was made of models, especially for study and design work. Albini paid close attention to the organization of the definitive drawing, which had to have a *logical* configuration: because "there is only one logic."

It is easy to imagine the sensation of his intolerance: for Villa Zambelli in Forlì[27], a collaborator at the time, named Romanò, had submitted various sections regarding the movements of the sidewalks around the construction. Albini, justifiably, wanted their order to follow the established clockwise "sequence": but instead they had been made at random, in the characteristic points, and they triggered the statements on "logic" of the most dogged side of Albini.

This is why the draftsmen of the studio on Via Panizza were so talented: the drawings that emerged from the studio, under the guidance of Franca Helg, were never mere drawings, but veritable fighting machines.

Helg's presence in the studio on Via Panizza[28] coincided with a slimming of the work: Albini was very stubborn and also a bit captious about drawing, a factor Helg attributed in part to a lack of worksite experience (Albini had no great passion for construction sites, perhaps because he began to spend time at them later on in his career: often he went together with Helg, who helped him with the more difficult choices). Albini produced drawing after drawing, in some cases even making more than were really necessary. They were drawings that offered a glimpse of late-19th-century influences: the taste and pleasure of giving thicknesses to sections, of giving the stone its consistency, of placing the mortar, through its representation. His was a very advanced form of reasoning and of cognitive investigation transferred into drawing, which nevertheless conserved its aesthetic matrix, rather than stopping short at practical *worksite* draftsmanship.

On the other hand, this way he had of designing through sheets, panels, taut wires, to convey an ethereal and immaterial image of space, produced an irresistible urge in Albini to transfer what he envisioned into the drawing even more than into reality, since it was harder for him to imagine: in definitive terms, it was a consequence of his lack of attachment to things in the very moment in which, case by case, he was inventing his own ground.

The technological narrative

Albini worked personally on the materials, both in terms of selection from samples and for evaluation of their physical-mechanical characteristics: he was a strong advocate of the idea that it is necessary to recover the properties and characteristics of the "new technologies" of the past. What was needed was to regain from past generations that ability of ideal appropriation of the virtues possessed by materials: "we have to know about new materials, just as our predecessors new those of the past."

Albini urged a line of behavior that challenged the "capitulation" of the quality of materials – traditional or otherwise – utilizing them in an intentionally coherent, highly descriptive way.

We might say that where the material was seen as "amorphous" the work became weak. I remember an episode in this regard: a Japanese professional had come to the studio, who was working on a project for Olivetti for a series of single-family houses with just one above-ground level, to be made in brick masonry. This man did not understand the static performance of a continuous structure in an aseismic zone, so he could not grasp the lack of sizeable masonry interlocks. Albini was not able to address the theme, however, to make it "Albinian." The process was not facilitated by the help of his tired translator:

the explanations fell on deaf ears, regarding the size of the bricks, their vertical and horizontal assembly, the thickness of the walls, the interspaces, the physical plant systems, the placement of the windows. Everything was constantly called back into discussion, and became the cause of endless arguments; the fact that the masonry courses did not run on the horizontal plane, unlike the practice in his Japanese reality, filled the young architect with despair. Albini, nevertheless, was not able to make the representation of the architectural fact take form, due to the excessive simplification of the technological premises behind the project. The overall effect seemed opaque, to the dismay of all in the studio.

The subsequent technical studies (of the insulation, for example) utilizing the technology of masonry led to a total lack of definition, depriving the artifact of conceptual purity and uniqueness in material terms. A doubly indeterminate situation has developed, in opposition; his very nature as a composer (each work contains the opportunity to be a great work) threw Albini into a state of aphasia: a trauma caused by the need to specify, in a list, the basic constructive features. As for the Japanese collaborator (did he become famous?) the elementary scheme of the structure just was not part of his background. The program of the building had not taken on meanings; the occasional destruction of the structural hypothesis, caused by occasional factors, demonstrated how the structural phenomenon became "inconsistent" for Albini and "impossible" for the Japanese designer. Albini's axiom "there is only one logic" had not been fulfilled. The project did not meet with success, and the client did not put it into construction; but in definitive terms, it did not take off due to the lack of understanding of the static hypothesis of the building. A thousand drawings bore witness to amorphous definitions, without any driving expression. For Albini this implied the impossibility of using a material (the continuous masonry of traditional construction) that could not be decoded into recognizable parts, and thus remained without identity and articulation.

In Albini the structural program determined character to the extent in which it was a bearer of signs that could be combined through frameworks or other complex arrangements. His research began with a compositional plot of the support: the alternation between "supported" and "supporting" elements allowed the modular bearing parts to show through, revealing the inner geometry of a recurring process; of that *method* that relies on the invention of juxtaposed frameworks. A process approach that was already clear, for Albini, in Gropius at Torten, for example, where this technological sense of graduality emerges, expressing the growth of the artifact: this was a lesson that could be glimpsed in his work as an architecture, both in the initial period of rationalism and in that of his successive designs.

While the world of product design in the 1950s produced an elite group that postulated belonging to the world of the avant-garde *tout court,* the design of the years to follow continued with a partial, fragmented vision of the world of production and the role of the useful object. The rule of the image emerged in the absence of a specific market. An object by Albini could be found in museums scattered around the world, and in the most sophisticated places of sale: and this boosted his critical acclaim, as a result of several successful exhibitions. It was a surprise for me, walking together with Franca Helg through the streets of the Harvard campus, to see their rattan furniture on view in the orderly gardens, in search of an improbable market.

Although the production cycle remained indeterminate in its final segment – and that is no small matter – Albini focused on his professional-artisanal relationship with production by keeping his contribution exclusively within the design sphere. Even before the war he worked for the Parma company, which produced metal objects and furnishings. In my own right, spending time in the studio, I picked up on that earlier but technologically evolved research for the production of lockers to place in factory dressing rooms. For Albini, even such a simple theme became a source of multiple studies: the item was configured inside complex geometric assemblies. These were parallelepipeds with a rhomboid base that interlocked together (like the buildings of Cesate[29], to convey the idea). They had an angle of 45° with respect to the wall boundaries, in order to gain the coveted ten centimeters in thickness, thus passing from the usual 55 centimeters to the solution of 45. The parts interpenetrated diagonally, transforming a simple, faceless artifact into an object of great complexity, revealing the shrewdness underlined by the "compositional tremor" of his long black moustache.

Clarity in design, precision and an irresistible desire to invent were the characteristics that never failed him in his everyday practice. In his studio, in the practice of working, through the invention of useful objects – I remember, for example, a small wooden trolley designed for the company Poggi – I learned that attitude of research applied regardless of the scale of the project, extending to all the phases of the work, in a method of investigation that corresponded, in his view, to one and only one "logic." A hypothesis that set Albini apart from any other architect of the time, and of other times: each project, for him, gained certainty in the correspondence between the premises and their development, and he paid no attention to values that were not intrinsic to their own technology.

Albini, in his design, narrated his technological knowledge, concentrating on the instruments and tools, on their correct use in view of the operative implementation of a job (for the woodworking shop or the metal carpentry) that was still a matter of craft. It was from the craftsman's workshop, which we disciples jokingly called "*brianzola*," that he drew the efficiency of a proposal that reproduces, in detail, an "effect" in which the new creeps in. His narrative was precise, cunning at times: he transformed knowledge into a message: he used to "block" us, always regarding the devices, because for him we were not yet able to penetrate the construction, the composition, the ordering of the parts of the object.

The students who had to take the exam in Furnishing and Architecture of Interiors in Venice on the wrong day were truly to be pitied for their misfortune[30]. He challenged their knowledge of a technological character, regarding the functioning of the "machines" needed for the construction and finishing of an artifact: the type of interlock, the type of glue, the protection of the ends of the wood, and then the order, the constitution, the association of parts. In this regard, I remember one "poor" young lady who because she had drawn very normal shutters of a bow window – reminiscent of the early Gregotti in Novara – was literally bombarded with questions, most of which were pushed to a level of description that was objectively implausible in any usual educational context. Those simple shutters became restless, complex machines bristling with inextricable difficulties.

Fortune and misfortune in Art
Lingering over Albini the designer also means reference to a moment of reduction of his activity, following a "change in the weather" in the world of furniture production: a phenomenon observed through the evolution of the programming of the models of the Poggi company in Pavia[31] (the firm that starting in 1951 produced objects by Albini-Helg).

It is interesting to observe, in this regard, the relations between those like Albini, Gardella and BBPR, and the generation that came immediately after them.

Those who had the "misfortune-fortune" of belonging to this outstanding group of architects legitimately faced with the task of "reconstruction," in the end saw their efforts frustrated, and those of a generation compressed, as it happened, by the one to follow: that of the 1930s, which in practice denied what came before.

This group (I am speaking of architects with a Milanese background born in and around the 1920s) that had also come up on the wave of Albini's thinking, to serve in the reconstruction of the country after World War I, through the long-debated themes of industrialization of building, rationalization of the worksite, etc. (the ideals of the rationalist movement), saw its theoretical line crushed by its own fathers who had most authoritatively interpreted the revolutionary movement of those who came, in the European avant-garde, from more established, distant experimentations. The participation in the 1950s in the debate on the national tradition, rich even in the ambiguity of its highly innovative cultural (and political) references, was experienced *without quality*, along the years of the Cold War, by those who with generational ties to the 1920s did not actually interact very closely with it, favoring the attempt to grant survival to the pressures of the architectural avant-garde, at that time already translated into the "formalism of the Modern Movement." A generation, then, which suffered in its participation in architecture *tout court*.

Vico Magistretti, for example (to whom we will return later on), can certainly not be said to identify with this problematic emphasis. His activity was applied in the field of design, a natural refuge but also a successful result of this group positioned to the side of the architectural debate: I am referring to Zanuso, the Castiglioni brothers, Rosselli, all Milanese architects. With the exception, however, of Vittoriano Viganò, who remained the most qualified architect of the group because he was different and moved *against the current;* the only one able to outline and maintain a coherent career in the specific field of architecture. This way of going against the trend, a primary characteristic of Albini, indicates Viganò as a driving figure of his generation, through a hypothesis of work that was particularly sanctioned by the avant-gardes, seeking an identity of operation precisely in this loyalty.

The *mentor* of Viganò is Le Corbusier: but Le Corbusier is also the *mentor* of Rogers; with the difference that the latter, though after many years of respectful proximity, also manages to liberate the new formal hypothesis of architecture, precisely regarding the conceptual question of linguistic references. And this is done in a way that is neither convinced nor aware: a work of elusive mediations, also by attacking from under cover. But for those of the next generation, of the 1930s, the message was loud and clear. Loyalty to the origins, to the canonical continuation of an improbable avant-garde, seemed like an appeal to an utterly decontextualized order; a clear, distinct, but by then sterile expression. As a result, in this hypothesis of construction of a concrete work for architecture, most of the exponents of the "middle generation" saved itself from the wreckage by carving out a long-term niche (Magistretti too is part of this generation). When, in fact, the role of Albini as a product designer ran up against a changed relationship between design, execution and the market for useful objects (and a lack of support for his cultural operation on the part of manufacturers and operators in that sector), the result was the end of Albini's activity in this field. It was precisely the generation of the 1920s – Magistretti in particular, in the case of Poggi – that "took his place," glorifying him but translating his methods into a triumph of consumerism.

In and around the 1960s Poggi, at furniture fairs, displayed the elegant design of objects by Magistretti (also with an object by Albini in the background, but the works of the new direction were those of Magistretti), projects that were in tune with everything that was being done at the time, but with one substantial and not secondary characteristic: the appeared to be immaterial, "reflecting black" or "matte black," thus erasing the structural evidence – specific to Albini – of the form of the design and its material. The 1960s had come to an end.

Albini, as reported by Helg, regretted this "change of the wind" caused by the passage from an elite market to a mass market: it was in this way that his action as a *designer on pencil point,* practiced with a pedagogical intent, was shifted to worksite technology in a persevering approach that brought together, in the 1970s, the claims specific to the middle generation. I refer here to the research on modular elements and their coordination: from the Terme Zoja at Salsomaggiore to the SNAM at San Donato Milanese.

The evolution between the INA building in 1951 in Parma[32] and the spa building in 1967-70 can be seen in this augmented indication of a more complex, less simple modulation, which in the case of the building in the city is instead of lesser complexity, since it is summed up in a gradation of parts, therefore tending to configure the designed element as an object.

While at Salsomaggiore he was able to produce a "module-form," in Parma the single parts are instead broken down and reassembled, but in any case all deconstructed, autonomous, because the modular elements are interpreted more as variation rather than as uniformity.

Observe, for example, the modular arrangement of the windows of the INA building with respect to the "module-object" of the Terme Zoja building or, in parallel, of the Madre di Dio complex in Genoa, or again – in a different way – of the SNAM in San Donato, where the technological elements take on their own independence, a true configuration isolated by the *pan de verre* and its shaping, to overlap like a superimposed oversailing course – also similar to the "module-object" of the Rinascente building in Rome[33] – to permit the passage of conduits. At San Donato, furthermore, the use of different and innovative materials also appears, such as polycarbonate in place of the conglomerate surfaces, making this research even more explicit.

Albini's investigation clearly offers the multiple key of interpretation of a design poetics and, by reflection, its logical and methodological-operative concatenations: the wealth of meanings Albini represented and still represents today.

On the one hand, a formalization connected to a technology based on separate parts – the INA building; on the other, the deployment of a "module-object" that could be configured as if through a new, evolving technology – Terme Zoja, the SNAM building – technologies that to this end become "molded" or "pre-molded," objects for assembly, in practice.

Magistretti, therefore, does not lay claim to Albini's place as a designer, but "represses" it: finding in the 1970s a new relationship in the world of *production,* above all in the context of those islands of the same production towards which Albini had aimed his geometric perceptions and his refined relationships of textures, colors and materials. He certainly does not the place of Albini, of his restlessness, his problematic character. Albini translated the technical and technological difficulties that tormented him into creativity; not because he was unable to conclude his discourse of great design, but because he feared he would not manage to complete that operation with respect to the problematic boundaries assumed and the methodological levels he constantly sought. The generation of which Magistretti is the most genteel protagonist was not capable of formulating a proposal – also for design – of the depth achieved by Albini.

In conclusion, it should be emphasized that after a period of discordant contributions in the interpretation of the architectural phenomenon – and the direction of the research conducted here confirms this – a need is felt to review the complexity of the "differences" pursued and arduously achieved, through a revision of a theoretical character, to be carried out through the orientations of design research not in a passive way, but to understand *the step to be taken*. The crux of the issue – also regarding what we have outlined as the possible *cultural attitude* with respect to the architectural project – is the belonging or lack of belonging to modes of work we might define, beyond anodyne or commonplace classifications, as being of *consensus* or, vice versa, of *dissent*.

Without any intention of ranking or establishing particular merits, I will attempt to clarify the premise with another example. Ignazio Gardella – with the necessary personal particularities – Vittorio Gregotti, Gae Aulenti, as well as the already mentioned Vico Magistretti and the other protagonists of the second generation of "Milanese" architects, are architects who interpret the general *consensus* of the growth years; Franco Albini, Vittoriano Viganò, Giorgio Grassi, Guido Canella are architects of total *dissent*. Dissent that sets them against the current inside a uniform generational flux. In Aldo Rossi, instead, we can see a "different" intelligibility: a capacity for intuition equal to its comprehensibility. An acute artistic vein that expresses its own *engrossed reason*, accompanied as it is by a deep knowledge of respect for the "rule." A quality that is wrapped, however, by a veil of undeniable conformity with a fragmented knowledge. A discipline indifferent to material doing that limits and constrains application on the front of construction technique. Canella, on the other hand, coherently represents the meaning of an "architect of dissent." He has always been an architect "against," who nurtured his work through a sort of aggression against themes, setting them out, endorsing them in a redundant way; retracing in architecture that utterly Lombard path of an enrichment of languages that in the force of the argumentation does not shrink from discontinuity and a dialectical verbiage that feeds, oppositely, on enhanced philological notations.

To be *against the current* or to be *in consensus*, even today, means a transverse interpretation of references of a generational character, to fasten the before and after of our complex itineraries. Ernesto Nathan Rogers, in this context, presented himself as an intellectual who postulated and enacted a hopeless synthesis, in a mental game. His work becomes increasingly important for us precisely for its cultural formulation which always remains a bit hidden, due to the quality of the message placed between a historicized interpretation of the context and a hazarded architectural proposal.

To find other significant contributions, we should remember that Giovanni Michelucci, retracing an inner itinerary on the nature of materials, moved in an area very similar to that of BBPR, foreshadowing in his concrete approach Mario Ridolfi himself, one of the personalities that provided the most punctual responses in the field, and the widest openings. Openings tested even prior to the war in a "rural" culture that put to shame the quality of the monumental architecture championed by Piacentini, situating itself in that context of the "peasant" world that later took on force and expression through the movement of Realism.

Where the generation of the 1920s is concerned, it did not have a Rogers, namely someone to sum up the terms of its own internal debate: this is why it was overwhelmed by the architects of the generation to follow, who reasserted the identity of architecture or in any case its independence, autonomy and specificity, recovering from the past those references to a tradition with strong connotations of a regional character, which then resurfaced in an architectural localism that still remains to be studied. I have already spoken of the architects of the 1920s: Viganò, with his work, undoubtedly constitutes the most plausible reference; Marco Zanuso remains "halfway across the stream," falling back on product design in the Milanese manner, triumphant, intelligent and elaborate, but sterilized and without convictions; and with him, all the other designers, among whom the most outstanding is indubitably Castiglioni.

Architecture is going through a moment of flexion, of rethinking today, unlike the other "arts" which manage, instead, to produce flavors and products that are still convincing, all things considered: in music, in literature it is possible to identify at least ten names or so – we have even had prophets, such as Pier Paolo Pasolini – who manage to restore not only a legitimacy of the cultural product but also recognizable and transmittable tools. In architecture today this does not happen: the international uniformity of the habitual tools of communication provides alarming proof of this fact.

In any case, architecture exists, and even these attempts to hide and to conceal it – because in certain cases this is the intention – will be in vain, to the extent that architecture in the end physically progresses, and when it is there you can see it.

The present attempt to interpret architecture that also crosses this meditation on Albini can be seen in relation to the inadequacy and superficiality of analysis now evident in institutional criticism. Today a battle has broken out with the aim of reinventing and repositioning nomenclatures, not for the purpose of grasping the particularities of works of architecture, but in order to establish nuclei of belonging, schools, long-term trends, even if they have faded with the passing of time, apart from a responsible function of design criticism.

Our generation has had a troubled approach to education, but undoubtedly an easier one: to remain in its context, then, did not necessarily indicate a desire (wanting at all costs to remain), but was a coherent but extemporaneous way to learn through a cultural connection with certain protagonists. Where I am concerned, I recall in particular Franca Helg for her stubborn capacity for observation, and my mentor, Ernesto Nathan Rogers, for his cultural uniqueness and his imagination; and then, last but not least, Franco Albini, for the invention of a theorem that on every occasion, unconsciously, he managed to betray.

Parma, 6 February 1993 – Studio Cortesi
Parma, 6 August 1993 – Casa Cortesi
Parma, 9 August 1993 – Studio Cortesi

Notes

Aurelio Cortesi has given many lectures and written essays on the figure of Franco Albini, working in his studio at Via Panizza 4 in Milan from 1957 to 1959. The legacy of Albini – his design activity and his way of interacting with students and collaborators in the studio – still represents a solid, recognizable reference point for Cortesi in the conception and development of architectural projects. For the preparation of these notes, an important reference was the essay by Franca Helg Testimonianza su Franco Albini *published two years after his death in* L'Architettura. Cronache e storia *(no. 288, 1979), because among the various contributions on Albini this memoir of someone who worked with him for over 25 years seemed closest to the profile outlined by Aurelio Cortesi.*

1. Franco Albini was born in Brianza (at Robbiate) in 1905 and was trained in the context of Milanese culture. After his degree and a period of apprenticeship in the studio of Gio Ponti and Emilio Lancia, the encounter with Edoardo Persico and the acquaintance with Giuseppe Pagano and the young staff of *Casabella* with whom he took part in the 5th Milan Triennale represented the foundations of the abstract, purist research that went into Albini's early production.
"In the Department of Architecture of the Politecnico di Milano, a school that was among the most representative and vaunted structures for the entrepreneurial spirit of the Lombard bourgeoisie, the orientation towards eclecticism left little room for doubts. Professors and students of Architecture were placed in two large halls of the old Polytechnic at Piazza Cavour: the dean was Gaetano Moretti, who left plenty of leeway for Piero Portaluppi.
The teaching was based on the drawings of D'Espouy.
Franco Albini's degree project (1929), diligently developed and drawn, was plausibly aligned with the dominant approach taught at the school. After taking his degree Albini felt the urgent need to gain work experience, first as an intern with Lancia and Ponti, and then in 1931 with his own professional practice, shared with his friends Giancarlo Palanti and Renato Camus.
In 1928 Gio Ponti founded *Domus* and had a lively interest in crafts; he focused on a new design that would be "the art of luxury for the elegant home." Lancia, a professional of extensive knowledge, made his own drawings, testing solution after solution in the details of his works of architecture.
In their studio Albini probably had his first encounters with furniture manufacturers like Turri and Dessi, and the first international contacts came in Barcelona, where Gio Ponti was curator of the Italian pavilion and Mies van der Rohe made that of Germany, at the International Exposition of 1929. In Paris, again for Ponti, he visited the studio of Le Corbusier. [...] After the first constructed works of 1930, still in the guise of modernist decorativism, his research evolved towards the models developed and proposed by the Bauhaus: Albini very often recalled, though only in a few remarks, his initiation to such approaches on the part of Edoardo Persico (around 1932).
Persico's irony, his problematic way of weighing questions, his uncompromising lucidity, revealed to Albini the need to achieve "coherence between knowledge and language," and the pursuit of this coherence was to become another dominant motif of his method and his poetics" (F. Helg).

2. In the 1930s Albini, with Camus and Palanti, addressed the theme of low-cost housing in keeping with a method based on the "necessary and indispensable" derived from the teachings of Pagano. Like the other projects for residential developments done in that decade, the Fabio Filzi development on Viale Argonne in Milan (1936-39) commissioned by IFACP (Istituto Fascista Autonomo per le Case Popolari) came from research triggered by the polemic against buildings *in period style:* "a low-cost housing complex without monumental blemishes," Pagano himself wrote in *Casabella-Costruzioni* (no. 144, 1939) to describe the work featuring linear volumes of different sizes derived from the juxtaposition of equal building types.
"These were years of lively encounters and discussions: yet for me they seem like confused hears, full of misunderstanding. The young architects debated and collaborated on wide-ranging the-

oretical projects, but knowing that the big commissions would all go to the architects of the regime, in their constructed works they fell back on themes of a reduced scope that also had very temporary duration; while on the new themes, they engaged in passionate personal research.

In those years the controversy regarding architecture in period style, modernist or modern, reached the pages of the dailies: Guido Piovene commented on the pages of the *L'Ambrosiano* against the architect Broglio of IFACP who built low-cost housing of 'eclectic' taste: in 1932 there was the first IFACP competition for the San Siro district, with many participants: Albini, Camus, Palanti, Romano, etc. The completion in 1936 of the Fabio Filzi development on Viale Argonne was the result of this early research" (F. Helg).

3. "The profession was closed to young people, and the debut came in the field of furnishings. Furnishings, not design: the difference is significant. The creation of furniture and objects followed a praxis of craftsmanship with degrees of freedom and possibility of intervention connected with the abilities and versatility of the artisans. In this experience of work in contact with cabinetmakers and furniture producers, the focus on and love of 'perfect workmanship' developed, which was to become one of the dominant motifs of Albini's work" (F. Helg).

Albini's early activity, across the 1940s, was directly mainly towards the sectors of exhibitions and pavilions, furnishings, competitions and small buildings designed according to the principles of modern design methodology spread by Pagano. But from Pagano Albini also picked up and developed the interest in the recovery of humble craftsmanship and spontaneous architecture.

The Pirovano youth hostel (1949-51, with Luigi Colombini) took form around the line of research aimed at the values of vernacular architecture, and thus at an interpretation of history (Pagano in 1935 had published the Domus notebook on "Rural Architecture"). Albini, an avid mountaineer, designed the hostel for his friend Giuseppe Pirovano by focusing on the typological features and construction methods of Alpine rural architecture, "almost as an exercise on the recovery of spontaneous elements" (F. Helg).

In spite of its different purpose, the hostel came from the same logic as the typological and constructive features of rural buildings in Valle d'Aosta: the Pirovano stands on a steep slope, following its shape with a jagged plan in which wood and masonry alternate in the load-bearing structure.

The building in Cervinia is one of the few works about which Albini wrote, presenting it in *Edilizia Moderna* (no. 47, 1951) with an article that underlines how "the programmatic limitation to traditional means of construction and natural materials sets out to accentuate the need for a deeper adaptation to nature and to the customs of the place. There is clearly no need to state that this is not a matter of folklore, but of an architecture that will not be environmentally, and therefore urbanistically, undifferentiated; and once again, to say that modern architecture does not consist in the use of new materials and construction procedures, because all constructive means are valid in all times as long as they are logical and still efficient."

4. "From the start of his activity Albini was driven by an interest in architecture that bordered on obsession. He concentrated his interest on architecture, on the way it was made, on the possibility and capacity to express himself through the concrete character of the proposal defined in terms of form, space, size. He was informed about achievements, claims, controversies, but he looked on without taking part in the theoretical debate, somewhat dismayed by the quantity of words, the wealth of terms that intertwined around themes and problems he preferred to approach by doing" (F. Helg).

In the period prior to the war the bond among the young rationalist architects stayed alive through encounters and discussions on shared works, installations and Triennale exhibitions, but above all in the context of the editorial staff of the magazine *Casabella*.

The Milanese school of Pagano, Persico and Galli used the publication as a fundamental means of asserting and absorbing the principles and language of the Modern Movement. The magazine founded in 1928 was directed from 1933 to 1943 by Giuseppe Pagano (first as *Casabella Costruzioni* and then as *Costruzioni-Casabella*): though having strong cultural ties to the members of the editorial staff, Albini seems to have preferred communicating through the publication of his works of architecture rather than through writings; he did direct the magazine – after two years of suspension of publication, in 1946 – in collaboration with Giancarlo Palanti, but only for a span of three issues (from no. 193 to no. 195-198, under the name *Casabella Construzioni*), after which the issues were interrupted until *Casabella-Continuità* directed by Rogers.

Later, after some experience in the field of journalism with various sector magazines, Albini opted for a sort of voluntary renunciation of the publication of writings, with the exception of a few pieces for educational purposes. Critics have often pointed out how "Albini, a reserved man, severe above all with himself, never concerned himself with recouping these works of his, nor did he endeavor – even in moments of great professional success – to publicize his output" (C. De Seta, *Franco Albini architetto, fra razionalismo e tecnologia*, in the anthology *Franco Albini 1930-1970*, exhibition catalogue, Centro Di, Firenze 1979).

One of the most significant pieces of his writing remains the short lecture delivered for the debate on tradition in architecture organized by the Movimento Studi sull'Architettura (founded in 1945 by a group that also included Albini) and published in *Casabella* in 1955 (F. Albini, contribution to "Un dibattito sulla tradizione in architettura svoltosi a Milano nella sede dell'MSA la sera del 14 giugno 1955," in *Casabella-Continuità* no. 205, 1955).

5. Albini took part in the 6th Milan Triennale (1936) with the installation, in the pavilion designed by Pagano, of the Mostra dell'Abitazione – which received the Diploma d'Onore – in collaboration with R. Camus. P. Clausetti, I. Gardella, G. Mazzoleni, G. Minoletti, G. Mucchi, G. Palanti, G. Romano; with the installation "Stanza per un Uomo"; and the exhibit design of the "Mostra dell'Oreficeria Antica," with G. Romano.

"The Milanese school strives to assert the principles and language of the Modern Movement, but also due to the conditions of limited cultural information imposed by the regime, there is no clarification of the relations between production, economy, society and architectural definition. Instead, especially around Pagano, there is clarification of the driving motivations behind modern architecture. Concepts of modular and serial design intervene to define taste, language and rhythms: that of functionality, the connection of spaces, and that of rationality, the modes of construction.

Collaboration and occasional disputes were aspects of the habitual condition of the young group of architects.

Albini, quiet and faithful, participated in the work of the group, contributing with all his energy to demonstrative projects and undertakings (Milano Verde, Mostra dell'Abitazione), but he developed his own poetics with greater freedom when the collaboration was limited to fewer participants (the Mostra dell'Oreficeria with Giovanni Romano) or when – even better – he could work on his own. Also in these personal experiences (Stanza per un Uomo, Soggiorno per una Villa alle Triennali, the INA pavilion of the Fiera Campionaria di Milano), he complied with firm conviction with the principles and tenets of the Modern Movement, as they were then expressed by the Milanese school that had taken form around Giuseppe Pagano, but he also enhanced his research with his own personal interests and his own particular sensibility" (F. Helg).

6. The Museum of the Treasure of San Lorenzo in Genoa (1952-56) – together with the refurbishing of the municipal galleries of Palazzo Bianco and the restoration of Palazzo Rosso in Genoa (1952-62) – represents one of the most significant achievements of Albini in the field of museum design. The project by Franco Albini for the Treasure Museum, commissioned by Caterina Marcenaro (director of the Department of Galleries and Fine Arts of the municipal government of Genoa), involved a "fixed" installation (without foreseen extensions or flexibility) to display selected pieces from the collection of the cathedral of San Lorenzo (from the Early Middle Ages to the 13th century). In a space created for the purpose in the basement of the Arcivescovado (archbishop's palace), Albini completed his experience in the field of "religious" architecture: a lone episode, comprising the repetition of cells in the circular layout covered by radial concrete vaults, an evocative and austere image for a definitive, eternal arrangement created for viewing.

"It should be noted that in all of his museum design experience, Albini never expressed an opinion on the work to be displayed, but concentrated only on the best way of doing it: at the beginning of my work with him at the time of the exhibition of Italian Decorative Art in Stockholm, I remember one of the paradoxes he often used to express himself succinctly: "there are no ugly objects, you just have to display them properly."
This was not an agnostic position, but his totally engaged way of understanding his own role, his own professionalism: it was not his habit to gaze in ecstasy at a piece, to take a critical stance; it was his habit (his "craft") to make his technical knowledge available, all of his ability to understand a problem and to solve it" (F. Helg).

7. F. Albini, "Quattro opere di un architetto emiliano: Asilo ad Aiola in Emilia, Agenzia di Automobili a Reggio Emilia, Ricovero per Vecchi a Montecchio, Seminario Vescovile a Reggio Emilia di Enea Manfredini," in *Casabella-Continuità* no. 206, 1955.

8. G. Samonà, "Franco Albini e la cultura architettonica in Italia", in *Zodiac* no. 3, 1958.

9. "Though with greater fluency and experience, in the new works the architect has not gotten beyond that almost programmatic rigidity that in the earlier works accompanied the functional rigor of each part of the building, both in the coherent arrangement of the spaces in relation to each other, and in the technical accuracy of the construction. A more fluid naturalness grants the simplicity of the new works a singular emotional enrichment, a fullness of their interpretation and assimilation, which makes them feel intimate to us, like the things that are most familiar. The Pirovano hostel in Cervinia, the housing construction in the Mangiagalli complex [...], the homes of the INA Casa area at Cesate, and of the INA-INCIS development at Milano Vialba, the building for the employees of the Società del Grès at Colognola; and for certain aspects related to their function, the office building of INA in Parma and the one for the technical and legal departments of the City of Genoa, a work of extraordinary volumetric coherence, all express this flat, serene and almost free simplicity, which is even more emotional the more it is able to reach that balanced organization of structure, function and form with which every excess of external uniqueness – from which Albini fled almost as if it were a crime - is neutralized or attenuated. Alongside these works, as if to bring out their human commitment and didactic value, stand the exceptional ones, the works that exist on an artistic level among the highest ever achieved in Italy in this postwar period. But the refurbishing of the municipal galleries of Palazzo Bianco in Genoa, and even more so, in that same city, the Museum of the Treasure of San Lorenzo, are works that are too well-known and admired, and repeatedly put into focus by perceptive criticism in its judgments of value, for us to return to them here, repeating penetrating critical interpretations that have already been formulated in an exhaustive manner. For us it will suffice to point out that their exceptional status sheds light on the continuity of the work of this great Italian architect of today, because it makes the values even more operative and concrete, showing us that Albini possesses extraordinary lyrical abilities, but ones that are expressed in exceptional poetry only in the rare themes that justify an exceptional abandon to pure imagination" (G. Samonà).

10. "In Albini, the feeling for horizontal and vertical frameworks means designing pure rhythms in incisive depth, in order to insert planar figures there at the right point, in keeping with a given purpose; and at the same time, it is a voluntary renunciation of the principles, though general in nature, that exist outside the internal reasoning. Therefore he overlooks the sense of the continuous, abstract surface, the complacency of the interlock and the juxtaposed forms in themselves, like thematic vibrations sliding on the plane to construct it in a material without thickness, without weight. Instead, his space is profoundly alive, because the various depths are logical givens of the theme; they become eloquent with the richness of the multiple perspective dimensions, but they conserve the composure of modular reasoning. The lines that run vertically and horizontally across the space are the parameters of this shaped depth, the very lively indications of a limit that corresponds to necessities rigorously controlled to construct volumetric extensions from specific functions. There are rarely diaphragms that separate the space into distinct zones without transparency, due to a poetic need to coordinate the extensions and to multiply their encounters.

Generally these diaphragms are rectangular extensions spreading horizontally or vertically and floating in the space, suspended from a thread-like weave, in keeping with a reasoned tension of the parts where signifying and functional values are most concentrated. Nevertheless, a grid of other linear structures is overlaid on them, attenuating any excess of violence and destroying the expressionistic effects of the dynamism the artist clearly abhors. An almost craftsmanlike desire strives to construct the form of every part of the space in the simplest way, in its various articulations and structures, in the interlocks, in the framework of suspensions and supports" (G. Samonà).

11. F. Tentori, "Opere recenti dello studio Albini-Helg," in *Zodiac* no. 14, 1965.

12. "I will therefore provide a clearly problematic, conversational, polemical type of answer, weighed down perhaps by all the baggage of someone who in these years has had to move forward with a certain action of cultural policy, though without the aid and encouragement of systematic visions of a dogmatic nature. [...] I disagree, in fact, with Samonà when for the postwar period of Albini he states: 'in his new furnishings that critical tension that made them a very effective tool of history has fallen by the wayside.' I believe the misunderstanding stems from the fact that the 'temporary' installations – of the exhibition on Antique Jewelry at the 6th Milan Triennale (1936) and of the exhibition on Scipione in Brera (1941) – can now be judged only on the basis of drawings and photographs: all documents that logically separate those installations from the situation of the temporary function, making us perceive them only as fragments of stylistic virtuosity" (F. Tentori).

13. "Thus it happens to rediscover the value of certain works, even recent ones, from a distance, and always through indirect documents. Browsing through a magazine, the gauze and threads and display cases of the exhibition in Stockholm (1953), of the exhibition "Venezia Viva" (1954), the red space of the hall of the 10th Milan Triennale (1954), and all the other installations return to take on a symbolic value that links them more closely to the main works: to Palazzo Bianco, Palazzo Rosso, the Museum of the Treasure of San Lorenzo. Overturning Samonà's conclusion, we might say that the 'extraordinary lyrical abilities' of this artist express themselves *not* 'only in the rare themes that justify an exceptional abandon to pure imagination'" (F. Tentori).

14. "Still in pursuit of the definition of this expressive center [...] I can add that certain famous 'installation pieces' by Albini have reminded me of Odradek, the disquieting character in Kafka (*The Cares of a Family Man*, 1919): 'No one, of course, would occupy himself with such studies if there were not a creature called Odradek. At first glance, it looks like a flat star-shaped spool of thread, and indeed it does seem to have thread wound upon it ... But it is not only a spool, for a small wooden crossbar sticks out of the middle of the star, and another small rod is joined to that at a right angle ... the whole thing can stand upright as if on two legs ... the whole think looks senseless enough, but in its own way perfectly finished ... and laughs; but it is only the kind of laughter that has no lungs behind it.' In Albini's exhibit designs, we find the same intricacy, the same clearly perceptible constitution in which the most natural materials take on a new, disturbing appearance: which may seem 'senseless enough' but is 'in its own way perfectly finished'" (F. Tentori).

15. M. Fagiolo, "L'astrattismo magico di Albini. Strutture del linguaggio dalle prime mostre alla Rinascente," in *Ottagono* no. 37, 1975. The same issue of the magazine also contained an essay on Albini by Aurelio Cortesi, "Lo studio Albini & Helg e la questione della tecnologia negli anni '60," which attempts to contextualize the activity of Franco Albini and Franca Helg in a perspective of "utilization of technique as a material that sets the orientation of a process in which technique is totally internal to a cultural context implicitly defined by the experience-new reality relationship; a new reality that experience and technique direct towards a phenomenal representation that takes on form and fulfillment in the new architectural image."

16. G.C. Argan, *Ignazio Gardella,* Ed. Comunità, Milano 1959. Gardella won the first edition of the Olivetti Prize for architecture and urban planning in 1959.

17. "The man who constitutes his own fate with his own hands: that *artifex* lives in Albini in its most ancient and authentic forms. Albini was above all a great craftsman: later he became an architect and 'designer' in the sense of those terms as we use them today: even his ongoing, severe technical updating was strictly at the service of an object, a work of architecture, a piece of furniture, and did not contain the seed of serial production" (C. De Seta, "Franco Albini architetto, fra razionalismo e tecnologia," in *Franco Albini 1930-1970*, exhibition catalogue, Centro Di, Firenze 1979).

18. "Albini's achievement in the building for La Rinascente, constructed at Piazza Fiume facing the Aurelian Walls, thus conveys the dual interest of a conversation resumed after a gap of centuries [...]. It should first be said that the graft was done with great ability, and we would not have called upon the precedent of the Lombard master builders to whom the visage of Rome owes so much, were it not for the fact that the new building reveals sensitive care for the setting, a hesitance to intervene at the margins of such a rich, characteristic urban context, which somehow suggests that immediate Roman adaptation that was once the prerogative of those who arrived in the city after having dreamt of it at length [...]. At the end of the 1500s and in the golden age of the Baroque, the Lombard architects were at home in Rome. In the circles of builders they had gained a very solid position, and together with the contractors, the stonecutters, the plasterers, they constituted a sort of city in the city" (P. Portoghesi, "La Rinascente in piazza Fiume a Roma," in *L'Architettura. Cronache e storia* no. 75, 1962).

19. This was the master plan for Habana del Este in Cuba, developed starting in 1955 in collaboration with Enea Manfredini. Albini's experiences in urban planning began in the mid-1940s with the Milano Verde project and the master plan of Milan in 1945, known as the AR plan (Architetti Riuniti, i.e. the Italian CIAM group, F. Albini, BBPR, P. Bottoni, E. Cerutti, I. Gardella, G. Mucchi, G. Palanti, M. Pucci, A. Putelli). That same year, he also took first place in the competition for the master plan of the Angeli district in Genoa (1946-47, with I. Gardella, G. Palanti and M. Tevarotto). "Just after World War II the master plan of Reggio Emilia (with Enea Manfredini, Luisa Castiglioni and Giancarlo De Carlo) was the first opportunity to develop a suitable method of complete and complex investigation that could support decisions that were no longer simply spatial in character. Immediately after that came the experience of the detail plans for Genoa, a relationship of work and often of collaboration with old friends, also in contact with Genoa-based architects (Eugenio Fuselli, Mario Zappa), and with functionaries and administrators of the city government. I believe these experiences marked a turning point in Albini's professional career" (F. Helg).

20. In the postwar period the activity of the studio expanded its range to an international scale: some furniture for MoMA New York (1948), and the design of many exhibitions in Paris, Berlin, London (all in 1952), Stockholm (1953), and Sao Paulo in Brazil (1954).

21. The project for Villa Olivetti in Ivrea was in 1956.

22. The design experience at the end of the 1960s and the early 1970s mainly involved the Terme Zoja at Salsomaggiore Terme (1963-70) and the third office building for SNAM at San Donato Milanese (1970-72).

The commission for the design of a new hot springs facility assigned to Studio Albini dates back to 1963: the initiative that began more than a year earlier with a competition that led to no results called for the construction of a new spa facility combined with a convention center, a library and an auditorium. The first proposals by Studio Albini-Helg, though developed for a different area than the one eventually utilized, reflected a typological analysis that set out to generate a highly innovative, unprecedented result.

The episode of the "Luigi Zoja" complex came in a moment of sweeping transformation of the concept and use of hot springs facilities, shifting from an elite context for the wealthy to a "social" service for purposes of healthcare open to all classes, leading to the need for new functional features and hospitality solutions.

The definitive project was completed towards the end of 1966: the layout in three portions, besides solving the problem of variations in the number of visitors, permitting use of the facility in proportion to seasonal requirements, also made it possible to construct and deploy the building in three distinct phases (from the summer of 1968 to the spring of 1970), rationalizing worksite timing.

In 1969 the studio of Albini-Helg-Piva was commissioned to design the third office building of SNAM, a company of the ENI group that supplied, transported and distributed methane gas in Italy, whose headquarters since its founding in 1941 was located in an area of the township of San Donato Milanese. The first "*palazzo uffici*" by the architects Nizzoli and Olivieri had launched a sort of "cycle" of constructions designed by outstanding professionals on the architecture scene. From the outside, the characteristic feature of the building is the fairing in self-extinguishing polyester resin reinforced with fiberglass, in a red color, that tops each level throughout the horizontal extension, and contains the physical plant systems. The various successive phases of redesign of these fairings confirm the technical-rational intent of Albini's design process; in the latter period of his production, he paid increasingly close attention to technological construction solutions.

23. The solution of the roof of the multifunctional hall of Terme Zoja (illustrated in *Domus* no. 513, 1972) consists of external terracing organized so as to create stands for spectators of outdoor events. In practice, instead of the functional role for which it was initially designed, the solution took on a sculptural connotation of connection with the surrounding landscape.

24. "The dining hall is defined by the perception of the serration of the roof, which is seen from the inside of the offices themselves, rather than from the canonical vantage points of the office building."

25. The Veliero bookcase with tensile structure was designed in 1938 and produced by Poggi for Albini's own apartment: only one specimen exists, left by Albini to Poggi himself. The Fiorenza armchair, still in production, comes from the design of the armchairs for the living area of Albini's home (1940). The famous Luisa chair, whose prototype dates back to 1949, was put into production in 1955. The glass radio cabinet is from 1938.

26. The new municipal offices of Genoa were completed in 1962 (Targa In/Arch in 1965).

27. Villa Zambelli in Forlì dates back to 1956.

28. Franca Helg writes: "In 1950 I began my collaboration with him, first as an 'external' consultant (the first version of the Museum of the Treasure of San Lorenzo in Genoa was done in my small studio) and then 'in-house' starting in 1952, working full time and with a widening range of responsibilities."

In 1953 the name of the studio was changed to Albini & Helg. Many critics have interpreted the presence of Franca Helg as a very important turning point in Albini's production, especially regarding his position with respect to technology, which from a strict focus on craftsmanship evolved into research on innovation in construction.

From 1962 the studio also relied on the collaboration of Antonio Piva, and from 1965 of Marco Albini, leading in 1975 to the name "Studio di architettura Franco Albini, Franca Helg, Antonio Piva, Marco Albini."

29. The INA-Casa complex at Cesate (Milan, 1951-54, with G. Albricci, L. Belgiojoso, I. Gardella, E. Peressutti, E.N. Rogers): Albini designed the single-family houses on two levels, an example of his innovative morphological approach. The duplex units are organized in rows based on the grouping of modules with L-shaped plans derived from a rounded and rotated square part.

30. Franco Albini began his academic career in 1949-50 as a lecturer on Interior Architecture, Furnishings and Decoration at the Istituto Universitario di Architettura in Venice (IUAV). In 1952 he obtained qualification to teach Architectural Composition and Interior Architecture. He gained a tenured professorship in 1954, teaching for one year at the Turin Polytechnic, 1955-56, then in 1962-63 at the IUAV and in 1963-64 in the department of Architecture of the Politecnico di Milano, as chair of the department of Architectural Composition.

From 1952 to 1956, with Ignazio Gardella, he directed the international summer school of

CIAM at the IUAV. Regarding the teaching experience and contribution of Franco Albini see: M. Baffa Rivolta, "Significato della didattica di Albini," in *Franco Albini 1930-1970,* exhibition catalogue, Centro Di, Firenze 1979, and F. Drugman, "Franco Albini: memoria e ragione," in the anthology *10 maestri dell'architettura italiana,* ed. M. Montuori, Electa, Milano 1994.

31. The encounter between Roberto Poggi and Franco Albini came in 1948-49 at the time of the production of the furnishings for the Pirovano hostel, and marked the start of a collaboration that continued until Albini's death and then continued with Franca Helg, Marco Albini, Antonio Piva. The first experiments were conducted on the famous Luisa chair, and most of the objects designed by Albini are still in production.

32. In 1950, a few months after the Pirovano hostel, where the context in its physical-environmental and technological-productive values constitutes one of the keys of interpretation of the project, Albini again approached a theme in which environmental insertion was of particular importance, and creating one of the most famous buildings of the Italian postwar era in this architectural episode.

The building of the Istituto Nazionale Assicurazioni in Parma, constructed from 1951 to 1954, was inserted on the corner of one of the oldest lots of the urban fabric, left vacant by bombing during the war. Albini's building is a volume of five stories "set" on a load-bearing system of large fair-face reinforced concrete portals, held by a regular grid of pillars and slabs that with the alternation of the openings rhythmically paces the enclosure of exposed brick.

33. The commission assigned to Studio Albini-Helg in 1957 by La Rinascente to design a headquarters in Rome on Piazza Fiume, a space featuring vivid historical landmarks, led to the completion of one of the most often published and studied buildings in the history of Italian modern architecture.

The episode is laden with meaning not just for the innovative results achieved by the designers, but also due to the fact that it represents the first time the Milan-based studio had worked in the capital, a territory which in the 1950s was dominated precisely by the ranks of opposition to Milanese architectural culture.

The studio developed an initial project, assessed by De Seta as "one of the finest works of architecture designed in Italy towards the end of the 1950s," but this version was not implemented due to changes in the requirements of the client.

In the Rinascente facility completed in 1961, we can see what was to become one of the most immediate and legible features of Albini's subsequent work: "that composition based on stacked trabeations, almost a memory of the architectural orders captured in their initial matrix" (A. Cortesi), which inserts itself in the theme of the spatial grid which is fundamental for Lombard Rationalism (from Terragni to Persico, BBPR and Gardella).

Lodovico Barbiano di Belgiojoso

Pluralist Architecture.
BBPR

Architecture, material and immaterial art.
The example of the Torre Velasca
On the one hand, architecture is an almost immaterial, only mental discipline; on the other, it has a strong relationship with matter, with the constructive act. Through the use of memory and poetry, I have often mentally traced back through the history of architecture myself, to consider – also in an ironically provocative way – the effective value of making what I have produced in thought. In one of my poems published in 1992[1] I reached the point of underlining the idea that the effort of construction would be worthwhile perhaps only for the Parthenon. A literary suggestion, ironic and aimed at simplifying and downplaying certain themes of architecture that have always been of great importance and complexity.

A poetic image, in any case, which after two or three years I still consider valid in its contents and essence: for me, expressing such a concept through a tool like poetry, which has its own techniques and its own inspirations means reinforcing the ideal axis that connects two complementary arts. Formulas and tools of extreme simplicity, which often conceal contents and values of absolute meaning.

At times, certain arts can represent and express values and thoughts arriving from other disciplines. With this, I do not want to state that so-called "art" is but one single thing: but there is no doubt that its practice implies a way of thinking about reality that can be shared, in fact, by *literature,* by *music,* and indeed by *architecture.* A clear separation can never exist between the arts: they constitute different ways of expressing the same concept.

Let's take the case of the Torre Velasca, for example, for which I think I can say that the result – going back to the question posed in my poem – has fully justified and compensated for the efforts that went into its making: I think it was truly worth the trouble to make the Torre Velasca[2].

In this architectural episode the discourse, also in terms of construction – and not just of the project, then – was very complex: the design, in fact, was developed over a span of eight years[3]. The importance of the location of the architectural object is a priority: the architecture can be seen as the outcome of many components and influences, some from within, some from the outside. In the case of the Torre Velasca the intervention was on a site in which the existing lot – between Via Velasca, Via Pantano and Corso di Porta Romana – had been destroyed by bombing, with the inevitable difficulties of coming to terms with a surrounding context of forceful historical character and meaning.

Given the fact that for this area the AR plan and the plan of 1953 provided mainly indications of a quantitative nature – cubic meters permitted to be built – there were two alternative paths open to us: the first was to "reconstruct" the buildings existing prior to the war, not so much in terms of style as of size and planimetric arrangement "in courtyards," therefore not altering the volumetric and morphological-typological characteristics of the area; the second was to make an ulterior effort, to try to concentrate the volume in a single body, taking the hypothesis of a "vertical" extension of the building into consideration.

Obviously we opted for the second hypothesis, which in our opinion could be more interesting and above all more stimulating from the viewpoint of architectural research: moreover, the previous organization of the area was rather ineffective, composed of small houses placed on the site in a rather random way, with the exception of those facing Via Velasca and Corso di Porta Romana.

The solution utilized was the result of intense, fertile dialogue with the municipal authorities: a sort of compromise was reached between our volumetric and typological choice – clearly more profitable in economic terms, because unlike the previous situation it made it possible to have windows on all four sides, eliminating the presence of blank walls and thus increasing the usable area – and the quantitative limitations specified by the existing planning: the building was made as a tower, taking advantage of a potential for development that as I recall was set at a level of just 10% less than the existing one[4].

This sacrifice of volume, was accepted in any case with the aim of being able to achieve our "vertical idea": an *idea* which from that moment on took concrete form in the choice of the architectural object itself, i.e. becoming *architecture.*

In agreement with Samaritani, who at the time was the general director of the Società Immobiliare in Rome, the owner of the area that commissioned the project, we also defined the functional characteristics of the building, the so-called "usage functions": one part had to be for offices, another part for residences, while a third portion had to have characteristics of mixed function, including offices with connected lodgings, a situation much in demand at the time[5].

The response to these needs led to the stacking of three distinct, recognizable elements: further design explorations, especially in terms of the plan, revealed the practical necessity and linguistic aim of widening the upper part of the building. The residential function, in fact, called for a larger area, to which the presence of the famous loggias had to be added, an element we felt was very interesting to have in the upper part of the building. It seems that over time these loggias have been closed, which is a true insult to their very purpose.

So the Torre Velasca was born, and so it evolved.

Function and volume

The architectural message was thought out and formulated in such a way as to have significant and clear relations with the Lombard tradition, and that of Milan in particular, but without resorting to stylistic or historical references. Quite the opposite: the volume, form and language embody real functional needs expressed by the client and materially translated by the designers in keeping with a design process marked by successive simplifications and interpretations. The needs led to the creation of two planimetric schemes of different sizes, with the result of an overlay of two different volumes, a factor that undoubtedly constitutes the main characteristics of the artifact: offices below and apartments above as basic logic, also in terms of the market, suggested. Hence the volumetric appearance of the tower: *function* and *volume,* closely connected to each other.

The work is therefore the result of studies conducted one after the other, each closely linked to its predecessor. Initially a project was developed whose structure, as is known, was conceived in iron; this was subsequently transformed into reinforced concrete because reasons of an economic order suggested this change of direction. The use of concrete, besides being advantageous in economic terms, also implied fewer issues regarding expansion and elasticity of the material. This combination of motives justified the modification during the course of the design[6].

Composition and technology

The architectural episode of the Torre Velasca was also useful to us in order to interpret – in an appropriate way, in my view – the problem of the relationship between the *compositional* and *technological* spheres in architecture.

As a group, when we approached any design theme or experience, the involvement of the technological aspect was simultaneously to that of the architectural research: for the Torre Velasca project, from the outset we worked closely and in dialogue with people having technical roles within Società Generale Immobiliare; in particular, I remember the engineer Danusso[7] who did the structural calculations, and at the time was a teacher at the Politecnico di Milano, holding the chair in Science of Constructions. He was a man of great depth with whom I was already acquainted because I had taken his course. Professor Danusso did his job in a truly exemplary manner, fully carrying out his role as structural engineer, but always attempting to adapt it and to make it coincide with our requests of a more formal nature.

Technology is and should be, in my view, the science that grants architecture *substance* and *support,* providing the tools for its technical implementation; at the same time, the essence of architecture is to be the inspiration that gives form to those tools. The tools are not only material in character – beams, pillars, slabs – but also methodological, ruled by a clear constructive rationale.

In the project for the Torre Velasca we were able to experience these concepts in parallel, making *theory* and *practice* interpenetrate to perfection. During the construction[8], when the underground part of the building had been completed, the work had to be interrupted due to problems connected with financing. This apparently negative episode actually allowed us to make a complete pilastrade below ground level – placed horizontally, because it was not possible to do it vertically – which enabled us to exhaustively study the design and dimensioning of that tapered pilaster that is one of the features of the building's expressive language. The particular form and the characteristic tapering of the pilaster are obviously based on reasons of a static nature, though always observed and judged from an architectural standpoint, in terms of the form we were trying to achieve. *Technology* is therefore at the service of *form,* without any contradiction between the two terms: in the design, it is necessary to make technology never constitute an absolute fact, an end in itself, a process that gives rise to forms that are likely to be schematic in most cases, never architectural.

Likewise, and reversing the terms of the equation, the research on architectural language has to respect technology, since it could never exist without it.

To design: a *global* activity

I think the approach certain designers have to the world of architecture, focusing exclusively on partial factors such as those of a technical or economic nature, and then putting them together as if in a "final copy," is a mistake. All the parameters of architecture have to be born at the same time, because in design there is no rule, no constant and repeatable formula that can offer the solution to various situations. It often happens that there is an idea of form as a starting point, which is why the problem lies in finding a way to make it achievable through choices of a technical character. In other cases the precise opposite occurs: a form is given to an initial technical requirement, one that is convincing in that given contextual situation.

Architecture allows for different modes of expression and different zones of movement: I would say, in any case, that apart from certain particular architecture competitions where the need to express an idea also leaves room for moments of free intuition and "inspiration" to liberate the form through studies of an almost exclusively aesthetic-formal character, architecture should always be conceived as a concrete entity to be realized: a true *global* activity.

As happens in most cases, to design always means thinking about the implementation of what is being envisioned, giving substance to the simultaneity of the *theoretical factor* and the *practical factor.*

Approaching various design themes, at least on a theoretical level, the BBPR group did not have internal divisions, specific tasks or roles linked to one or another of its members: design was a global, all-encompassing activity. We might say that Rogers was the one who had the most independent formal intuitions, while Banfi, Peressutti and I were more closely linked to the need to develop matters of a more technical character and to transform them into architectural forms. There were no conflicts: it was a succession of reciprocal assistance in a productive complementary relationship of aptitudes and abilities. Furthermore, though in different ways and forms, we were all engaged on different fronts, divided between *school* and *studio;* in particular, in the field of teaching, *theory,* and in the more strictly professional sphere, *practice.* Rather than talking about a relationship between two separate spheres, I would speak of a coexistence of two areas that inevitably have to move forward together, and for us – also from an ethical standpoint – represented the verification of each other.

School and profession

I think it is a mistake to assign priority to one sphere or the other: inside BBPR, for reasons that were also a bit coincidental, perhaps, I was the one who spent more time on worksites. This was also because Peressutti and Rogers were often busy abroad, where they had been invited to teach and where they sometimes remained for months at a time: Rogers was frequently in the United States, in Argentina, London, etc.; Peressutti began in London and ended up teaching in America[9].

On the other hand, I gave up the opportunity to teach abroad: in 1955 I was asked to teach a course in the United States, but it was precisely in the period of construction of the Torre Velasca, so I did not accept the offer.

For a certain period I was teaching in Venice, together with Franco Albini: those were the years in which Giuseppe Samonà invited to Venice personalities like Albini, Ignazio Gardella, Bruno Zevi for history, yours truly and the Venetian architect Carlo Scarpa[10]. I have fond memories of Franco Albini: he was a truly exceptional man, with a great ability to invent things. His inventions involved both interiors and exteriors: I think some of his interior designs are the result of brilliant intuitions.

I also remember that Albini was a very tough teacher, very strict with his students: he had a unique kind of rigidity that did not exist, for example, in other personalities like Gardella, who was more of an improviser, if you will, less tied to a method to be followed at all costs. Albini was bound to a sort of self-discipline, of great rigor, the same rigor that can be seen in his works of architecture: his teaching was therefore very meticulous and rigid, and he held himself to that same rigidity, in his life and with respect to the things he did.

Albini, like many others of that generation, was a person engaged on an equal level in *teaching* and in *professional practice*[11].

BBPR always existed in these two worlds, which for us were not only similar but also absolutely complementary: in effect, in teaching you had to accentuate the critical aspect regarding what you were doing, and this aspect automatically translated into a sort of positive self-critique of the design practice that was unfolding at the time.

Today the situation has substantially changed: in universities, as in other institutions, we are seeing the presence of different professors who *teach* without *designing* or at least without *building:* at the same time, there are many architects who work and practice architecture without teaching it, without transmitting knowledge that at times could be of great didactic interest.

For the generation of architects to which I belong, this double activity has been very important: I think it could be decisive to ensure that part of the ranks of teachers be more deeply involved with the problems of *real* design and not just what we might call the *academic* aspects.

Of course it would be unthinkable, and wrong, to oblige or force a situation that for many reasons has changed over time.

In any case, I think the main error that has led to today's disorientation is that of the enormous number of students now enrolled in Italian architecture schools, also in the light of the related factor of the percentage who take a degree, which is remarkably low. I think young people could easily find work in the field of building in other roles: it is not necessary for everyone to have an architecture degree and a professional practice, especially if they do not have a true faith in the discipline. I therefore think that in *making* architecture there is also an ethical factor: *to make* architecture means *being* an architect.

In the years to come much will have to be done in order to have a smaller number of students in architecture schools, and at the same time a smaller number of graduates in this subject.

When the partners of BBPR took their degrees there were eight of us, all together: the next year there were twelve, then fifteen. Soon after that, the number rose to forty, then fifty: after 1968, a trend towards bigger numbers has led to unstoppable crowding and a situation that is hard to keep under control.

Magazines and architecture

Besides teaching, we were all also involved in directing or contributing to a number of architecture magazines[12].

It is important to emphasize, furthermore, that a profound difference can be seen between the magazines of my era and those of the present. The architectural production of the time, and the quantity of professionals involved, were numerically much smaller, and the job of the magazines was to identify and publish the works that deserved such attention: today the approach is less rigorous on a critical level, and as a result the publications tend to chase after fashions and trends.

I do not think that today's architectural production, as it can be seen through direct experience or through sector publications – obviously taking into account the numbers and the evolution of the world of design in general – is better or worse than it was several decades ago: of course today we are looking at a more industrialized kind of production, a factor due to the more general evolution of economics.

To offer some example of those who more than others – among those who logically come to mind – can be said to have continued the discourse taken forward by us as BBPR or by other architects of the generation of postwar Italy, I can mention the Turin-based architects Gabetti & Isola, though it should be said that they are somewhat linked to the dictates of *postmodernism*, to use this term in a way that is not widespread today. They have never been completely faithful to the rationalist teachings as we understood them back then, and it is precisely in this matter that we can observe their coherent progress over the years.

Among the personalities who spent time and grew up in the editorial staff of *Casabella* when the magazine was directed by Ernesto Rogers[13], I can mention Aldo Rossi: an intelligent man, though I do not totally agree with his choices, and I have never been fully convinced by his architecture, because it is perhaps too tied to a certain type of neo-classicism; nevertheless, in his operation I can recognize a great capacity for control. Another architect I recall with pleasure is Guido Canella: an erudite and at the same time capable personality.

The studio: structure and responsibilities

In the 1950s the BBPR studio operated with no more than four or five people on hand: generally there was one more experienced architect and a younger one, flanked by three or four geometers. Two of them are still here working for our studio: at the time it was normal for everyone to wear a white smock, a lab coat that is still worn in our studio today. I remember that they were also worn in Franco Albini's studio.

To describe a typical day at BBPR, where the design operation is concerned, it should be said that we often had meetings, right in this room, around the table where we are now: these meetings generally focused on questions of a general character. Subsequently, also for reasons of a practical nature – and thus not just of aptitude – or stemming from specific knowledge of the client or of the theme to be addressed, one member of the group would take greater responsibility than the others for the development of a particular aspect or a particular project.

The objective was always group interaction. We had established a sort of rule – I don't want to call it a "religion," but it was almost a "credo" – which in any case was an important, particularly heartfelt agreement: no one of us would ever say "*I* did this, this is *my* project, *my* idea." Instead we would always use the plural: "*We* did this, it is *our* project, *our* idea." This turned out to be a very important factor, stimulating that need for ongoing discussion that became the characteristic that more than all others set BBPR apart from other architects, especially in those days: the continuing and active verification of the group also had to do with the simplest projects, which involved the contributions of all.

A sort of *in-house* review of projects, as we were used to doing with the students in our work as teachers: a little university inside the studio.

When I spoke of divisions of tasks based on motives also of a practical nature, I was referring to factors that emerged spontaneously, most of the time. For example: Ernesto was from Trieste. This meant that the projects connected to the Trieste area – like the one at Borgo San Sergio[14] and the organization of the coastline, though the latter was never implemented[15] – were carried out mostly by him: for specifically practical reasons. This did not mean, however, that the rest of us were completely excluded from the work. So it often happened that Peressutti or I would sometimes go to Trieste, to better understand the context, or to solve certain problems of a purely technical nature.

Travel, for us in the group, was a relatively normal factor, apart from the commitments of teaching: for example, in the period of the Torre Velasca, accompanied by an engineer of the Società Immobiliare, the client for the project, I went to Brazil to observe the performance of reinforced concrete structures. In those years the tall buildings and skyscrapers in the United States were made in steel: given our desire, as I said, to change the construction technology by passing from metal to concrete – I think it was Rogers who was the first to have this intuition – I went to Brazil, a country that was in the avant-garde at the moment in the area of tall buildings made with reinforced concrete.

There were examples of high quality, to visit and to study: in particular, a number of works by Oscar Niemeyer, whom I also had the pleasure of meeting; we planned to do a project together, though afterwards the idea fell through[16].

The trip was a great opportunity to visit various architecture firms, and to directly observe how reinforced concrete was designed and built: a study tour organized to learn about technologies that were still in the early phases in our country, while in other apparently poorer nations they were instead fully established. After the return from Brazil, together with Professor Danusso we developed the structural design.

A posteriori, having to assess the activity and the production of many years of practice, I can certainly state that the Torre Velasca, also on the level of personal gratification, is the episode I recall with greatest affection, without any regrets in terms of either the concept or the execution. The client – a very important factor in architecture – was farsighted, permitting us to fully express our intentions in various situations: first of all by choosing the tower solution, for a matter of prestige, and thus encouraging and stimulating our architectural research.

On the topic of the client and its importance, I remember that Rogers liked to say that the relationship between the client and the architect is the same one that exists between father and mother: the client is the father, the architect the mother. The latter, inspired by the father, carries the fruit of that relationship in her womb, and then gives birth to the object born of that relation.

In our case, the *architectural project*.

Milan, 13 December 1994 – Studio BBPR

Notes

1. The poem – published in its entirety at the start of this book – is dated January 1989 and comes from the anthology L.B. Belgiojoso, *Come niente fosse,* Milano 1992.

2. The Torre Velasca, a skyscraper for offices, apartments, shops and an underground garage designed for RICE – Ricostruzione Comparti Edilizi S.p.a. – in an area destroyed by bombing in the center of Milan, is still the most famous and often studied project completed by the group formed by Gianluigi Banfi (1910-1945), Lodovico Barbiano Belgiojoso (1909-2004), Enrico Peressutti (1908-1976) and Ernesto Nathan Rogers (1909-1969). Designed in the first half of the 1950s, Torre Velasca becomes the high point of the process of reassessment of the rationalist language launched by BBPR from the start of their partnership, which began even before they took their degrees in architecture at the Politecnico di Milano in 1932. The activity of the group over a span of nearly half a century ranged through various design sectors (furnishings, installations, competitions, renovations, residential buildings, urban planning, product design) and areas of theory, with intense participation in the critical debate and constant contributions in terms of teaching, all on an international scale.

3. The first architectural hypotheses for the Torre Velasca date back to 1950-51: though the project took on definitive form in the time span from 1952 to 1955, the preliminary studies already envisioned the future construction to a great extent.

4. The new solution reduced the volume by 12% – bringing it to 126,000 cubic meters for the entire complex – granting the municipality 1650 square meters, free of charge, for use as a parking facility: with this compromise, the authorities granted permission for the unusual height of 87.5 meters above ground.

Thanks to these agreements, the designers were able to immediately put aside the municipal project with a continuous wall and internal courtyard, in order to investigate the idea of vertical development, in a deliberate refusal to carry out an operation of "mending" of the bombed urban fabric.

After some very short preliminary investigations on the theme of the skyscraper, examining the various typologies, both established (slab and T arrangements) and alternative (the first studies include solutions with oblique facades), the group chose the direction of a compact volume instead of one based on slabs, accentuating the character of separation from the surroundings and from the past, which was already implicit in the choice of a vertical volume, giving rise to the characteristic "mushroom" shape of the building. The tower, in fact, is configured as the composition of a vertical block on which to place a horizontal volume with a constant overhang of about three meters, in keeping with a scheme that overturns the classic arrangement of the skyscraper that tapers towards the top.

5. The building has 29 levels, reaching a total height of 99 meters with the technical gear. Of the 29 floors, two are underground and contain technological systems and a parking facility; the ground and first floors are for commercial activities; nine (2nd to 10th) are for offices; seven (11th to 17th) for studios with apartments; one (the 18th, separating the base of the tower from the upper portion) for mixed use; eight (19th to 25th) are for apartments of different sizes. At every level the layout develops around a central core containing the vertical access systems.

6. The solution calling for a metal structure and many of the facings in glass, developed in collaboration with a specialized firm in the United States, was discarded because it implied a cost 25% higher with respect to the use of reinforced concrete.

The change of the material, of course, implied greater bulk in terms of dimensioning of the load-bearing structure, a series of perimeter pylons with a variable section, and a central core to contain staircases and elevators; all this was organized by a hierarchy of elements that emphasizes the pilasters, left visible as opposed to the horizontal beams that are concealed by cladding in prefabricated parts. The vertical ribs contribute to the continuity between the two volumes that make up the building: sloping in the void and splitting to support the overhang, they resolve the most delicate moment (and thus the most thorough studied, with the aid of models of all types and sizes, all the way to actual size) of the architectural organism, i.e. that of the attachment between the lower block and the overhanging volume.

7. Società Generale Immobiliare of Rome – with which BBPR had already worked from the early postwar period on projects of urban and real estate reconstruction – besides acting as the client and owner of the area, took direct part in the design and construction of the Torre Velasca: the technical division of the company handled the definitive design of the structures formulated by the engineer Arturo Danusso, the physical plant systems and the technical-economic management of the entire operation.

8. Sogene was the contractor that built the Torre Velasca, also providing all the technological data on the project. The worksite began in February 1956 and required about two years.

9. Ernesto N. Rogers had an intense university teaching career and conducted lectures, seminars and debates in Italy and abroad, especially in North and South America: Tucuman in Argentina, Lima in Peru, Santiago in Chile, Chicago, London, Harvard, Berkeley. From 1952 to 1959 he was co-director of the CIAM summer school. At the School of Architecture in Milan, where he taught until the year of his death, and held the chair in Stylistic Characteristics (1952 to 1962) and later in Elements of Composition, where he became a full professor in 1964. Enrico Peressutti, in 1950-52, taught at the Architectural Association School in London, and later at MIT in Boston (1952), Princeton University (1953-59), Yale University (1957 and 1962) and in 1968 at the University of Illinois. He held seminars and lectures at the University Institute of Architecture in Venice, in Europe and in the United States.

10. Franco Albini was a tenured professor at the Istituto Universitario di Architettura (IUAV) in Venice from 1955 to 1964, about the same years in which Lodovico Belgiojoso was teaching at the same school (1954 to 1963). Both were then invited to Milan as full professors in Architectural Competition.

11. Besides the relationships that developed in the academic context, BBPR had professional relations with Franco Albini during the development of the AR Plan for Milan in 1945, the project for the administrative center of Milan in 1946, and the construction of the INA-Casa complex at Cesate (Milan) in 1951.

12. From the start of their careers the members of BBPR were active in the field of publishing, working with many magazines including *Quadrante, Casabella, Domus, Rassegna d'architettura, L'albergo in Italia*, and *L'Ambrosiano*. From the first postwar years, Belgiojoso, Peressutti and Rogers resumed their activity as critics: together they directed the book series "Architetti del Movimento Moderno" from 1947 to 1950; Peressutti worked in the editorial staff of *Metron*; Rogers, after two years at the helm of *Domus* (1946-47), directed *Casabella* from December 1953 to January 1965, introducing the programmatic term "Continuità" in its name.

13. Also with reference to other contributions that form this publication, we feel it is useful to indicate the main episodes – without delving into the matter of the different "editorial philosophies" connected with cultural directions and influences – of the history of the architecture magazine still published today under the name of *Casabella*, because the magazine has been a particularly important means of transmission of the ideas of many of the protagonists of Italian modern architecture, and of these *Dialogues*. The publication of the magazine *La Casa Bella* began in 1928. The editor for the first two years (1928-30) was G. Marangoni, followed by A. Bonfiglioli (1930-32). Starting in 1933, the year in which Giuseppe Pagano became the editor, joined by Edoardo Persico as writer, editor-in-chief and then co-editor (until 1936), the magazine was called *Casabella*. In 1938 Pagano changed the name to *Casabella-Costruzioni* and in 1940 it became *Costruzioni-Casabella*. In December 1943, after Pagano had been deported, publication was interrupted by order of the Ministero della Cultura Popolare. This suspension lasted two years (1944-45), but after an attempt to resume publication in 1946, with just three issues under the direction of Franco Albini and Giancarlo Palanti, the magazine again vanished for seven years. The rebirth came in December 1953, with the release of the first issue of

Casabella-Continuità, first every two months and then as a monthly, directed by Ernesto N. Rogers. Rogers remained as editor for over ten years, until January 1964 (from issue no. 199 to no. 294/95). In the period between Rogers and Vittorio Gregotti (director from 1982), the sequence of editors was: Gian Antonio Bernasconi (1965-70), Alessandro Mendini (1970-76), Bruno Alfieri (1976) and Tomás Maldonado (1977-81).

14. This was a low-cost housing complex for employees in the industrial zone of EPIT, a project commissioned to Rogers in 1955, in which the studio BBPR was hired for the urban planning and coordination of the architectural design of the Romita Act and INA-Casa developments, and later for the design of the civic center and church.

15. The project that was never implemented of the Landscape Plan for the western waterfront of Trieste was prepared in collaboration with L. Semerani and P. Cosulich by order of the Chamber of Commerce, Industry and Agriculture of Trieste in 1957.

16. In 1936-44 Brazil went through a moment of decisive transformation in terms of architectural culture, a process triggered by the presence and influence of a great master of the Modern Movement: Le Corbusier. The first important work by Oscar Niemeyer (born in 1907) was the Ministry of Education and Health Care in Rio de Janeiro, built from 1936 to 1943 thanks to the collaboration of a group of South American architects, with the consulting of Le Corbusier.

The teachings of the European mentor regarding design method, plastic expressive impact and utilization of local productive resources led to a fundamental breakthrough in the training of young Brazilian architects, which was to contribute to make Brazilian architecture better known abroad, thanks to its characteristics of autonomy following World War II.

At the moment of Belgiojoso's journey in Brazil, Niemeyer had already done constructions that experimented with the potential of reinforced concrete in various locations in the country, and in the course of a few years he was to work, with the other protagonist of Brazilian architecture Lucio Costa, on the colossal undertaking of Brasilia, built in the late 1950s and early 1960s. Observing some of the achievements of Niemeyer in the 1940s, it is not hard to identify compositional features and formal solutions, especially in the treatment of vertical structural members in reinforced concrete, that the Milanese group would later reinterpret in the Torre Velasca.

Ignazio Gardella

Choral architecture

The project: analysis and synthesis
I have always split my activity as an architect between professional practice, through intense design activity, and the parallel pursuit of university teaching: this has given me a chance to come directly to terms with both theoretical and practical aspects, the latter closely linked to the material implementation of the architectural object.

In this regard, I think it is interesting to develop certain reflections on my way of designing and approaching practice in the wider sense of the term. I think that an architectural project, pertaining to a specific topic, can never be considered unique and immovable: I don't believe that in the face of a given theme and a given project to address it, there can exist an optimal project, hidden in a corner, to discover through a series of cognitive investigations, very lengthy ones perhaps. Investigations that are useful and necessary, but do not solve the overall problem of the design. I believe the project does not exist *a priori*. I do not think that in the moment in which one approaches a design experience related to a particular sphere, that there can exist a complete example, or a project to which to make reference, from which to take inspiration: instead, a project exists that can be constructed as it develops.

Consistent with the method I use in my university teaching, I believe it is best to always start from an initial, still generic, not all-encompassing idea: generic in the sense that it does not have to arise as an exclusively abstract idea, but has to be based on a background of technical and architectural information derived from the cultural base each of us possesses, which grows with the progress of years of practice. An initial idea, then, of the complete project: not totally defined, but in any case already thought through in all its aspects, of circulation, form and structure. Thus it is possible to work on this idea, developing it and then transforming it, at times reaching solutions that are completely different, distant from that initial idea. This happens particularly in the early years of professional practice, or when one is still in school, moments in which one does not yet have the technical-cultural background sufficiently vast to immediately find the path of the solution that will be developed.

To have an initial idea, however immature, also serves as a "crutch," as a first object on which to make variations, to already have a reference to something concrete from the start. In this way, you have the opportunity to avoid the risk of continuing in the vain pursuit of the optimal without knowing to what it can be compared.

Also where cognitive research to conduct in greater depth is concerned, having already indicated an initial idea helps you to understand in advance – avoiding the danger of not pursuing them – which studies are indispensable and should not be postponed, as opposed to all those that do not pertain to the specific aims of the project. A sort of case of "choices in progress", useful and quite precise. For example – to make the discourse border on the elementary – if in the preparation of a master plan one initially makes the decision to demolish certain buildings, it is logically useless to program a precise survey of those buildings themselves.

The design work takes the form of a continuous approach through a symbiosis of "analysis" and "synthesis" to the *truth,* constituted in our case by the project to be achieved. After many years of professional practice, having gained by now an established level of experience, I believe more and more that the right path to be taken is that of always and in any case working on an idea, without waiting in vain for an improbable and at best occasional "illumination": now, on the basis of this gained experience, it is spontaneous for me to summarize many variables almost immediately, which is why an initial idea can turn out to be not so distant from the final one.

Designing to "understand further"

I have always had a very intimate relationship with the project, one that is not limited to a rough idea, but either due to my innate curiosity or to the cultural background provided by training also in engineering has always pushed me towards both theoretical and very detailed graphic scales of the work.

I have always developed my projects all the way to the study of the details: above all in the early years, when I was personally involved in the complete preparation of the project – drawings, detail studies, development of particular construction aspects – I have always attempted to "understand further," analyzing the project in a complete way.

An analysis of the particular that should never lose sight of the global, the overall objective of the project: an investigation of the particular that is never an end in itself, but always pertains to a mental program of work connected to the initial idea. These in-depth studies also have to do with the *genius loci,* as well as the area of physical plant systems. Or the thoughts turn to the mason who will have to carry out the idea, on a daily basis: all the elements of architecture are called into play in the study of the detail, as an integral part. The *particular* is and has to be a *particular:* a part, that is, of the whole. The detail is not something that can be added, but something that has to be thought of as being part of the total construction.

Undoubtedly the relationship between drawing and work has changed over the years. When I began working, in 1930[1], technology (as might be logically surmised) was not particularly advanced, which was why the project, also for construction, supplied for the tender, was simple, because it was lacking in many features that were then incorporated in a subsequent phase, during the construction, also taking into account the factors associated with the "moods" of the worksite.

Today, instead, since technology has advanced greatly in the meantime, the drawings and graphic materials are in any case much more detailed: there is a demand for greater depth of information. Technical-executive drawing and architectural drawing compensate for each other, becoming reciprocal keys of interpretation. I believe this is why two types of drawings exist: one that can be an end in itself, which however cannot be considered an architectural drawing; and one that in my view should be pursued and utilized, namely the true "architectural drawing" that serves to transmit the orders for the construction. A tool, then, that is capable of supplying all the information for those who make the construction.

In the first years of teaching at the Department of Architecture I often came across students – it was frequent at the time – who came from art high schools, students who due to their educational background already had advanced drawing skills, but more connected with a practice of *beaux arts* – what we used to call a "*smaffera,*" a drawing made with charcoal and the fingers – rather than an appropriate form of technical-architectural representation. I remember repeating that in my view a good architect does not have to know how to draw. At the School of Architecture in Venice there was Mario De Luigi, who taught Life Drawing in those years, and one day he came to me in a friendly way and said: "listen, stop telling that to the students, otherwise they arrive in my class and they don't value the discipline; they say there is no reason to make an effort, because Gardella says there is no need to learn how to draw." In the light of the way the discipline has evolved, this episode now seems rather extreme and ironically paradoxical.

Getting back to the types of drawing and their necessary "overlapping," we are now designing an addition to Bocconi University in Milan[2], where alongside the structural problem – a theme that has always existed – the problem of physical plant becomes important, with the design and positioning of the climate control systems. This is a very complicated issue that has a deep impact on design practice, and above all on design choices.

Nevertheless, I believe that the gap and separation between the drawn project and the construction is not as big as some people say: the drawn project has to already contain all the responses to design questions, which is why during the construction the choices to be made will always be of a marginal, not substantial nature. Of course choices like the color of the brick, the stucco or the window frames can be made – and usually that is the case – on the worksite; but I believe the general idea has to already be there, as a whole, in the project.

Getting past the myth of Technique

Where my thinking on the relationship between architecture and technique is concerned, one aspect should be emphasize: I am part of a family of architects, because my father, grandfather and great-grandfather were architects, and today both my son and my grandson are architects too, for a total of six generation. I began investigating architecture when I was a boy, copying from books by Vignola, Canina, and the classical treatises. My grandfather guided me step by step as I remade the drawings of the masters, and of my father, who had a great passion for the discipline, would take me to visit monuments and buildings, not just in Milan but also in Verona, Vicenza and Rome.

Due to these family-related reasons, and because the cultural thinking in circulation in the period in which I enrolled – the year was 1924 – was quite distant from the modernist vision of architecture that had already stimulated the enthusiasm of people like me, it came naturally to reject the type of schooling that was available at the time: a school that more closely resembled an academy than a Department of Architecture as we would envision it today. This aspect led me to focus, in new architecture, not only on the functional element but also and above all on the technical side: due to this series of circumstances, I entered the Department of Engineering of the Politecnico di Milano[3]. Only later – it was a rather complicated story – did I also enroll in the Department of Architecture, where at first I did only two years, because I got into conflict with some of the professors – back then I was already part of the group of Milanese architects who had embraced the cause of the Modern Movement – after which I went to Venice, where I took a degree and began teaching[4].

So I completed two degrees, at least from a more "formal" than substantial standpoint, because we might say that the "real" degree in architecture I earned at home, in the period in which as a boy my grandfather revealed to me the mysteries of the main sacred texts of architecture.

Thinking now about my situation and the academic path I took in the early years of my training, I can say that I am very pleased to have completed both courses of study, which implied a cultural interpenetration I think is positive.

This in spite of some of my engineer friends who never miss a chance to ironically remind me that I am "also an engineer," using a sympathetically jesting tone regarding the category of the architects.

Having this dual educational background, and especially the degree in engineering, has been useful – besides the obvious factor of specific knowledge of the discipline – in order to get past the "myth of technique," a myth that has had a great influence over many architects of the Modern Movement. In the period in which this myth held sway, above all in terms of a cultural logic certain architects continue to sustain, I think there was a remarkable expenditure of energy and time: time that was "lost" and will have to be recovered as soon as possible in the architectural debate.

From the postwar era to the present, except for the period of the 1950s and a good part of the 1960s, we can say that Technology and Architectural Composition took two different paths that have rarely intersected.

I am an architect born and raised in the Modern Movement, particularly that of Milan, marked by figures like Albini, Rogers, Palanti, Figini & Pollini, who coexisted with architects like Terragni and Cattaneo; although in effect the Modern Movement was fundamentally the pursuit of a new language that could in any case justify the terms *functionality* or *technology*. It was no coincidence that slogans were in vogue such as: "the function determines the form," or "everything that is useful is beautiful." Concepts I have always tried to turn on their heads or at least to adapt: just as it is wrong to insist in an extreme way that function determines form, so it is equally wrong to say that form determines function. Were I to have to paraphrase a slogan, I would rather say, "everything that is beautiful is useful": the category of beauty, in fact, contains that of utility. Plato is quite convincing on this score, in some of his dialogues on beauty.

This interpretation of the phenomenon is obviously only partial: I believe that some of the disciplines approached in a school of engineering, such as mathematics, which digs deeper to know the mysteries of logic or of infinitesimal analysis – and is thus a teaching of a philosophical order – are also extremely useful for architects.

In short, I believe the existing relationship between technique – and therefore technology – and architecture is one of absolute integration. It is hard to find an architect today who contains the figure of the structural engineer inside himself, and is thus capable of doing structural calculations and those regarding technological systems.

The project for the Bocconi University I am developing in this period, for example, is a work of a certain importance and complexity, and where the structures are concerned I am working with Eng. Amman, for the technological systems, and Eng. Morini, professionals who fill out the frame of expertise around the figure of the architect[5].

Choral architecture

I would underline that in my judgment – a totally personal one – the figure of the civil engineer, especially today that we are living in an epoch of great specialization, has no reason to exist. There should be just two figures, with specific responsibilities and roles: the architect and the calculation engineer, joined by the engineer specialized in physical plant systems. The possibility, however, of having a sort of common language, as Weber urged, is a very important factor.

Though it often happens in common practice, I do not believe one can set off on a design adventure by thinking, as do many, about making a project and then filling it out and completing it with structures and physical plant. Certain "old" engineers, of bygone days – still with a pioneering mentality – interpret the profession in this way: they leave complete freedom of expression to the architect and then intervene in a subsequent phase, convinced that they can solve any type of technical-structural issue. This approach is certainly a mistake, and not in touch with the times.

It is a mistake in two ways: first, because it is not realistically possible to think about having a sort of magic wand that solves all problems in one fell swoop, without compromises; second, because technique, in its most general sense – structures, physical plant, components – influences architecture, in the positive interpretation of the term.

I rarely think about technology as an essential factor in my design work, a factor without which the meaning of my architecture would vanish. It seems quite clear that technology can and should round out the project and its intrinsic choices; if instead it is seen as a starting point of the entire design phenomenon, it becomes a type of approach that is not mine, which I think is too limiting. Though I have never had the opportunity to design works or structures – like a stadium or a bridge – where the technical-technological contribution must be expressed at its highest levels, since it is predominant, it has never happened in the field where I most often operate, that of both private and public civil constructions, that I have thought about a *technological form* from which to begin to make the architecture.

In the project, you have to take into account the specificities and particularities of the design experience in progress, to avoid that uniformity and "depersonalization" that tend to be caused by the increasingly sophisticated technology and ever less romantic logic that lie behind design operations.

Technology should not provoke architecture, on a par with a mass medium, a homogenization of languages, making information and therefore solutions more uniform.

There are other factors that contribute to a meaningful architectural result: one decisive design aspect to which I always pay particular attention, for example, is undoubtedly light: its potentialities are fundamental for my architecture. As in classical architecture certain choices were made for greater enhancement of the requirements of light – just consider the fact that most of the moldings of facades and their constituent elements were developed precisely in terms of careful consideration of the element "light" – so in my architecture the focus on light has always been very strong.

Between *history* and *criticism*. The relationship with the other protagonists

Having had the good fortune of being able to cross the architecture of the entire century, it has been possible for me to know and spend time with exponents of the architectural world with remarkable cultural personalities, hailing from different generations. I have also been lucky to work with many accomplished colleagues to whom I have given much, and from whom I have received a great deal on a personal level. Even before taking my degree in engineering I was a close friend of personalities like Franco Albini and Giovanni Romano: a group of friends that mainly gravitated around the figure of Edoardo Persico, who at the time was the binding element. It was thanks to him that one year we were able, all together, to give form to a section of the Milan Triennale[6].

In the context of my friendship with certain colleagues who have left an important message in the architectural debate in Italy and the world, Franco Albini is undoubtedly the personality of whom I cherish the most vivid, profound memories[7]. I recall him very fondly because our bond was like that between two brothers, even if our ideas on specific themes and our works of architecture were partially different.

Albini, among the people I spent time with, was the architect that more than the others fostered a close, constant relationship with technology, or more precisely with *technological research*. For him, technological input was very important, although in the end Albini was an artist: what interested him most was the problem of language. Besides Albini, my most heartfelt memories are of Ernesto Rogers and the friendship after the war with Lodovico Belgiojoso.

To have had the opportunity to spend time and above all to work together with figures of this stature was a great privilege for me, because from each of them – though we all had personal ideas that at times were also forcefully in contrast – I was able to intercept profound messages on a theoretical plane and on that of actual design practice. I believe we had a very solid, constructive relationship: back then there were only a few of us, which led to greater complicity in our field; furthermore, we lived surrounded by a climate of widespread hostility arriving not only from Fascism but also from representatives of the civil society, who were not willing to accept the architecture of the Modern Movement, or accepted it only in a very partial and reductive way, i.e. for limited themes such as bathrooms, kitchens and other very precise problematic areas. All this stimulated and favored the creation among us of a true, deep friendship, a relationship that was not limited to superficial interaction, but took the form of continual, stimulating gatherings and discussions. We tended to meet for lunch once a week, an excellent opportunity to discuss architecture: we debated things, even hotly, but always in a productive way, oriented in a certain direction.

We were a small group, so we were very united and compact, and above all very active on the level of interpersonal relations: I believe that today this type of relationship on a personal-professional level no longer exists, and unfortunately this absence has its effects, above all on a cultural level and one of peer-to-peer exchanges of views on architecture. An absence that can be attributed, on the one hand, to the exorbitant number of architects that has now entered the market, and on the other by a more widespread lack of interest in dialogue and debate.

Design and the spread of information

Debate, seen as dialogue, is now relegated only to the magazines, though in my view they constitute an altered form of debate itself, distorted by the form and contents presented in the critical analysis of projects. Just consider the limited dimensions and lack of "real" information through which projects are illustrated and presented to the specialized audience by the magazines in circulation on the market today.

I am more convinced than ever that an architecture magazine has the duty to publish things in a less superficial way, providing more information than what is made available today: the magazines should publish fewer projects – in a more selective way – and above all should cover them on a more legible scale. Today's projects are presented like postage stamps from which it is physically impossible to glean the meaning and to appreciate the content.

I believe that architectural criticism, especially that aimed at the sector magazines, has the power to strongly influence architectural thinking, and through the illustration of design results it can set trends inside the architectural debate: prior to the war, besides the much sought-after foreign architectural reviews which for our generation represented a coveted reference point, in particular *Casabella-Costruzioni* stood out – the second part of the name was added by Pagano when he took the reins at *Casabella* – as a very valid magazine, interpreted by the most perceptive observers as a true manual[8]. The magazines were the only places, together with the Triennale, where we could show our projects: the only moments, in the end, in which the Modern Movement could fully express itself and spread its thinking[9].

Antidogmatism and order in architecture

Among the architect-friends I spent time with, Franco Albini was undoubtedly the most Calvinist; Rogers, and all told the entire BBPR group, were instead less rigid and perhaps less orthodox. I too, from the outset, think I was quite free of overly rigid schemes: from my first steps, taken in relation to the Modern Movement, I understood that I wanted to remain free of obligations to preset canons.

When, for example, I did the Dispensario in Alessandria[10], Giulio Carlo Argan emphasized more than once that in his view the building was simultaneously heretical and very new in the scene of modern architecture, particularly due to the use of brick in a lattice format[11], a feature with which I experimented not as an attempt to recoup a certain type of rural tradition, but as a construction technique I thought was ideal for that specific place[12].

I have always been rather distrustful of dogmas, an opposition to them that is still part of my character today, at the age of 90. Those same canons of the Modern Movement, but also the more recent ones of the Post-Modern, do not belong to my way of interpreting the profession and, as a result, of interpreting architecture. I always try to be myself, without having at all costs to seek on all occasions a ranking that is often forced or does not reflect the reality of things, and is often useless.

Precisely in reference to the difficulty of sticking to specific schemes and currents, I have always had my doubts about the attempt made by critics – an effort useful to understand the architectural phenomenon but dangerous when it is superficial and simplistic – to find labels for my architecture, and for the architecture of others. In the exhibition held in Venice in 1980[13] I was inserted in the group of the Post-Modern architects. From a certain standpoint I might share in this interpretation of events, because my architecture has always attempted to transmit the rejection of a precise dogma: this is why I can be considered a forerunner of certain movements that emerged later. Nevertheless, in my rejection of dogma I do not automatically accept the fact that everything is possible: my rejection of dogmas, in any case, conceals the desire to insist on an order possessed by architecture, which in my view represents its highest value. The five orders, after all, can be transformed into a sort of metaphor of *order in architecture.*

I love music, an art I think is closely linked to our world. Were I to have to say what music I believe or at least hope is comparable to my architecture, I would choose the music of Antonio Vivaldi, a music with its own precise order, but without rigid dogmas. Paul Valéry in *Eupalines* draws a close relationship between architecture and music, revealing their similarities and differences, a relationship that has always fascinated me and convinced me. Effectively, as in all correspondences, there exists a natural difference between the two arts, though it is a difference that is not as pronounced as it might seem. Music too, like architecture, needs the *fourth dimension* represented by time. Listening to music means listening to a series of sounds, or tones, of rests, which together constitute a musical composition. The same thing happens in architecture: I do not believe it is possible to see a work only through the photograph of a facade. A work of architecture, to be truly seen, perceived and understood, must also be absorbed, walking around it, entering inside it, moving through its spaces, using them. It is a perception, then, that happens through the dimension of time. The time variable is an integral part of a work of architecture, as of a musical score: a shared component that is perhaps less apparent in the viewing of a painting.

Therefore it is not by chance that I may draw with greater emphasis and engagement if I am working with a musical backdrop. While I draw I find it fascinating to listen to a symphony by Vivaldi, which besides giving me great enjoyment also helps me in my concentration, in the composition. This is how I strive, in my projects, to reach that purity and clarity that exist in the sound of the *Four Seasons* and in all of Vivaldi's music. A purity of language without sedimentation, without compromises.

Architecture as a choral phenomenon

Like music, the art of poetry also goes through moments of great creative tension that are strictly comparable to certain phases of the design process.

I have recently read the book of poems *Come se niente fosse* by my friend Lodovico Belgiojoso, which was also the source of the poem at the start of this volume, and I must admit that although I have known Lodovico for ages, I was surprised: I knew him as an architect, not as a poet. Fortunately his poetry is crossed by a thin vein of irony, when it raises doubts about the necessity of transforming ideas into matter: I say fortunately because otherwise we architects might as well do something else. Ironic brilliance, then, that conceals a very clear bond and attunement of intentions between poetry and architecture. Relationships of similarity exist that perhaps are incorrectly overlooked: today's architecture, which is not necessarily that of temples or cathedrals, is increasingly a matter of a *choral effort*.

A cultural sphere that differs from other forms of artistic expression that achieve concrete results through autonomous working methods. A *writer* sits down at a desk and writes his poem or his novel, in a direct relationship between himself and the work; an *architect* cannot build a house on his own. Today an architect needs a choral effort of various contributions, ranging from the engineer to the mason, just as in the Middle Ages constructions were choral undertakings, though with different figures involved.

Ignazio Gardella

This is why I believe a process of integration has to exist in design and then in construction; this type of collaboration has to be established from the beginning of the evolution of the design, working with the help of a team of experts in other neighboring disciplines. In the light of these phenomena, today the architect has a role of orchestration: effectively, precisely due to this factor, having a background that also includes the study of engineering permits an overall perspective on problems, of greater breadth and greater depth.

The architecture of differences

Architecture, to live and to survive, has to rely on a very large number of contacts with other disciplines or institutions, while at the same time it needs to establish a close, meaningful relationship with the context in which it is inserted.

From the outset, from the beginning of my career as an architect – a job that permits you to come to terms with reality, to stay in touch with reality – I have believed that the relationship with the site and, as a result, with its history – with what we commonly define as the *genius loci* – is of fundamental importance. I have never thought that a building could be transported to a location different from the one for which it was designed. I believe – and a few decades ago this concept was not taken for granted as it is today – that the relationship between place, history and project is a very close, inseparable one.

Another type of bond with the site exists, namely the relationship the designer and the project establish with a multitude of specific factors of the context: people, materials, users, administrators, local production in the general sense of the term. This type of contact, to achieve optimal results, has to be very close. I have had the good fortune to work in many different contexts, coming to grips with different customs, different ways of using both intellectual and material resources. An architect has to be able to adapt to *differences* because they are what gives architecture its force.

Architecture and place must therefore become two elements in the project that are part of a single cultural discourse, but also and above all a technical discourse. You cannot think of designing without knowing and considering the products that come from the context, and the way of approaching the design problem in that place.

I have a very close relationship with Venice, for example: I have made weekly visits to that city for over 25 years. Before designing the Casa alle Zattere, I roamed the city far and wide, not to visit the monuments or other specific episodes, but to try to fully absorb that *Venetian flavor*, a very particular atmosphere. I remember that building in Venice with great clarity, because it brought me a lot of criticism[14]. That was the only work for which I received letters of praise, but also true insults, mostly from the Venetians themselves: I remember one such missive because it was full of abuse, and therefore it was hard to forget.

My architecture tends to change in relation to places and situations. When I built the Terme di Ischia[15] for example, I came to terms with the local methods and customs. They have a very particular habit, there: also for therapeutic purposes, they make vaults using volcanic stone, features that are very characteristic in that place. At the same time, the locals also do a sort of dance, a true ritual, wearing typical local costumes, to ensure the solidity of the structure of the vaults themselves. I mention this episode to emphasize, with an extreme example, how architecture often exists in symbiosis with the essence of a place, also in its most spontaneous and natural forms.

Architecture as unique experience

Every project is different from what came before it: every approach to design, for me, is a new and in some ways unique experience. It would be hard for me to desire *a posteriori* not to have made one of my works: it is almost unnatural for an architect to renounce or reject one of his own creations. On the other hand, were I to have to choose one constructed building to save above all others, one to which I have a particularly strong bond, I think the Dispensario Antitubercolare in Alessandria, though it was one of my first works, represents a truly important step along my personal path of growth.

If I had to choose one project that was never built, I would say that the Teatro di Vicenza represents my dream that did not come true. A dream I was never able to build: a project widely published, widely discussed, but which only reached the phase of the contract bidding, and then collapsed due to a political crisis in that municipality[16]. This shows how external factors absolutely beyond the will and work of the designer can constitute an imposing presence that has an impact on architecture, shaping it or at times even disrupting and spoiling it.

Being an architect today: study and worksite

Usually my studio has a relative small staff, though their numbers can rise in moments of upcoming deadlines.

So it is an "elastic" studio in terms of management, suited in my view to the type of work an architect has to do today in Italy. Being an architect in a country like ours has become very difficult, because you never have certainties on which to base a correct organization of resources. Projects drag on for years in a latent state, hampered by very slow processes and procedures: this means that for certain projects the architect lives in a constant state of impending alarm, and for entire periods the work makes no substantial progress. Then the news suddenly arrives of a very close deadline that forces you, as I was saying, to gear up in order to respond to such "urgency." Furthermore, the continuous overlapping of different regulations, arriving from different spheres – municipality, fire brigades, and so on – means that the project has to be assessed by many different entities, causing long delays in the process of implementation. We are at a point in which the progressive increase in the "effort of interpretation" of regulations runs the risk of having a negative effect on the formal results of the artifact. Designing is important, but defending yourself from attacks from the outside is equally important.

I have always spent lots of time in the studio, though to describe a typical day, my professional work begins even before I physically reach the studio, because with the accumulation of experiences and the increased background of design practice, you reach the point of being able to reconstruct a plan or an elevation on a purely mental level. I have always had the tendency not to get up too early in the morning, though when I went to Venice to teach I had to take a train at 6.30; much of the thinking and reasoning on projects was developed – though it might seem paradoxical – in the morning when I was still in bed. When you are looking at a drawing you concentrate on that specific piece of paper; but if I do not have a drawing in front of me, I still have the construction in my mind, and for me it has always been easier to work on it when I am away from the graphic conventions that can at times influence certain choices. This means not seeing just the plan, or just the cross-section, but being able to think about the whole, simultaneously, without physical limits.

In any case, I have spent much of my time in the studio: I preferred not to arrive to early in the morning, but I would stay there later in the evening, even quite late, to draw with that concentration you can only have in the evening-night period. I have always tried to safeguard – except in cases of true necessity – Sundays and holidays against the "attacks" this profession "without regular hours" automatically implies; I have always attempted to take my mind off work problems for an entire day, perhaps by doing something else – for example, I liked to ski and to play tennis – and this was very useful to help me find new stimuli in the following week.

I have always loved spending time on worksites, as well: I believe worksite visits are a very useful tool for an understanding of most of the phenomena that can then be analyzed in the studio.

Teaching and testing yourself

In my view, there is a very close bond between professional practice – in the noble sense of the term – and teaching, an area where I hope and think I have transferred meaningful cultural and design experiences, derived from knowledge gained in the field[17]. At the same time, the school has given me a lot: in our sector, and in the academic world in particular, giving and taking exist on a par. The contact with young people and above all the shared necessity to precisely clarify the project phases and some of their particular issues – processes that when they are individually carried out in your own studio never reach the same level of stimuli – make the research on the project arrive at very high levels. The fact of having to critically justify the various phases, to make them explicit for the students, is decisive for clarification of our own ideas: a sort of self-testing that in the school, thanks to the school, becomes punctual and fertile, because you live in a situation of ongoing discussion.

Being architects, being ourselves: a thought for young people

Given my family origins, and seen in a wider scenario, my experience has been relatively unusual, which is why today it is not easy for me to understand the true origin of *being an architect.* Since I was born into a family that had always lived inside the myth of architecture – my great-grandfather Jacopo was a rather well-known architect in Genoa in the first half of the 1800s, who worked with figures like Barabino – my personal observatory might be very subjective. Architects are not born: but one can be born with the possibility of *becoming an architect.*

Architecture demands a high level of effort, of application to the specificities of the discipline. I requires tenacity and a desire to understand phenomena, implying constant curiosity and constant updating.

Being an architect means having your own way of seeing and managing space; and making an effort, in this context, to be coherent in what you do. Being coherent does not mean repeating yourself; it means changing, being in tune with the different space-time situations that arise case by case and are never identical. If a river does not flow, it runs the risk of becoming a swamp: a risk certainly not run by those who are always ready – without discarding their principles – to change their projects in relation to different situations. Aldo Rossi, if we look for examples in the present panorama of architectural culture, is one of those rivers that do not run the risk of getting "stagnant." In fact, though I do not fully agree with his works of architecture, I have the awareness that he is a true architect. Aldo Rossi truly senses architecture: this impression of mine was confirmed when I worked with him[18]. Paolo Portoghesi, to mention another protagonist of these *Dialogues*, is an architect of great intelligence and theoretical brilliance, and I admire various works of his, especially the early ones like Casa Baldi. Portoghesi has also had an undeniable influence in the break with a certain type of conformism intrinsic to the International Style, and a certain type of imitation of the Modern Movement.

Were I to give some advice to a young architecture student or a recent graduate, first of all I would tell them they should be themselves: a phrase that might seem rhetorical and banal, but in my view can be very useful and profound, if interpreted in the right way. I believe that in all of us, and above all in young people, there is a certain tendency to accept certain forms, a phenomenon that may be related to a kind of intellectual laziness and adaptation that leads young people to acritically rely on a certain way of designing.

To have reference points is legitimate and indispensable: reference points of both a linguistic and a methodological nature, of emulation of an architect one admires. But there should always be characteristics of critical analysis and objectivity of judgment. If, instead, the reference is only and exclusive strategic, called upon in order to obtain a shortcut, to reach the preparation of a "design" more rapidly, then the approach is incorrect and also very dangerous. Architecture is not a tendency, it is the expression of the self, in all senses.

Milan, 28 February 1995 – Studio Gardella

Note

The text Choral Architecture *was prepared by the editors of the book after a long, intense conversation with the architect Ignazio Gardella in his studio in Milan.*

1. Ignazio Gardella, born in Milan in 1905 to a family from Genoa, began his career in his father's studio after taking a degree in engineering in 1930. In the early years he developed many projects, including the work that brought him renown in the world of contemporary architectural culture: the Dispensario of Alessandria (1933-38).

2. Gardella's project for the expansion of Università Commerciale "Luigi Bocconi" in Milan began in the early 1990s (in collaboration with his son Jacopo). The project calls for a building with parallel wings developed around two semi-courtyards, connected to another volume with an elliptical plan, again organized around a small internal courtyard.

3. It is interesting to note that in the interviews, and in Gardella's writings, but also in the many biographies, there is often an accent on this aspect of his training, namely his "engineering" background, as if to constantly bear witness, in his personality, to an attitude that encourages interpenetration and interaction between the *professional-architect* and the *professional-engineer*.

4. Three years after the degree in Engineering at the Politecnico di Milano, Gardella enrolled in the School of Architecture at the same institute, though he did not complete his studies there. He took a degree in Architecture at the IUAV University of Venice in 1949, the year that was also the start of his teaching career. Nevertheless, his training as an architect, apart from the influence of his family, had already begun in the years in which he not only studied Engineering, but also spent time with friends at the Polytechnic such as Franco Albini, Lodovico Belgiojoso, Ernesto Rogers and Giovanni Romano, who were also students at the time. Together with this core group of young architects, just after World War II Gardella founded the Movimento Studi Architettura (MSA), oriented towards a critical reassessment and activist interpretation of the message of the Modern Movement.

5. Amman Progetti, for the technological systems, and the engineer Franco Morini for structural consulting, had already worked with Gardella on the definitive project for the Teatro di Vicenza, in 1979-80.

6. This was the display design of the Mostra dell'Abitazione, which was assigned the Diploma of Honor at the 6th Milan Triennale in 1936.

7. Many works were done in collaboration with Franco Albini: plans on an urban scale such as the project "Milano Verde" for the organization of the Sempione/Fiera rail yard in Milan (with R. Camus, G. Mazzoleni, G. Pagano, G. Palanti; 1938); the scheme of the Piano Regolatore A.R. of Milan (with BBPR, P. Bottoni, E. Cerutti, G. Mucchi, G. Palanti, M. Pucci, A. Putelli; 1945); the project for a residential district and detailed Master Plan for the Angeli zone in Genoa (with G. Palanti and M. Tevarotto; 1946); competition projects such as those for the "Palazzo della Civiltà Italiana" (with G. Palanti, G. Romano; 1937) and the "Palazzo dell'acqua e della luce" (with G. Minoletti, G. Palanti, G. Romano; 1939), both for E42 in Rome; the low-cost housing projects like the IACP "Mangiagalli" complex in Milan (1950-52) and the urban and housing plan for an INA Casa complex for 6000 inhabitants (with A. Albricci and BBPR: 1951-53); studies for the industrial production of construction parts for Società Ansaldo of Genoa (1944-45). With Samonà, Albini and Rogers, Ignazio Gardella directed the CIAM summer school from 1952 to 1956 in Venice; with the group BBPR he also designed the Italian Pavilion at the Brussels Expo (1957-58).

8. In Gardella's case, the connection with the sphere of architectural culture was also based on relationships with figures on the editorial staff of *Casabella* in the 1930s, such as Giuseppe Pagano, Edoardo Persico and Raffaello Giolli. In that period, for *Casabella*, Pagano and Persico were respectively the director from 1933 to 1943 and the contributor, editor-in-chief and co-director from 1933 to 1936. In 1938 Pagano changed the title to *Casabella Costruzioni* and in 1940 to *Costruzioni Casabella*.

9. From his early career Gardella was involved – especially in the first decade – with the milieu of the Milan Triennale: in 1936 he received two gold medals at the 6th Triennale for the display design of the "Mostra dell'Abitazione," with Albini, Camus, Clausetti, Mazzoleni, Minoletti, Mucchi, Palanti and Romano: in 1940 he took part in the 7th Triennale with the installation of the "Mostra del Vetro e della Ceramica." Later he also participated in the 8th edition, in 1946, with the installation of the "Mostra della Prefabbricazione," and in the 9th Triennale, in 1951, with the design of the "Mostra della Sedia Italiana nei Secoli."

10. The first project (in collaboration with Eng. L. Martini) for the Dispensario Antitubercolare of Alessandria was in 1933; the definitive design dates back to 1936-37. The building was completed in 1938. The project was published that same year in no. 128 of *Casabella-Costruzioni*, with an article by Raffaello Giolli. The building, a compact block on two levels in reinforced concrete, was the focus of extensive debate due to the presence of an external partition wall in exposed brick, an intentional contrast with the clear rationalist lines of the construction.

11. Giulio Carlo Argan published a monographic volume on Gardella's work in 1959, at the time of the assignment of the Premio Olivetti – first edition – to the Milanese architect.

12. This statement is confirmed by the words of Gardella: "Of course when applied to the compositional context of the Dispensario the grille no longer had anything of the rural character in which it was originally applied, and that was fine with me. The material had been selected in terms of the natural concrete and technological availability offered by the place: at the same time, its shift into a different design context interrupted any imitative reference to a naive use in a vernacular tone. In a certain sense it was dematerialized, from the viewpoint of its original content, but it offered a different continuity with technical history, based on what was suggested by the site" (I. Gardella, "Materiale e immateriale," in *Materia* no. 5, 1990).

13. This was the international architecture exhibition titled "La presenza del passato" organized in the context of the Venice Biennale in 1980: the central core including 76 architects was introduced by a section of "tributes" that included, besides Ignazio Gardella, Philip Johnson and Mario Ridolfi, "as recognition of the importance of their work in the perspective of a creative recovery of historical heritage, and the disavowal of the constraining orthodoxy of the International Style" (P. Portoghesi, *Postmodern. L'architettura nella società post-industriale,* Electa, Milano 1982, p. 29).

14. The Cicogna apartment building, known as "Casa alle Zattere" in Venice (1953-58), together with two other works by Gardella, the workers' housing of Borsalino in Alessandria (1950-52) and the Mensa Olivetti at Ivrea (1954-58), represents a milestone of the path of critical reassessment of the international Modern Movement. The house facing the Canale della Giudecca was designed in 1953, but was not built until 1958 due to the long procedures required for the approval of the authorities, which imposed significant modifications, above all for the facade on the canal. This work inserted Gardella in the debate – that began precisely in those years – on the theme of existing contextual features: the architect's position was dictated by the desire to establish a dialogue with the historical context, drawing compositional stimuli from it, while at the same time rejecting any form of imitation of the historical fabric, declaring total independence of the language utilized.

15. Terme Regina Isabella, Lacco Ameno d'Ischia (NA), 1950-54, with E. Balsari Berrone. The hot springs facility – initially a renovation, and then a new project – was part of a wider-ranging program of interventions designed by Gardella but never implemented, commissioned by a group of Milanese physicians. Of the existing 19th-century building, Gardella conserved only the colonnade of the main facade, making it become a contrasting feature with the new project in concrete with a pink stucco finish. The building was the result of a complex series of revisions caused by uncertainties on the part of the client, and stands out for the diverging lines of the plan and a markedly asymmetrical arrangement; in terms of layout, it has two levels – plus a basement for storage – reception spaces and lounge areas, treatment rooms, medical clinics, offices, research laboratories, a library and lodgings for doctors and nurses.

16. The project for the Teatro di Vicenza took 2nd place in an invitational competition announced in 1968, with the participation of Ignazio Gardella, Franco Albini – whose project was the winner – and Carlo Scarpa. The competition had no further development in terms of refinement of the design or construction until 1979, the year in which the municipality of Vicenza hired Ignazio Gardella – Albini had passed away in 1977 – to proceed with the executive project based on the same general idea that had been submitted 11 years earlier. The building – never constructed – had the form of an extremely compact square block, incisively cut by the staircases placed diagonally in the volume. The two almost independent parts would have contained a horse-shoe-shaped theater for 1262 seats and the foyer below it, in one volume, and the stage and all the service structures in the other, for a forcefully symmetrical scheme.

17. In 1947 Gardella was invited by Giuseppe Samonà to teach at the Istituto Universitario di Architettura di Venezia: his activity in that school extended from the academic year 1949/50 all the way to 1975. In 1952 obtained a lecturing post, and in 1962 he became a full professor of Architectural Composition.

18. The collaboration with Aldo Rossi had to do with the project for the reconstruction of Teatro Carlo Felice in Genoa: the two Milanese architects, together with Fabio Reinhart and Angelo Sibilla – in a group reporting to Mario Valle Engineering, formed by Gardella himself in partnership with the contractor Mario Valle – won the competition in 1982. The work was completed in 1990.

Roberto Gabetti
Aimaro Isola

Conversational Architecture

Architecture of Interpretation
The complaint of anyone asked to answer a precise question usually goes like this: "it is not easy to respond, it is a complex matter." And we react in the same way, when Emilio Faroldi asks us to chime in on "architectural design today."

We could also dodge the question, not talking about the difficulties of architecture, but about the difficulties of the present: putting ourselves together with the others, without precise boundaries of responsibility. But there is something correct about not closing us off in a definite, conclusive professional role. While an initial boundary exists between office work and time at the worksite, between our job and education, one clear opening is towards the place in which we work, where the project comes into being and coagulates; another opening is in our everyday life, which has to do with Turin, with Piedmont, as with the rest of the planet[1]. The difficulty of opening and closing the view, of aligning a point or an entire piece of the world, is also operative in character; among many conditions at the limit, there is the need to outline an image, a figure that is not merely an arabesque.

Everyone wants to know how to walk in the woods without getting lost. We might mention many proven measures: our advice is to enter the forest and try to get back out. Often, after a long excursion, amidst promising trails and unexpected obstacles, even the seeker who gets lost in the woods returns to his own starting point: this is already a useful experience, because it leads you to discard that intuitive hope, to put it aside. Of course you will have to start out again: but courage cannot be given to those who don't have it, or even the desire to start all over again each time.

At the start of any design itinerary one has the sensation of having to delve into chaotic, elusive material: and the temptation of immediately trying to find the right thread is an illusion. The same is true of success in this profession: a project immediately approved by a hasty client, a competition won at the first shot, the drawings immediately accepted by the planning board; these are all starts that all for caution. Opposition to the project and requested variations can, through our choice, become phases of enhancement or sources of frustration.

We think you make fewer mistakes whenever you go back to the ways of life of the so-called users, to their requirements, to what they feel are their "real" needs, to the consolidated intense debate that follows, to put necessity to the test: which is often hidden.

We think you make fewer mistakes when you think of that construction that has to be conceived as being there, for that place; it has to have a form, colors, materials or other factors suitable to interpret that place. The point is to interpret: because this might mean recognizing presences to be approached through continuity, or presences to be approached by opposition. These are not alternatives, one or the other, almost dictated by luck or fate; continuity and opposition are influenced by our will, our choice: which also means simply by our ability to conclude, continue, complete a discourse, or to the contrary our total inability to follow the discourse of others, recent, past, remote, to continue it in a different way. In this manner, something can arise in us that is a far cry from passive listening, though neither is it outcry – in the sense that we try to contain our reactions within the boundaries of good sense or good taste, without exceeding any common limit.

The project path, which we do not like to define as *creative,* but simply indicate as *mnemonic,* suggested by memory, or *intentional,* driven beyond the concrete present, does not necessarily coincide with the bureaucratic itinerary of the project: in fact it proceeds in leaps, on that almost continuous line that marks the passages from the rough design to the definitive project.

Often it is the detail close to reality that solves our rough project, but in other cases the opposite takes place: an initial thought governs every subsequent specification. The first case might apply to the "overturned pyramids" of Via Sant'Agostino in Turin[2], while the second applies to the first project for the competition of the theater of Parma[3].

Perhaps it is honest to talk about "our attitude": "our" means shared only in the sense that it has become such after active interchanges between the two of us, in an attempt to choose or to eliminate a proposal, to make it resurface or retreat once again. At times one of us may be attached to a personal idea: often each of us is attached to his own. But this is in the game of exchanges, never in certainties. To speak of attitude is also correct, perhaps, first of all so as not to say too much; to suggest that every time we design we are there to work, always with something inside that has already been there, and is there once more. Without thinking that just because we have already rounded some dangerous cape we are now closer to safety; always sensing, with pleasure, that moment in which the anchor is raised and navigation resumes. Of course we often

Roberto Gabetti and Aimaro Isola

think of others, those who have come before us in our work: they are recurring thoughts, constructed by our memory. Only rarely might they seem like critical formulations, because they exist inside immediate memories, thoughts pondered at length.

If we remember Franco Albini, it seems we are evoking a technological solution of felicitous invention, applied to a project conducted with admirable concentration in its necessary phases.

So it is a strong, evocative thought, connected to present or latent technologies[4].

Albini offers us another suggestion: to think of the architecture of the building just as one thinks about the furniture, trusting that we can identify a technology that solves the problem. We meditated for a long time on the INA offices in Parma, or the Rinascente in Rome: those two isolated "types" led us to a strong indication for action; an encouragement driven by the means available at the worksite, or only perceptible from inside the worksite. We experienced this sensation firsthand, in the work for the SNAM at San Donato Milanese[5].

Here we are talking above all about first impressions. Of course we can surprise them in the theme itself, as soon as the client somehow delineates them: of course we immediately seek them at the site, to gather a result of our first impressions.

To tame, not to challenge: to challenge, not to tame. Or: to continue, not to interrupt. To choose forms and colors and arrangements or to determine them outside a vocabulary of immediate use, are other possible alternatives.

The impression, the first one and all those subsequent, soon involves needs of life, forms, materials, without ever attempting to operate in terms of separate parts.

The chosen material, its positioning in the technological context, becomes a prevalent reference as the phases of the project gradually evolve. So the material is definitely, on its own, a medium of expression: precisely because it is inserted in a context rich in results. The possibilities that remain open come from history and the present; their coagulation in prevailing impressions can be a fixed point from which to continue – or from which to decide to turn back.

Those who look to us for a recipe to design quickly and well should keep their distance.

We work a lot and slowly, along uncertain trajectories. This is not a sign of our age, but it comes from our many youthful, much more youthful experiences: at the origin.

The architectural idea as an "art" of ongoing research

Representing this concept implies an attempt to interpret the potential of a theme, questioning it in a continual shift from particular to general, tracing forward and backward through the project. This continuous tracing means trying to effect a hermeneutic operation, which like all hermeneutics encounters obstacles, moments of backtracking, erasures. As happens with every hermeneutic idea, any questioning, any interpretation, these factors can call the entire system back into play, the entire series of variables, present, intuitively glimpsed, recalled.

We do not know if at a certain point along this path we can continue, or if we will find the path blocked and have to begin all over again, from scratch. The hermeneutic line may represent an idea of architecture seen as interpretation and formulation of a strong hypothesis that can sustain a system for the project.

Also on the worksite, you have to have the courage to forget the basic idea of the building, to challenge what has already been defined, critically rethinking every preset variable: all this in the perspective and the full awareness, which we tenaciously pursue, of having to intervene with caution in this phase: as little as possible.

We are architects who on the worksite tend not to even consider the idea of demolishing something: if anything, we tend to add, to perfect, acting by "addition" rather than "correction": although we know that obstacles may always arise in the work.

As a metaphor – a rather banal one, perhaps – we often speak of *silence:* when we are faced by an empty piece of paper we go through moments of true panic. This is a problem that might seem to plague only the young, but that is not the case: not only novice architects – who logically have a moment of impasse dictated by lack of experience – feel the responsibility of setting forth on a project: even today, when we approach a project, we feel this tragic moment of the blank sheet of paper. Many "experts" pretend they do not feel it: but it is actually an essential moment, shared by all true researchers. It is a phase in which each person lays his being on the line: "am I or I am not an architect? Am I able to fill up this paper, or not?"

It is a wager that is "tragic" each time, a wager that is repeated, almost a ritual: the challenge is tragic in the sense that our very being, existing in balance, can weaken, can erase itself. In these situations we are wrapped in that silence that detaches us from any previous conceptual construct, from that trail we had followed up to that moment: in short, manuals work, it is true; but they do no work on their own; things we have already done are precisely that, "already done," and can almost become a disadvantage. The experience that has surrounded us up to that point seems to melt away. A moment of silence: nothing more. A moment of solitude as well. Moments that are hard to include in current professional practice: fundamental moments.

This silence that corresponds to the white page is not just an initial moment: it spreads throughout the span of the project. It returns, even when we are at the worksite. Most times, we feel the terror of having to immediately choose. The choice of a color, which perhaps is a recurring, elementary choice – in certain particular contexts it becomes a basic issue: each time, we feel the terror of not knowing how to begin again. These episodes, connected with even very small choices, take us each time back into that initial moment of silence, scattered or diluted in time, which has a dramatic impact across the entire project.

Meek courage: a question of method

The metaphor or in any case the concept we would like to express is that of slow reasoning, carried out "in the negative" more through silences, gaps, than through positive contributions, though they do exist. We mustn't linger in this silence: through it we live an experience, we encounter courage.

Little is said in architecture about the concept of "courage": when it is mentioned, it is approached in a form with which we do not agree. Courage, for us, does not mean a daring structure or the novelty of exceptional forms, as avant-garde architects have long insisted, along with engineers bent on performing feats. It is the courage to risk our very being, and as a result the being of others. Quality is the outcome of this courage; just as it leads to the variation of apparently definitive choices, which also happen along the path of implementation, guiding the revisions without leaving any trace of the struggle.

Having to change what has been decided, what has been designed, does not always imply making the work "worse."

Knowing how to adapt can at times also be a virtue: an adaptation can happen along the initial phases of the design, or after visiting a worksite, but it always happens in the studio: we don't trust the brilliant solutions that are hatched before the eyes of businessmen and craftsmen. Let's take the SNAM building, for example: when the construction began – after a year and a half of development – the project was complete down to the last nails, the last components. But it had not been defined through separate choices, but through intense dialogue with suppliers, contractors, etc., in front of both of us, always bent on achieving an idea through multiple variables.

In a certain sense, then, the building already existed. But during the design you cannot foresee all the future steps; you can avoid allowing significant problems to arise, you can launch the construction process on the right path, which incorporates the concept of the completed work. But the unexpected exists: it is therefore important, also on the worksite, to have a network of preset relationships, to guarantee good results: at San Donato there were few modifications, mostly imposed by the client. The project was organized in such a way that the system for making necessary modifications was already set up in advance: some of the variations actually improved the project during the construction phases[6]. As far as "method" is concerned, in the sense of a preset working praxis, as an *a priori* description of what should be done, we can say that we have never taken that into account: we undoubtedly approach the elaboration of individual, different themes along a line we might define as "spoken." Of course the drawing, the sketch, the scrap of paper, can help us: but from the outset we always discuss everything, talking about everything, trying to formulate our own conventions.

The first part of the design happens through ongoing exchanges, intense conversations, plot lines of reference, merely allusive perhaps, for what we intend to do. When our discussion is sufficiently advanced, sustained by the indispensable drawings, we support the results, the provisional conclusions we have reached, also in relation to the client, the contractor, our colleagues.

Of course drawing is important, but in most cases it belongs to an *a posteriori* phase, an event that serves to organize ideas systematically. The drawing is obviously not just the pretty sketch, an end in itself; it involves testing of congruencies, emerging from the conversational approach, which does not stand still until the end of the project: and it even continues after that, because the project continues to be discussed, when it is spread out on the table, in front of the critics.

Perhaps – and this should not seem like a paradox – at a certain point a project grows even more after it has been completed. So our "method" – if we have a "method" – may lie precisely in this process of dialogue: a conversation between us and with things, from the outset, a conversation with technologies, with past experiences and new counterparts: the timing is spaced by moments of silence, in which we try to create that detachment between us and things, which is necessary to move forward with our theme.

The concept of landscape in the "conversation" with personalities and production

Recent years have been marked by profound rethinking of the relationship architecture establishes with external factors, with the "context": almost as if this were a discovery. Not for us: we have been the main advocates of this singular interest in places: or at least the critics seem to think so. Today, more than talking about context, about the *genius loci,* we would like to rectify the discourse, introducing the concept of "landscape," meaning not simply the mountains, the city, the historical center, but also the climate, the neighboring situations, the place and time in which we come to grips with the theme. An image, that is, where this scenario takes on a more complex meaning: it becomes society, economics, production.

To insert a building in a "landscape" – in a context – does not mean operating through mimesis with respect to places: we do not favor a constant "matching," but where necessary we follow a line of differentiation, of separation: separation is certainly a dramatic event, so it must be measured. This "landscape" seen as a way of establishing a relationship with the outside, introduces elements of novelty, of richness, inserted case by case in the various situations we encounter, which time then changes.

There is little doubt that at the time of the Bottega di Erasmo[7] in Turin we were faced by a type of craftsmanship that was slowly vanishing, and that we thought – in a rather Morris-like vision – could find new possibilities of expression. And what was possible then took place; from that time to the present, after the terrible events in which the city seemed to gobble up and destroy that evoked world. In any case, we were operating them in a different climate from the one we encountered a few years later – twenty years later – when we built the Residenziale Ovest[8], or even further on when we did the Quinto Palazzo Uffici at San Donato Milanese. There too we can see skillfully crafted solutions, traditional and new, because parallel to the mutation of the situations caused by time, we tried to train ourselves in the sense of combining changes caused by the particular and specific situations with our own proposals, suitable to position the building in space and time. With meaningful signs – at least that was our intention[9].

In definitive terms, we have not underestimated the fact that so-called "innovative" technologies, materials and processes might not be abstract entities, detached from the real world, but can represent people, companies, technical systems, authors and co-authors present in our operative sector. We have to be careful in the theorizing of a discourse, setting a gap between *technology* and *personalities:* the theoretical knowledge of a given technical potential is one thing, while the concrete human capacity to convey and interpret a complex assumption, a plot traced by the architectural project, is another.

The architect, the designer has to take the responsibility of understanding – through painstaking knowledge of the situation in which he moves, but above all of the counterparts with whom he has to come to terms – the real possibilities of transfer of every contribution towards implementation, of translating his ideas into matter: and it is not so rare to come across personalities who do not understand or know about a given technology, but want to utilize it in any case. This inevitably leads to a clash.

This is why in design it is very important to precisely know the character of every company, of craftsman or otherwise, large or small: their strong points, their particular abilities.

Even in an age of advanced technology, such as the one we are crossing today, if we find ourselves dealing with a company that is not capable of handling certain types of technology it is better to put an idea aside, to seek another that is more feasible. The point lies in knowing how to recognize a possible lack of resources, taking it as a constraint that is not insurmountable, as design input to be taken into account: which means designing and redesigning each time, for the occasion.

In the Quinto Palazzo Uffici of SNAM our partner-counterpart, the client with whom to discuss the project, was represented by a group of technicians or in any case employees of "SNAM Progetti" or SNAM: very well-informed, flexible people who had the fundamental capacities to grasp a certain type of intelligent – "culture" – dialogue on the ways of choosing technologies, of clarifying construction processes, from the drawing to the implementation; this building can certainly be defined as the product of a conversation[10].

Our way of working, of "communicating" through architecture starts from this indispensable state of openness to dialogue: we speak with manuals, catalogues, technical notions, literary citations. Everything is mediated through personal relationships, which we set at the basis of any design or worksite operation: they are the true guarantee of good results. We closely rely on the efforts of worksite assistants, geometers, mason, or a great engineer for calculations regarding reinforced concrete: personalities we appreciate and admire precisely because with them it is possible to establish this essential phase of dialogue.

Perhaps this is the recipe, if we can use that term, behind our architecture: not so much as a proposal, as *a priori* action, but as an unspecified openness to dialogue with places, technologies and above all with people, with the client, with the various protagonists.

From idea to implementation: clientele, production

We spoke about "mimesis," identifying a meaning of uniformity: we do not want to simply pursue a logic of mimesis with what has already been determined, but with what has been established through meaningful conversations, through discussions that enter into the production cycle, through relationships, also strong ones, from which we hope to gain positive results for the project. Conversations we see not as attempts to match our intentions, but as tools of mutual growth.

This reasoning connected with places, with the productive resources in which the project unfolds, should not be extended only to projects above a certain size, or beyond a certain level of complexity – as in the cases of the constantly referenced "Quinto" at San Donato, the Uffici Giudiziari in Alba[11], the Centro Residenziale Olivetti in Ivrea, the residential complex at Sestriére[12], or – going back in time – the Bottega di Erasmo. It should also be applied to smaller projects, in identical form and with the same intensity, though with a shift of scale.

Let's take the Tuminera[13] as an example, a work designed for a producer of cheeses. We did this in Isola's home town. The initial input came from the fact that the client had a bit of money to make a building with an extremely simple form. An industrial shed with a length of ten meters, which would be adaptable, later on, to another function; a shed for which the client had the desire to somehow display the facade towards the street, to represent the various productive activities for which he wanted to create a certain image.

The client had these simple, apparently clear ideas: for us, they were points that spoke of the "vernacular," that led us towards American models.

This is an extreme but indicative case. That back part, as you can see, is a very simple shed faced in brick. The front portico, on the other hand, is made of wood and stone: the client practically made it with his own hands, and for this reason we designed it entirely with elementary pieces, which he then assembled, one by one. Other examples: the monument in honor of the Partisans at Prarostino[14], or the church-sanctuary of Montoso[15]. Except for certain parts for which a local company with a bit more equipment intervened, these works of architecture were built by volunteers: partisans who were comrades of Isola during the Resistance, parishioners of Bagnolo Piemonte. They also went there on Sundays, for two or three years, putting one stone on top of another.

These projects too, these constructions, came about from forms of dialogue, connected with specific counterparts. Passing to the phase of implementation means having people between us, the designers, and the work of architecture: the client and the contractor are the main counterparts, with which to come to terms in different episodes, different situations.

These relationships do not always go through situations of antagonism, but at the same time they do not always proceed smoothly, in an idyllic way: there can be disagreements, even clashes. But we believe that dialogue, talking things over, sorting things out, is always the best way to approach a work, to avoid the battle, the big difference of opinion, the obstacle. Of course there are also humorous situations that may arise. Isola recalls a remark by Gabetti, when at the start of our activity we were still uncertain about what path to take: we had to design the Bottega d'Erasmo, commissioned by the owner of a store specializing in antique books which had the same name, and we were discussing the characteristics of the building.

Given the particular location of the project[16], Gabetti mentioned the Mole Antonelliana, thinking that would please the client who was also from Turin, and closely connected to our own cultural circles. As soon as the client heard that reference, he frankly stated that of all the buildings in Turin, the Mole was the one he simply couldn't stand; so much so that he had hesitated at length before purchasing that lot for construction, because it was too close to that monument. "For my building, I imagine a Renaissance palace, with capitals and columns," he said. At that point Gabetti played what he thought was a trump card, replying: "Sir, do you have any idea what it costs today to make a capital, or a column?" So the Bottega di Erasmo was born as you can still see it today: or, more precisely as the result of that idea after various modifications.

The Bottega d'Erasmo, while construction was in progress, was raised twice, because first it was supposed to have two floors, since at first we thought only about the bookstore, without the residential portion. Then we added another level, for the owner's lodgings, and then an upper story with a setback[17].

Of course in those moments we were not pleased to have to rethink and re-discuss the whole project: but such detours are frequent in the making of architecture. The project, in its initial conception, becomes a landscape, a scenario, where you can step in to conduct further work.

This relationship between the idea and the implementation leads to continuous mutation, to the extent – as our first important experience demonstrates – that there can never be a moment of complete, frozen, immutable formalization. The designed architecture, in its encounter with reality, inevitably undergoes modifications, which in one way or another the designer has to take into account. From this standpoint, we have never made a drama out of new situations, even those that seemed to upset our previous plans.

We think that already, in moments of training, one should receive and at the same time transmit the habit of always and in any case identifying an escape route for the idea, for any new idea. Isola specifies that in the School of Architecture of Turin he teaches a course[18] in which – on the basis of a constructive idea – the students have to reach a deeper level of the project, a true definitive design, all the way to the nails; starting with the urban layout, all the phases of the worksite are simulated. This happens even in the case of risky hypotheses, for which the range of solutions would be very large; but it is necessary to know where a certain project is heading: to know how to rethink your project, to start over again, from the beginning.

Isola is convinced of the value of initial ideas: he believes that this aspect is of great importance because – as Borges says – "the paths are infinite," and it is also true that following one allows you to glimpse a way out. This is a fundamental experience. In the students this idea of having to strive towards the implementation has to take form, at least in the study of a path that leads to the completed work.

Given the way certain things are heading today, it should be said that we are not very pleased – I imagine no one would be – when we are invited to take part in a competition we know we will lose from the outset; we take part in competitions with the goal of winning them, not so much for the victory itself, as to be able to experiment with new paths, new solutions, in the real world. The relationship with the execution, with what we have defined as the "production side," is a constructive one, which case by case we orient with respect to the particularities of the situation: this is true both for operations of a "serial" type and for those involving "craftsmanship."

We are quite willing to use industrial objects – standard "catalogue" items – also because the catalogues at this point are so complete that they can respond to a very wide range of needs.

The main thrust, instead, has to do with the study and exploration of the points of contact, of interaction between various serial items, various construction systems and ways of connecting the components of the architecture: this is the true crux of the issue today. It is also true that the whole history of architecture, where technologies and construction systems are concerned, reveals marked discontinuities of choice, differences in contributions firmly rooted in the worksite: these differences, seen as variety, constitute the technical and formal wealth of individual buildings and of the city as a whole.

In the development of our building for SNAM, the question of the window frames was agreed upon with the client, as an element that had to be completely reinvented with respect to current production: above all, it was necessary to produce a number of pieces that no industrial company, at the time, could have manufactured on its own in the required quantities.

We thus conducted a study of thicknesses, of the dimensioning of the object[19]. Though it was a complex artifact, and called for a high level of specialization, we were able to define it through exchange of information between us and the producers. We believe that it is still possible to have a conversation with companies today. We have only rarely found this not to be the case.

For the building in Alba, perhaps: this was one of the few instances when the dialogue with the contractor became very difficult. We were faced with a rather strange initial situation, because certain members of the clientele had not understood the characteristics of the project connected with the surrounding greenery, and in the end, though with regrets, we had to limit the project to the only lot that had been assigned to us[20]. The contractor was used to working in the context of large infrastructural projects, and was quite indifferent to the matter of making one building as opposed to another.

As soon as construction began we found ourselves having to cope above all with legal, regulatory and economic issues: an immediate accent was on the new costs involved in the variations made during construction.

This put the two of us and Giuseppe Varaldo, as supervisors of the work, in the position of having to judge the validity of the requests advanced by the contractor.

Turning to another topic, we have always had a good relationship with technicians; each of them, in a latent way, has his own *Kunstwollen:* a very strong artistic urge is also present in those who think of themselves as pure technicians, such as those who make structural calculations for reinforced concrete. Precisely in the case of the Quinto, at the start we had an excellent and very sensitive engineer on the job, with whom we had an intense and erudite dialogue regarding the type of structure to be used: unfortunately that conversation was interrupted due to the death of this precious collaborator.

Designing in tune with the times means using the tools of design in an appropriate way, responding to the needs expressed by the cultural climate. In this regard we think the times have changed quite a bit: for the Bottega d'Erasmo we designed even the tiniest details, precisely because many construction systems were flexible, at the service of the designers and the project managers. Following a trail that was also perhaps that of Ridolfi, we sat down at the drawing table, designing every part much more than we would today: the joint of a window frame, the seam between the stone and the frame, the bolt, the brick that had to interlock in the stone, etc[21]. The drawings were rather refined, due to the fact that at the time the carpenter, the smith, the mason had a certain willingness to accept that type of drawing: they were also linked to a technological tradition of the 1800s and 1900s, which was still very much alive in Turin in those days. But times have changed a lot. Today it would be absurd to design a window frame, when we know very well that it would be like designing a car: in the past it was still possible to make a variation of the bodywork, but today you buy the car and accept it as is, without even considering the problem of how you would like it to be.

Production has been oriented towards macro-systems that are much more given, more complete: our action is conducted through these macro-systems. It would be wrong and useless to disrupt them through a design that might put the implementation of a work into crisis. We are not urging a passive position regarding the *elements to be designed:* in any case, we want to underline the usefulness of specific interventions only when that action produces a significant, indispensable improvement of the product. In our case, we try to choose what we need from what already exists, inside production, without emphasizing the so-called high-tech aspect that often relies on acritical worship of anything that is innovative.

For us, what is innovative and what used to be can only have different meanings: we do not focus on innovative use, but on aware use of the essential elements, which can be very new or very traditional.

Certainly there are new developments we could not rely on yesterday, and so our language tends to expand; but we are not enthused by the neologism as such: what is important is its meaning.

The elements of design as elements of habitation

The same plot, the same tissues, the same symbols can be read in the territory: when we have to think about a settlement, we try to put back together various situations of land registry, various shapes of streets, rivers, certain shifts of altitude. The same sort of permanence constitutes a landscape we believe can also be found in materials and technologies.

Every element of old and new technologies, every trace of landscape brings with it a long history, which is the history of how they have been used, how they have been assembled and above all deployed, and how they have been experienced in time, how the lines of the surrounding environment have been followed. It is about recognizing that these pieces have their own historical depth, their own weight, also in philosophical terms. All too often we forget these aspects, treating them simply as means, as tools.

We forget that every element has its content of history, its own and that of the place it represents. This is the true meaning of materials and the technology created to assemble them – the wooden boards used at Sestriére are not the same ones used in another location: the stone gathered at the site is not the same as stone procured from other parts.

These elements all connect together with a discourse on "form," a discourse that possesses its spatial and typological attributes extended to the landscape.

Also at school, with the students, we often express serious doubts about the meaning of terms like *typology, type*. Terms about which rivers of ink have been spilled. We want to make an impact on the specific characteristics of change, because it seems to us that in these years, also from a historical viewpoint, there has been a "hyperstaticity" of the typology: a tendency to fill the typology with too many constraints. A greater value has been attributed to the type than it should have: the typology should be considered by placing the focus on the true meaning of *habitation*, therefore in a logic that more thoroughly engages the viewpoint of the receiver. Those who speak of type, of typology as an autonomous science capable of moving forward on its own, are quite mistaken.

We prefer to insist on the fact that all of architecture today, like philosophy, should pay greater attention to use, to what should be done for something else, without closing ourselves off in our own disciplinary fields, through logics that exist for the most part inside them.

In philosophy we think about Gadamer, Lévinas, Cioran, who accentuate the theme of "how we can live," of hospitality. For this – Isola points out – it is important to always think about places, about continuity between inside and outside, between corridors, streets, squares, and the resulting voids: the typology, seen not only as a memory of historical continuity, but as a space to be inhabited.

In these dramatic moments in which everything seems to come to an end, in which ideology no longer has a strong meaning, habitation – our way of living – coincides somewhat with our way of being. Not much is left to us today, besides habitation: so it would be sad to inhabit places that are not "ours." This is why the typology is – and must be – always connected to a fact of habitation, in the wider sense of the term: connected to places of life. In this sense, we have to free it from too many constraints, propose it in the form of a feasible model.

Of course, design also means transforming and revising models: this operation should be carried out with particular care with respect to "magnitudes" and "quantities." On multiple occasions there has been talk of typology, rightfully also linking the discourse to technologies: this is a significant theme. Likewise, however, the discussion should be widened to the spaces of mediation, which are important from both a technological and a typological standpoint. Presenting the problem in typological terms has fostered a design practice that tends to put the focus above all on the planimetric layout, while overlooking different design aspects of at least equal importance. Isola, in this sense, refers precisely to the above-mentioned spaces of mediation: the staircase, the lobby, the balcony, the portico, the entrance to the house, to remain in the residential ambit.

We believe the reconnection of typology, like technology, should be pursued in these terms.

As a result, many elements of design, the module, geometry, typology itself, should be considered not as events detached from the reality of the project – metaphysical, *a priori* events on which much philosophy and much architecture have journeyed – but as tools closely tied to the ultimate aim and concept of architecture: "habitation."

Turin, 1 March 1993 – Studio Gabetti & Isola

Notes

1. Roberto Gabetti and Aimaro Isola, born respectively in 1925 and 1928, both in Turin where they both completed their studies, confirm this background across the full span of their career with an intellectual approach typical of that city, in which *technique* and *production* play a fundamental role, also in the world of culture. In 1950 their competition project for the Galleria d'Arte Moderna in Turin marked the start of their partnership, which still continues today.

2. The project of residences for the company Centro Storico Torinese (Turin 1978-84, with Guido Drocco) involved the reconstruction of part of a block inside a regeneration plan for four blocks in the historical center of Turin. The rough project was presented in 1980 and called for the completion with four segments of pyramids placed at the corners of the destroyed area, marked by an appearance of closure to the outside and openness to the inside of the block thanks to terraced arrangement of continuous loggias, tapering the volumes towards the top. Themes already explored by Gabetti & Isola, such as the stepped arrangement and the loggias, were joined by solutions that went completely against the current, especially the volumetric order that made a break with the traditional unity of the historical block.

3. Halfway through the 1960s Gabetti & Isola took part in two important competitions, one for the Teatro Paganini in Parma (1964-65 with Luciano Re) – a work that was never built – and one held by the Comunità Europea del Carbone e dell'Acciaio for the design of prefabricated modular residences (1965-66, with Loris Garda and Luciano Re). In the invitational competition held in 1963 for a cinema-theater in the center of Parma – besides Gabetti & Isola, the participants were Carlo Aymonino, Luigi Caccia Dominioni, Vittorio Gandolfi, Luigi Pellegrin, Paolo Portoghesi and Aldo Rossi – the duo presented a project with a simple geometric volume, a cylinder on an elliptical base paced by the steel posts of the ground floor portico, which in the second phase of the competition took on a more complex, jagged appearance.

4. The retrospective investigation of rationalist architecture conducted by Gabetti & Isola from their first years of activity was accompanied by complementary but independent research on the artifact and on techniques, especially on Gabetti's part.

The interest in Perret – in the wake of Rogers – also points to the desire for a new, transverse interpretation of the Modern Movement, in a perspective that tends to connect *constructive innovation* and *formal tradition*. The reference to Albini is no coincidence: the investigation of Roberto Gabetti on the mountainous context of the Alps and the related technical and technological legacy has a place in the wake of the studies conducted by the architects who made Alpine architecture a special observatory – just consider, amongst the others, Carlo Mollino and, as mentioned, Franco Albini – leading to conferences held precisely on this theme, where Gabetti himself was the secretary.

5. The project for the Quinto Palazzo Uffici of SNAM at San Donato Milanese (Milan 1986-91, with Guido Drocco) arose from an invitational ideas competition – with the participation of eleven groups of architects – announced in July 1985, for the creation of an office building and related services. Gabetti & Isola were the winners with the project "I giardini di ...", marked by an accentuated focus on the use of plantings, and by a volumetric arrangement developed on the basis of a cubic module of 3.6 meters. The overall layout calls for an amphitheater building formed by two polyhedra in glass of different heights, in an oblong curved form, that meet at two nodal points to enclose a large green area. These two bodies undergo narrowing at each level, in keeping with a modular scheme, with an irregular stepped and sloping space covered by roof gardens. The modular pattern is revealed on the facade and the roof thanks to a framework of pipes in green aluminium.

6. The competition guidelines, given the complexity of the theme, required submission of essentially qualitative indications, with the prospect of delegating the solutions to the problems the project presented, relying on the various forms of expertise involved. The successive municipal project – submitted in January 1988 – was to make certain modifications to the initial

design: first of all the planimetric reversal, the loss of a structural function for the metal grid on the facade, and the creation of a perimeter ring running along the outer elevations.

7. After the first project of importance – the proposal for the Turin Bourse (with Giorgio and Giuseppe Raineri, 1953-56) – Gabetti & Isola leapt to the forefront of the architectural debate with the project of the Bottega d'Erasmo, a building made on a lot in the historical center of Turin for a bookstore specializing in antique volumes – on the lower levels – and apartments, featuring a structure in fair-face reinforced concrete alternating with brick walls and portions in Luserna stone, such as the base and the parapets of the balconies.

Designed in 1953, terminated in 1956 and published in *Casabella-Continuità* in 1957 (no. 215), the Bottega, with its detachment from preset models and references to the host context, triggered a debate on the process of revision of Rationalism, becoming an unintentional manifesto of the so-called *Neo-Liberty* turn (on the role of Gabetti & Isola in the polemic around *Neo-Liberty* see F. Cellini, C. D'Amato, *Gabetti e Isola. Progetti e Architetture 1950-1985*, Electa, Milano 1985, pp. 138-142).

8. After the research on the tradition launched through the Bottega, the Unità Residenziale Ovest in Ivrea (1968-71, with Luciano Re) represents a recognizable signal of a turnaround in the design research of Gabetti & Isola. On 20 September 1968 a letter from Olivetti confirmed the commission assigned to the two architects from Turin for the design of a building of mini-lodgings for recent graduates hired by the company based in Ivrea.

Challenging current residential types – the tower or the row house – and with the aim of solving the problem of insertion in the context, the design research of Gabetti & Isola shifted towards a building that makes the natural setting the main premise of the project: a constructed volume with a depth of 11 meters and a semicircular shape – set on a circumference of almost 70 meters in radius – resting on a slope in the terrain that covers the outer side, making the roof into a terrace that could be utilized. The sizing of the apartments, composed of minimum units, called for simplex and duplex lodgings. The inner side of the two levels of apartments features a continuous glass wall paced by a dense series of aluminium posts.

9. The experimentation of Gabetti & Isola continues in the second half of the 1970s with different solutions and results, even in similar contexts. Often in the architecture of the Turin-based duo we see highly innovative technological solutions (for example, in the Casa Solare at Orbassano, 1982-85), though they do not represent the prevalent compositional motif.

The theoretical activity of the two designers continues across the entire span of their production, revealing a progressively clearer distinction between poetic writings and an increasingly independent reflection on design culture. The theme of the antithesis between tradition and innovation remains one of the most stimulating over the years. Their investigation on the possible interpretations of tradition goes beyond design activity, involving the cultural sphere of writings, publications and criticism. Their writings are prolific, especially in the case of Gabetti: a literary output that reveals an attitude that tends to place the written text at the same level of importance as designed production. The writings, nevertheless, almost never take the form of a theoretical justification of the architecture, accompanying it in a parallel but independent way.

10. In the case of the "Quinto," already in the development of the rough project Gabetti & Isola were flanked by specialists from various disciplines – energy, physical plant, security – as well as the constant presence of experts directly hired by the client. The computer development of the executive drawings – an operation made necessary by the complexity of the project – was done by Snarnprogetti, outside the studio of Gabetti & Isola: the designers always took part in the choices, though at the moment of the construction their presence gradually diminished.

11. Gabetti & Isola approached the question of urban design in the project for the Palazzo di Giustizia in Alba (1982-87, together with Giuseppe Varaldo and with G. Drocco, E. Moncalvo and R. Fassino), in which they returned to the familiar themes of the portico-gallery, terraced buildings and underground extension. The building in fact presents itself "by subtraction" as a parallelepiped of terraces covered with greenery, sloping towards an internal courtyard-street.

12. The project for the residential complex at Sestrière (Turin 1973-80, with Guido Drocco) constitutes the natural next phase, after the Residenziale Ovest in Ivrea, of the process of experimentation with the combination of simplex and duplex layouts connected by a covered walkway. The allotment plan that generates the building called for the creation of a volume capable of containing apartments, shops and sporting facilities. From the roof terrace placed at street level, the building faces towards the valley and follows the slope of the terrain through a composition "in leaps" with a constant depth of two meters. The perimeter walls are clad in fir planks, while the roofing of the stairwells, galleries and loggias of the apartments is in curved pieces of methacrylate like plexiglas, sustained by a structure in galvanized iron.

13. The project for the "La Tuminera" cheese dairy and residence (1978-80, with Guido Drocco) is part of a group of works of architecture made at Bagnolo Piemonte (Cuneo) in the second half of the 1970s (from 1974 to 1978), with very significant results on the level of expressive solutions in relation to the regional culture. La Tuminera is a building composed of two distinct volumes – one for the production of cheese, one for the residence of the owner – connected by a volume with a portico that makes the overall image uniform, in keeping with a simple horizontal layout scheme, in reference to the tradition of the Prairie House. All the volumes have a structure in reinforced concrete and outer cladding in exposed brick masonry with a stone base; the Luserna stone of the roof forms a contrast with the raw wood posts of the portico, "signs" of the traditional architecture of the town.

14. The monument commemorating the fallen heroes of the Resistance at San Bartolomeo di Prarostino (Pinerolo, Turin, 1965-67) was commissioned to Gabetti & Isola by a volunteer committee that carried out the implementation of the design.

15. The theme of recovery of the tradition was further developed in the Santuario dell'Assunta at Montoso (Bagnolo Piemonte, Cuneo 1963-67, with Giorgio De Ferrari), with a focus on small buildings located in highly traditional contexts, also in terms of production. The church at Montoso was designed to be built directly by the congregation that had commissioned the work. The compact and plastically shaped architectural organism has a rectangular plan whose axis of symmetry coincides with the short side of the rectangle: the space of worship, introduced by a narrow portico, flexes outward at the altar to form a niche flanked on one side by the volumes of the sacristy and the steeple. The structure is mixed: brick pillars and walls in exposed stone, inside and outside. The windows are set off by smooth white stucco, in tune with a typical characteristic of local rural architecture; the roof in Luserna stone has a steep pitch.

16. The area purchased by Angelo Barrera, who commissioned the Bottega d'Erasmo, is located very near the Mole Antonelliana; furthermore, the inclined form of the lot creates a clear connection between the building by Gabetti & Isola and the famous monument in Turin.

17. The first project for the Bottega – approved in July 1954 – was for a building with three above-ground levels and a basement, all set aside for the antiquarian bookstore, apart from the upper level which contained an apartment. In December 1954, when construction was already in progress, the client requested five above-ground stories plus one that would be set back, as permitted by the building regulations, extending the bookstore to the third level and inserting apartments in the upper levels.

18. Since 1967 Roberto Gabetti has been a full professor of Architectural Composition at the Turin Polytechnic; Aimaro Isola has held the same position since 1977.

19. The outer facades of the Quinto are formed by double, completely glazed walls with an aluminium framework structure, forming a continuous interspace along the perimeter with a width of 90 cm to provide optimal environmental comfort, while permitting ease of maintenance of the physical plant systems inserted in the suspended ceilings and raised floors. The design of this facade system was developed based on in-depth study of energy use, to achieve excellent results in terms of consumption and thermal/visual wellbeing. The tight construction schedule called for the use of prefabricated industrial parts and of special machinery designed for the occasion.

20. When the municipal government of Alba, in 1981, commissioned Gabetti & Isola with Giuseppe Varaldo to design the Palazzo di Giustizia, the project also included the design of a new piazza that would set the urban character of a marginal area lacking in identity. This part of the project was suspended in 1985 by choice of the designers themselves.

21. For the Bottega d'Erasmo, besides the refined construction details, in 1956 Gabetti & Isola designed the furnishings of the bookstore; a few years later, in 1962, they also created furniture for the owner's apartment and the spaces on the ground floor.

Paolo Portoghesi

Material Architecture

Architecture, production, technology

I would like to begin by indicating that the problem of the relationship between architecture and resources of construction-production in Italy is particularly pertinent. This is for two reasons: one is probably the ambition of Italian architects to keep faith with a humanistic ideal of power to the imagination; the other is precisely the ambivalence of the productive system, which is more accentuated in Italy than elsewhere.

I became aware of this problem in my experiences of what could be called the myths of Italian architectural culture starting in the 1960s[1]. After the period of reconstruction, Italy was sorely burdened by its structural underdevelopment: at the time, prefabrication existed only in very basic terms, and it was not until this era that one began to talk about industrialization in construction.

For years architects had, in effect, preached the myth of industrialization as a sort of duty to adapt to laws of a productive character arriving from abroad. The patents for heavy prefabrication did indeed reach Italy from *abroad*, from France or the Soviet Union; these were the systems utilized in the 1960s and 1970s, often translated into backward formulations with respect to the progress that had brought them into being in their nations of origin.

I experienced this problem firsthand, the mythical interpretation Italian architects had assigned to questions of prefabrication, industrialization and macrostructure. When I had the chance to travel in the world halfway through the 1960s, I realized that this problem did not exist, or in any case was much less central in the other European countries and in other places like the United States, where instead the use of prefabrication or industrialization happened through a very precise orientation of research, without coming into conflict with architecture.

Even today in America construction takes place with the aid of very different technologies: the most common is wood, a technology we have always considered archaic; it has only been recently, through correct use of laminated wood, that we have been able to recoup certain values. The technology of wood, in fact, offers architecture a high level of experimentalism, though with the passage of time – not a secondary factor – there can be problems of durability. In American culture the "constraint" of prefabrication applies above all to large constructions, involving the system of procedures for the deployment of materials, rather than the operations that influence the architectural form. Stone cladding, for example, an element often used in the making of skyscrapers, has required very sophisticated construction and worksite technologies and a high level of safety measures (because there can be little doubt that a slab of marble with a weight of 100 kilos, falling from a height of 400 meters, constitutes a cataclysmic event).

In my view, this attitude has always reflected a correct interpretation of the relationship between *architectural research* and *technological research,* in the sense that technologies have mainly and almost exclusively focused on solving the problems raised by architecture. The problems of tall structures, for example, have never invaded the area of formal choice, or at least if they have done so this has happened in a specific territory, that of construction without qualification, i.e. "non-architecture," which in America is normally entrusted to specialized technicians who have nothing to do with the architectural establishment; the latter, instead, has reserved a very important right to freedom and autonomy.

Just observe architectural production in the USA over the last 30 years, and you will immediately realize – just by intuition – that their very refined technologies have always been utilized with great freedom by architects: even the curtain wall, which might be interpreted as the assumption of external rules on the part of designers, has actually been shaped to meet the widest range of expressive needs, with the result of an extraordinary wealth of technological solutions.

This *dictatorship* of technology over architecture is a factor we sense above all here in Italy, which went through a truly tragic moment in the 1960s when it was thought that everything should be designed on the basis of what was suggested by heavy prefabrication; as a result, joints were displayed in brutal form, and anything that could be a hindrance to production was absolutely eliminated, in favor of the choice of the quickest and most economical options. I remember that there was even the introduction of tunnel formwork: techniques and operations that by the time they reached Italy were already obsolete in France. Precisely in France, in the 1960s the industrialization of construction took on forms that left even too much up to the architects: incredible things were prefabricated, in the sense of absolutely arbitrary choices.

Clearly, in Italy there has been a particular regimen, which still continues to exist. We do not take an empirical approach to things, but neither do we have the rational approach of the French. We are rationalists, but rationalists *more royalist (realist) than the king.* The French, who are true rationalists, see both *esprit de géometrie* and *esprit de finesse* in reality; instead, at times we surrender to the *esprit de géometrie* while we forget about the *esprit de finesse*.

This issue is typically Italian and should be explored in order to free the architect from this sort of "straitjacket" that in many cases he wears of his own free will.

In my academic-professional experience[2], I have realized that only if we surrender for reasons that do not depend on us do we tend to suffer from the negative weight of technique. Instead, if there is the possibility of dialogue, of interaction, of reciprocal influence, this fragile problem melts like snow in the sun.

Technology – and by this term I mean the set of variables of the productive and constructive system – becomes a formidable tool to make things in a faster, more economical way: at the same time, technology proves to be quite willing to cooperate when the ideas of the architect are sufficiently clear, and above all when it is not asked to *take part in the invention,* but to *achieve a given idea* – and there is a substantial difference between the two.

I do not want to deny the existence of a share taken by technology in invention, because in certain circumstances invention is indubitably a factor; it is in any case an *invention* at the service of an *idea,* not a form of assistance offered to the architect to solve problems he does not know how to solve in that circumstance.

Getting beyond this conflict should imply better training for architects, to reach the point of possessing what Pier Luigi Nervi called *static sensibility,* as well as the conviction – not so much on the part of technologists as of producers and therefore builders – that "forcing" the architect to adapt to a system external to his expertise does not automatically lead to economic advantages.

The background of this misunderstanding should probably also be sought in the Italian economic system; although today it is no longer only a problem of an economic-productive character, for a long time that was certainly the case.

The architect has too often been put in a secondary position with respect to the privileged relationship between politics and the economic dimension of constructions.

Recent legal developments have shown that in the last few years, to have large margins of operative and therefore economic freedom, it was better to build a highway than to operate in other sectors of public works; there is a clear intention to transform public works – in the noblest sense of the term – into production similar to that of infrastructures, a production that is therefore totally quantitative in nature, in which the concept of quality is only secondary, and thus represents an insignificant parameter.

In definitive terms, beyond these problems at the margins of architecture, which nevertheless have their influence, my design approach in terms of the relationship between *technology* and *architecture* is not governed by this presumed "dualism." My attitude is instead one of acceptance of what the outside world, of technology and production, offers to support architecture, basing the success of the work on the ability of the architect to transmit his message also through a constant presence in the world of the construction site.

I believe that a certain type of world, which we can define as *academic*, ought to get back to "dirtying its shoes" and experiencing its own architecture, building it with its own hands.

The worksite and construction technologies

In my relationship with the worksite, and generally with the technological and productive variables connected with the post-design phase, I have been assisted by a useful family tradition: my father, an engineer, had a small construction company, and my first significant work, Casa Baldi[3], was done together with him, spending time at the worksite, knowing the work from the inside in terms of technology, production and economics.

For me this was a great lesson, because I could get acquainted with the *world of the worksite*, which is useful to evaluate all the phases and moments of design and implementation.

I fully feel like an heir to a culture closely connected to that of architectural neo-realism, for which Mario Ridolfi is undoubtedly the most representative figure. He always had a close relationship with the worksite, dictated by the conviction that the know-how and wisdom acquired in a traditional construction can be applied to any type of worksite, including those with a high level of industrialization[4]. Wisdom means skepticism regarding theoretical guarantees and the philosophical aspects of productivity.

I remember, in this regard, that living on the worksite in the 1950s allowed you to witness a series of absolutely irrational behaviors: every time an ulterior element was inserted in the architecture, which was essentially a matter of masonry, it caused a sort of micro-catastrophe. Some examples from memory: when they inserted the window casements, the frame and counterframe were assembled together; when the electrical system was installed, everything was ripped up to make gigantic channels; it was practically a way of starting all over again, through methods and operations that clearly went against any rationality. What I am saying can easily be checked and verified.

From this level and scale of problems to the solving of a matter such as the bathroom, with the insertion of a preassembled block, there is a big difference.

The bathroom block is already a sort of "pseudo-problem" in its own right, which through the merely apparent illusion of saving energy and money leads to an operation that is so complex – the installation of a foreign object – that it cancels out the supposed advantages: elements like the bathroom block or the tunnel have a logic when effectively – not just theoretically – the industrialization is total, also implying the entire assembly of a building. Their use, as a partial factor and episode, has always proven to be a disastrous operation inside the traditional logic of the worksite.

Concrete experiences have helped me a great deal, providing me with that minimum of expertise that allows the architect to defend himself, and to engage in an open dialogue with technicians and specialists in this sector.

Over the years I have observed, in the case of certain colleagues of indubitable value, that the inability of the architect to speak the same language as those who do the construction can cause an inferiority complex in the builder – which is actually quite rare – or much more frequently an arrogance on the part of the maker, to whom the designer ends up having to submit.

Dialogue is very useful because in the end the idea is to find the quickest and most economical solution to individual problems: in this the architect, if he has some vocation for the work, is as useful as the engineer, given the fact that contrary to what might be expected the engineer has a more theoretical approach than the architect, who by nature and history has a more practical way of dealing with problems.

Let's get back to the matter of design-implementation. Where "monumental" buildings are concerned, I have built only the Mosque of Rome. In the field of residential construction my experience is undoubtedly more extensive. In this area, for me to two low-cost housing complexes of Sesto San Giovanni represent one of the most significant episodes[5].

The first one was built with prefabrication, supplied by the company that won the bid, resulting from the period in which the Istituto Autonomo Case Popolari of Milan, like many other IACP agencies in Italy, held competitions not for architects but for contractors.

Each company usually presented its own method and its own patent, and only in a second phase was the winner of the contract joined by an architect, who therefore had to use the proposed construction technology. This is one of the most absurd things that can happen to an architect. In my case, only with enormous effort, and reaching an agreement, was it possible to make a building in which I designed the prefabricated panel in keeping with the contractor's patent, utilizing pressed cardboard walls as had been previously stipulated. The result is a parallelepiped with two towers, whose enclosure is made with paneling designed by an architect.

In the area that remained open next to the first building, given the fact that other contractors were not involved, we made a second building through a traditional construction system that involved – importantly enough – the same costs as the previous building.

The quality of the two artifacts is truly not comparable: on one side, you have one of the usual buildings found in our peripheries, though in this case it is decorated by a signature; on the other, there is a building with a central layout, designed and constructed with traditional methods, developed to take on a role as an urban volume, and a meaning as organized interior space: in my view, it is a successful work with sufficiently high levels of performance, though it complies with the IACP standards, which are extremely limiting and at times harmful. Above all, people feel good in the building, which is the greatest virtue of a residential complex. For example, the balconies have a size that permits dining outdoors. In short, it is a building that comes from a precise design idea, born and developed in the mind of an architect. Definitively, in spite of the imposed logic of the central plan – which was an added constraint – I am convinced that I was able to create an inhabitable residence.

The other building is there, bearing witness to the difference between two methodological approaches and two construction techniques: this does not mean that only a traditional construction technique can supply quality; but in any case it can underline and confirm, once again, that the way industrialization has been understood and formulated in Italy has served only to lower the qualitative level of architecture.

This does not rule out the idea that one could make a prefabricated building that is more beautiful than the one I made with traditional methods. But it is equally true, in short, that the mechanism of industrialization has served above all to increase profits, at the price of less control over quality. The most advanced technology is all to the good, but we should not make the mistake of discarding traditional technology, which is always the fundamental basis of architecture: America can teach us much in this regard. In the United States, to get back to the previous example, construction is done with the most advanced technologies, while continuing with the parallel use of "archaic" technologies, which would seem almost prehistoric to us.

The Mosque of Rome

Let's look at the Mosque[6] and the *monumental* experience: in 1974 I submitted a project in an international competition, and beyond what might have been an optimistic preview of the results, my proposal was based on the certainty of finding a suitable contractor later on.

I started from the intuition that interlocking arches – typical elements of the Islamic tradition – would be most effectively built with the technology of reinforced concrete, and in particular through a type of partial prefabrication.

I must admit that this was a case of good fortune, because I found excellent counterparts for the calculation of the structures, and for the engineer who then supervised the worksite: thanks to them, my intuition of using reinforced concrete as the ideal material for that construction system was completely fulfilled[7].

The interlocking arches represent the most characteristic feature of the spatial image of the building: the joints, which are the most complex parts in geometric terms, were made in the factory, while the rest of the concrete was poured on site. This is an important detail: it is evident, in fact, that the pieces poured in place are of such a size that they could not be done in the factory, and it is also clear that if the connection had only been based on tangency, the structure would not stand up. I believe that for the purpose of obtaining a convincing result this was the right way of using prefabrication.

In a later phase, to develop a rational and economical system of use of the formwork, we worked side by side with the builders to find the best solution: 17 domes were made with a single mold that was raised and lowered with hoists. To obtain a smooth concrete surface, which had to resemble stone or plaster, we used formwork made with formica, which could last for a maximum of four pours, after which it had to be resurfaced.

All this happened in an atmosphere of great cooperation, which is a fundamental aspect – and this is not a cliché – for the good outcome of operations like this one, marked by a high degree of complexity. The structure was developed for prefabrication, also because I have a certain amount of experience in this field: I worked for about ten years for a light prefabrication company, and that experience definitely helped me to understand the real problems of the assembly of the parts.

The intuition that a type of structure with those characteristics would achieve maximum expression only with reinforced concrete, and furthermore only with prefabrication, is undoubtedly the result of that collaboration. Perhaps we could also have utilized prestressing, in my view: when the tender guidelines were prepared, Riccardo Morandi[8] made a proposal that called for prestressing, but it was not possible to pursue it, though in any case we were able to conserve the sections we had designed in what became the definitive solutions, which was a source of great satisfaction for all.

If you consider the fact that the structure was calculated in keeping with antiseismic regulations, the wonder experienced when you enter the mosque and see the slender size of the structural parts is even greater, a dimensioning that makes you think of wood rather than concrete, but is actually simply based on the correct use of reinforced concrete.

I am very fascinated by the matter of *entasis,* of tapering: in effect, the cross-section of these prefabricated parts varies gradually towards the top, towards the extremity, and this could not have been done except in terms of industrial production.

The Mosque is an important example also due to the fact that together with modern techniques we applied archaic ones, or in any case archaic techniques done with modern means, as for example the use of brick cladding similar to what reaches us from classical antiquity, used in the tomb of Annia Regilla and then replicated in the Renaissance by Laurana, Michelangelo, Sangallo, Borromini. Reading the specifications from the time of Borromini, we learn that the bricks were obtained from large slabs, practically cut from roofing tiles, so as to have a very slim size, and were then honed on both sides with a sort of sandpaper, to make a geometric solid with perfectly parallel surfaces. This made it possible to rely on mortar joints with a thickness of less than one millimeter.

Today achieving this is much simpler: in the Mosque we applied a particular technique that called for the use of fired clay blocks cut in parallel "slices" so as to obtain perfectly smooth surfaces that would adhere firmly to each other. With this technique, one of the surfaces usually remains as it was after firing, and is thus used towards the inside: in this way precisely the "flesh" of the brick is used, achieving perfect installation. This also required training of the workers, who gradually learned the method: the first surfaces laid, in fact, especially those of the outer facade, are the ones in which the work is more irregular and sloppy, while the last portions to be installed were done very precisely.

Where the particular decorations are concerned, we relied on Islamic craftsmen who worked alongside the local team on the worksite: the constructive part was done by Impresa Federici of Rome, with its own workmen.

I already had experience in collaboration with specialized workers for the installation of Roman travertine, the stone taken from the "Cava del Barco" quarries, the same stone used to make the Colosseum. When the time came to do the decorations, Moroccan artisans entered the picture, capable of making ceramic mosaics with an extraordinary, fascinating technique: starting with a tile measuring 10 x 10, with their pounce they draw their "star", which can also be two millimeters per side, and then with a hammer they are able to cut this part and make it sufficiently rough on the back. After this, they lay the tile upside down: they pour cement on the panels resting on the floor, and then raised them and attach them to the walls. This is a very intriguing technique, because in those operations it reveals and ancient knowledge that has fortunately been conserved and passed on.

Just consider the fact that to control the intensity of the blow delivered on the ceramic part, to obtain these minimal forms, a sound amplifier is used to make it possible to gauge the strength, detecting it from the sound: the result is composed of small gems, much more similar to precious stones than to construction parts.

These details greatly enhanced the Mosque, giving it an unmistakably Islamic atmosphere.

The cultural attitude, the method

The experience gained in the Mosque reminds me in some ways of certain operations of Louis Kahn in some of his most important works, where to conserve a certain level of architectural semantics and not to lose its meaning, the worksite required workers who were "aware" of what they were doing. Passing from Casa Baldi to the present, through a numerous series of experiences of design and construction, I think I can say that the quality of an architect also lies in his capacity to adapt to the external world of production and the resources made available to him, grasping the right values of the environmental situation and the context, which is therefore not only historical, but also economic and productive.

For example, in the production of architects like Roberto Gabetti and Aimaro Isola, their continual changes of direction in terms of language are determined above all by the variable of resources, which for them constitutes a key of interpretation parallel to the traditional approach. The Mosque, in this sense, is undoubtedly very significant; also the above-mentioned buildings in Milan, precisely due to the different situations of production, led to a very different final result, not only from a technological standpoint but also and above all due to the resources available.

I trained myself in architecture – which should not seem like a paradox – reading the writings of Vitruvius and the *Eupalinos* of Valéry, therefore reaching the conviction that the architect is the catalyst that produces something unique, endowed with forceful unity, from things that were originally separate and extraneous to each other: it can be a work of art, but in many cases it is simply a stratagem.

The architect is above all the maker who solves problems, in the most general sense of the term, therefore focusing on everything, even military architecture. Once the architect was the technician par excellence, and today he has to return to that role, all the way to the military component.

The word "strategy" is very apt for the figure of the architect, who has to immediately take possession of the surrounding conditions, the economic character of the context, its productive character, to bring out its maximum potential: it is the question of the talents narrated in the Gospels.

In many cases, when people design they used tired formulas, a practice I feel is very negative. Faced with a particular situation or function, I usually try to bring out its specificities, drawing maximum benefit from the initial input.

"Post-Modern" is a term I have used, but it is time to put it aside[10]. The situation of great pluralism and experimentalism today is definitely not to be scorned: at present works of architecture are produced that have a maturity, a complexity and a richness that are clearly not possessed by previous works over the last two decades.

I am very much taken, for example, by the charm of the architecture of the

1920s, an avant-garde architecture that represented a high point of research, but it definitively create a language for the few, and later as it spread on a popular level it became banal, ridiculous, ineffective. It was an interesting elite operation, which the production system appropriated for purposes of profit.

Today there is an attempt to re-establish a "physiological regimen" in which architecture can spring from the relationship between needs, possibilities and conditions, thanks to the catalyst of architectural imagination.

We cannot avoid come to terms with the past, with the identity of places: it is pure illusion to think we can continue along the path of abstraction, as has recently been suggested by the deconstructivists, because in definitive terms there may still be some centimeters of leeway to discover, after which we will nevertheless "hit bottom" and then have to retrace our steps.

After all, design is truly an aware assumption of position of a cultural attitude that involves all the human senses, and that manifests itself – though with differing results – in the various projects and the various scales of design.

There is no doubt that every design operation has its own micro-history that does not depend only on the internal motivations of the architect, but also on surrounding situations dictated by economic reasons, the client, the operators involved.

In the design process the methodology and genesis of the project can be extremely variable: they range from the initial sketch to global ideas, only then to return to the detail or vice versa, as we have seen, the detail that is already born with the architecture.

There are those who imagine architecture that is always built specifically for each occasion, and those who consider architecture and its parts as a sort of catalogue that is the result of an increasingly vast range of choices offered today by the world of production.

I believe that whatever direction is taken, whatever the purpose of the job, when there is space for architecture the designer has to make a complete commitment to carry it out.

If I am able to choose the area in which to operate, I prefer design themes and works in which there is a real possibility of reaching completeness, of reaching the most detailed scale possible, thus to be able to design all the architectural elements; this does not mean that I exclude the catalogue *a priori*. I too, after all, have designed pieces for industrial production and as *components*, and for me this is a very interesting sector.

Context, materials, music

Material is an element connected with both the worksite and the place. Through the material, I have always felt a strong interest in the place. As a boy, visiting the towns of Lazio, I observed the diversity of architectural culture that can lead to the use, depending on the geographical zone, of limestone rather than tuff, or instead of peperino, and this aspect of the inseparability of *place* from *material* has always been very important for me.

Of course I have always had a tendency to interpret architecture *in toto,* in all its aspects, including tactile or olfactory considerations: works of architecture, especially when it rains, have their own fragrance that arises from the reaction between material and water. I learned this sensitivity from observation, and I have tried to transfer it into my architecture, just as I have applied my experience as a photographer to calculate the intensity of light, and the relationship between direct and reflected lighting.

Perhaps also for this reason, I love rugged materials that have an impact, a transmissible impression of a *materic* character; but I also appreciate precious materials, though I believe that one category without the other can soon lead to a sense of overkill.

Over the last few decades we have exaggerated with the rustic, the *brut,* because at a certain point this pervasive brutality has prevented us from grasping the true meaning of materials, which instead ought to be used like the notes utilized by a musician, in continual counterpoint and interweaving.

Attempting to interpret the particular moment we are crossing in the architectural debate with this musical metaphor, we can compare Rationalism to 12-tone composition, as a movement that pursues the aim of trying to create a musical category from scratch, in an artificial way – though absorbing something of the tradition, in limited form – thus also including the concept of dissonance in its expressive language.

All this has caused a radical break in relation to the audience: a gap that while it is less serious in the case of music, becomes a very serious matter when it comes to architecture.

At Montecatini, for example, an attempt was made to intervene in a container in which to insert a structure capable of creating an architecturally valid space. On that occasion I realized – and today I am even more convinced – that the material that more than others could give an identity to that space was wood. So I decided to use it in its laminated version, to free it from the traditional characteristics influenced by the technique of gluing, thus redeeming it from the trilithic dogma in which wood as used like stone.

Wood, with its fibers, its grain, its knots, in nature bends, frees itself, sinuously extending to embody the very expression of freedom and growth; but when it is cut and truncated into geometric solids, and thus used like stone, it is deprived of its nature.

This unnatural aspect can be avoided with lamellar wood: at Montecatini I used this technology, bending and branching the wooden pillars like tree trunks.

Material Architecture

In the architectural tradition it is rare to see such results: a log bent to construct a Gothic arch in some Norwegian church, or the marvelous irregular branches used in Japan as a merely decorative feature. However, I used wood, in the form of a tree, as a support, and this is possible only through the use of lamellar wood.

Perhaps not everyone has understood the philosophy behind that operation, which seemed to them to be only a flight of compositional fancy. For me this architectural episode represented a real experience in technology: the combination of the void created by the demolition and the idea of using wood led to the definition of a space I feel is very satisfying. I can see that the space today is utilized by the people who spend time at the Terme Tettuccio, as a characteristic moment: people have their pictures taken, they linger there to experience the atmosphere of the place.

The particular use of the wooden structure is inserted in a spatial sequence of great character – through zones of very high architectural quality, though academic in nature – also sustained by very apt, very rich decoration, in which it was certainly not easy to insert other elements; the operation was possible precisely thanks to an open relationship of familiarity with the technology and its expressive potential.

I must admit that *Holzbau*[12] responded very well to my design requirements: they might have been a bit dazed by such a different use of the material, but instead they made one of their representatives available, who came directly from Alto Adige, and thus worked with wood with the expertise of a woodsman: he achieved outstanding results.

Unfortunately – I say this regretfully – I have designed extensively with wood, but the project at Montecatini, for the moment, is the only project that has been implemented. Actually, in the zone there were precedents, namely the pillars of Giovanni Michelucci, which he has proposed and reworked on a number of occasions: first in the work on Pinocchio at Collodi, then in the Chiesa dell'Autostrada in Florence[13], both very interesting examples; his reinterpretation of the olive tree is brilliant, and it was a real shame that he was not able to built the theater in Olbia[14].

This relationship connected to the theme of *nature* and *architecture* is of particular interest in my design research, because I have always been fascinated by this continuous ability of nature to "suggest."

Detail

In these years there has been much debate regarding variables like memory and tradition, which have been and still are the central theme of the architectural discussion: technology, production, worksite and all the phases that connect design to implementation also have their own history and tradition.

But another aspect that cannot be overlooked in an interpretation of architecture presented in these terms is the relationship it has with *detail*, also in relation to those who produce architecture.

I believe that detail, as I have also said regarding the Mosque where it appears at a very high level, has to go beyond mere decoration, also in a not specifically technological way. At times architecture exists thanks to the assembly of a kind of "micro-parts": Franco Albini, or Mario Ridolfi, have made their works of architecture out of detail, or more precisely *from* detail.

There is a part of detail that arises together with the work, part of the idea itself, and is thus indispensable. But perhaps the most interesting aspect comes when the detail springs from the dialogue between the architect and the work.

On the modern worksite unfortunately the dialogue has significantly diminished, although this relationship of constant presence with the object, which was once above all *physical*, can now be shifted into a *mental* space, equally useful for the rethinking of the project.

It is important to realize that the work, at a certain point, breaks free of its author and takes on its own objectivity, even its own subjectivity: from this moment on the architect can and should above all be a good *listener*, an interpreter, and the detail represents the best way to interpret.

The experience of the worksite, seen in the traditional sense here, in which the architect can intervene also in subsequent, progressive moments, testing, attempting, verifying, is an experience that comes from a relationship of dialogue and comprehension between the *architect* and his *work* – not necessarily a relationship of "love" but also one of "hate." Making architecture thus becomes a marvelous operation: the opportunity of being able to operate through a type of detail we can define as "corrective" or in certain cases "expressive," at the maximum of the virtual logic of the work, is perhaps one of the most extraordinary aspects of architecture.

My architecture often springs from a detail: for example, the idea of the "adjectivized" corner – one of my obsessions – a bit in the manner of Hoffmann, is a matrix of detail that in some ways can solve any problem.

In this sense, a project could be based on the identification of this joint of three different planes, which I tend to interpret as a self-sufficient element of syntax.

In many episodes – I recall in this regard the project for a hospital in Agrigento[15] – the process of implementation is a fundamental moment: in this sense, the greater the volumetric complexity, the more problems will have to be solved, so the interest of the architect in different forms of detail is sharpened. This is often represented, in my case, by this all-inclusive joint. Once, I remember, there was the joint of Wachsmann; now Renzo Piano, to cite one example, works extensively in this direction.

This is the perspective through which to interpret the renovation of Palazzo Corrodi at Piazzale Flaminio[16] which I have recently completed: a building of great interest which I have attempted to bring back to life on the inside, since time had left behind only the enclosure – all the characteristic features of the interior space had vanished – thanks to specificities that while being filtered by my own personal history, have their origin precisely in that enclosure.

I thus had the rare opportunity to be able to design many details, going down to a very small scale, in great depth, even reaching the design of the fabrics: we would even have decided to design the handles, had there not been economic limitations, as often happens.

While on the one hand the lack of economic boundaries would be troubling, there is no doubt that such considerations have a way of limiting the degree of detail that is possible in the design.

Starting from a limitation, starting from a detail, are essential *mental* operations in design; the detail decided on *a posteriori,* or during the course of construction, or even after the work has been completed, comes instead from the practice of *listening* in a moment in which the detail itself takes charge of the testing and validity of intuitions: shedding light on this inner logic of the *work that narrates itself,* that uses the architect and at times forces him into acrobatic feats, represents the ultimate effort in our profession, its final act.

Rome, 3 March 1993 – Studio Portoghesi

Notes

1. Paolo Portoghesi was born in Rome in 1931, and took a degree there in 1957. His debut in construction came with the design of the interior of an office building for ENPAS in Pistoia, and the ENPAS headquarters in Lucca (1958-59), relying on the example of Ridolfi. At the start of his career, from the late 1950s to the early 1970s, Portoghesi worked above all on single-family homes: Casa Baldi (1959-61), Casa Papanice in Rome (1969-70), Casa Bevilacqua at Gaeta (1964-72), Casa Andreis in Scandriglia, near Rome (1965-67). Only later did he progress to the design of more complex works.

2. Paolo Portoghesi's activity has always been divided between teaching, historical research and architectural design, in keeping with an orientation towards the reabsorption of collective memory within the modern architectural tradition.
From 1967 to 1977 Portoghesi taught in the School of Architecture of the Politecnico di Milano, where he was Dean from 1968 to 1976. He is presently a full professor of Architectural History at Università La Sapienza in Rome. From 1983 to 1993 he was President of the Venice Biennale. As a historian and critic he has explored the urban history of Rome, some essential nodes of architectural history such as the Baroque and the Renaissance, and a number of personalities and episodes at the origins of the Modern, also finding fertile stimuli for his works of architecture in these studies. He has taken an active part in the discussion on the renewal of architecture, becoming a spokesman for the Post-Modern movement in Italy. Portoghesi has been the editor of several architecture magazines: he has also worked as a product designer; many essays have been published on his activity and his theoretical position. Portoghesi represents, in a sense pertinent to Borromini, a figure that aptly interprets the synthesis between design research and theoretical research-debate, between in-depth knowledge of historical issues and constructive architectural practice. In the 1960s and 1970s he was very close to avant-garde figures in the world of art and architecture – his encounter with Bruno Zevi was very important – though he did not take a direct part in groups, warily keeping his distance from proclaimed theories.

3. Casa Baldi, built in 1961 on Via Flaminia in Rome, was one of the first constructed works of Paolo Portoghesi: a small house designed for a filmmaker friend on a plateau of volcanic stone along the Tiber, adjacent to very ancient Roman ruins. The building became emblematic of his production because it launched experimentation with curved walls – revealing the passion for the spatial effects of Borromini – a prime linguistic reference of the project in which reflection on the use of reinforced concrete is combined with surfaces in brick and local stone.

4. During his university years and early career Portoghesi had a particular interest in Neo-Realism, interpreted in the sense of artistic expression based above all on the real needs of the society. For Portoghesi, the houses by Mario Ridolfi on Viale Etiopia (1951-54) constituted the most significant and interesting example of the production of those years.

5. The IACP buildings at Sesto San Giovanni (Milan) are a pair of neighboring artifacts, both made for the same client, but at different times. In the first experience, dated 1981, the design was asked to work as a consultant only in the final phases of the construction process: this commission was not so much for an architectural design as such, as for the setting of the character of the enclosure of the building, with all the limitations of a job in which the plan had already been determined, and the constraints of the standards imposed by IACP. While the first building was made with the prefabrication technique, the second (1984-85), due to the wishes of the designer, was built with traditional techniques. This structure with a central plan called in typological terms for vertical connections placed exactly at the geometric center of the building, to serve the four apartments of a standard floor. The building with six stories as well as the ground level and the mansards has a brick red color, paced by exposed vertical pillars, gables at different levels over the higher part of the building, and loggias that indicate the central axis of the facades.

6. The Islamic Cultural Center and connected Mosque of Rome constitute one of the largest construction initiatives undertaken in Italy since 1975, the year in which the "Centro Islamico

Culturale d'Italia" announced an international architecture competition for the construction of a *mosque* and a *cultural center* to be built on an area of 30,000 square meters donated by the municipality, at the foot of Monte Antenne. The 40 projects submitted by architects from Europe and the Islamic countries were examined by a commission of experts on architecture and Islamic culture, after which two projects were selected, that of the Portoghesi-Gigliotti group and that of the Iraqi architect Sami Mousawi, who later joined forces with the Italian group in a relationship of collaboration for the preparation of the definitive project. The entire complex included the main mosque, with a capacity of 2000 worshippers, and the cultural center, with a small prayer room for daily use, a library with a vast collection of books on Islamic culture in the West, an auditorium for 400 persons, exhibition spaces, official spaces, meeting rooms, offices, large parking areas and gardens.

The layout called for a typology from the archaic and classical period of Islamic architecture: the central volume – set aside for men's prayer – is a block with a square plan, topped by a large central dome and 16 lateral domes, directly connected to a courtyard with porticos. The layout organization takes its cue from basic geometric forms, the circle and the square, elements of the design of the temple which along with forceful symmetry grant the facility a role as a monument with respect to the city. The indoor and outdoor spaces are shaped and organized by a series of polystyle pillars that branch out at the upper extremity to form the ribbing of the interlocking arches that support the domes. Light plays a leading role: a ribbon cornice decorated with verses from the Koran emphasizes it to create an effect of suspension for the entire structure.

7. Portoghesi's project was selected due to two factors: the achievement, above all in the prayer hall, of a typically Islamic atmosphere, and the proposal of advanced construction technologies; these factors were maintained and developed in the definitive design and the construction. This worksite brought together sophisticated research related to engineering for technologies of prefabrication, and painstaking study of crafts techniques. Strategically placed next to the main worksite, another site was used for the production of the parts of the load-bearing structure, partially prefabricated and partially poured in place through the use of formwork developed to achieve an effect similar to stone for the concrete. Both the pillars and the arches were made with mixtures of white concrete and Carrara marble dust, making the structural members into an element that brings character to the architectural space, also on a decorative level.

8. The projects of the engineer Riccardo Morandi (Rome, 1902-89) were inventive experiments, above all in the field of prestressed reinforced concrete: he is famous for his bridges, built all over the world.

9. The Mosque project was approved in 1983 and assigned during the next year to the Roman contractor headed by the engineer Fortunato Federici: the worksite continued for eleven years, from 1984 to 1995, making it the largest and most important in Rome in recent decades. The complex was opened in June 1995, in a ceremony attended by the Italian and Islamic authorities.

10. Critics assign Paolo Portoghesi the responsibility for the introduction in Italy of the "Post-Modern" – a term originating in the English-speaking world – thanks to the installation of the exhibition *Strada Novissima* in the architecture section of the Venice Biennale in 1980, on the theme *The Presence of the Past*. It is nevertheless important to emphasize, to avoid the generic kind of judgment that selected him as the spokesman of this presumed current, together with other exponents of Italian architecture in the 1980s, that Portoghesi has always spoken of a "postmodern condition" in reference to an extensive cultural phenomenon, rather than recognizable or encoded linguistic formulas, or ideologically defined objectives.

11. The project by Paolo Portoghesi for the Padiglione Termale of Montecatini (Pistoia) dates back to 1987 and addressed the creation of a structure for a reception and waiting area inside the existing building of the Terme Tettuccio, a hot springs facility on two levels. Portoghesi's project is inserted in the larger volume, taking advantage of the height made available following the demolition of the floor slabs, and setting the tone of the single space with a forest of wooden pillars that sustain a perimeter balcony walkway and a roof in colored glass.

12. The Holzbau company, located in the industrial zone of Bressanone, specializes in the

design, production and installation of lamellar beams and structures. Founded in 1974 thanks to the collaboration of several local entrepreneurs with a German company, it was the first in Italy to experiment with and develop woodworking techniques to achieve higher levels of mechanical performance than those of solid wood, and formal quality of a very high level and flexibility.

13. In the project for the restaurant, hotel, bar and tavern complex "Osteria del Gambero Rosso" located in the Parco di Pinocchio at Collodi (Pistoia), and completed by Giovanni Michelucci in the period 1958-63, a structural solution appears of a branching pillar, an element that was to become a constant in the research of Michelucci, appearing in many of his works, including the church of San Giovanni Battista at Campi Bisenzio (Florence), better known as the Chiesa dell'Autostrada (1960-64).

14. In 1989 Michelucci was hired by the municipality of Olbia to design a complex including an indoor theater, an outdoor theater, a theater workshop and a service area equipped for crafts activities. Michelucci developed only a rough project, after a long series of hypotheses whose sketches offer the best documentation of the architect's design idea after his death at the end of 1990.

15. Competition project for the new hospital of Agrigento (1986).

16. The intervention by Portoghesi at Palazzo Corrodi in Rome has to do with the internal transformation of a 20th-century building into spaces for offices. The operation is full of references, both in the key elements of the building (like the monumental helical staircase inspired by Borromini) and in the details and finishes (like the floors and suspended ceilings with classical and Baroque geometries).

Aldo Rossi

Architecture
of the idea

Architecture based on an idea

I believe I certainly did not begin by planning my professional life: I have nevertheless made choices, in the sense that I thought it would be better to study a foundation, a theory, on the basis of which I could then *begin* architecture.

When I completed my studies, the state of architecture, what today is defined as the architecture of the 1960s, was at truly low levels.

Already in the 1950s, when I studied without much continuity at the Politecnico di Milano[1], what had struck me most was the insufficiency and lack of preparation of the professors who were teaching there at the time. At the Department of Architecture I went through moments of great crisis, and my relationships with many of the teachers were almost "traumatic": only certain cases were exceptions, like Prof. Luigi Dodi, I remember, and Prof. Portaluppi, though he was always being attacked and criticized, and of course Ernesto Rogers, whom I got to know in the final phase of my degree program[2].

Over the span of my career I have therefore crossed different phases, and I believe it is for this reason that over time I have been the architect with the most designations: from "politico" to "man of letters," "painter" to "architect," and now even "professional"; I have always paid little attention to these adjectival formulas, which after all are simply different aspects of a whole; I have instead tried to coherently follow one linear path. Even this ultimate phase of mine, the professional phase, marked by very intense production, should be interpreted within a process aimed at continuity between theoretical study and construction; time and luck have contributed, as at the start of an avalanche, to foster the intensification of the projects and achievements in recent years[3].

In any case, there never exists – at least not intentionally – a perceptible break between the two types of activity: the boundaries between the disciplines are very blurry, and even today, if I fall in love with a project, I like to make a nice drawing, to write an essay, apart from the "professional" phase I am going through.

The most important thing in the work of an architect is to offer an idea: an idea that demonstrates a certain superiority to a sketch tossed off on the fly, or a note hastily jotted down. Architecture comes from an image, a precise image that is taken into our depths and translated, precisely, into the drawing, into the construction. The most important moment is precisely the *idea of the architecture*. Only when you have this idea in your head can you begin to draw it and, as a result, to perfect it. To those who ask me if I am against computers and their use in design, I respond that progress marches on and it is right for it to advance more and more, but the human mind still takes precedence – and I hope it will always be so – in a very important way for the verification, reproduction, refinement of the idea. Without a basic idea you cannot advance in architecture; I also think that this discourse, once again, is not valid only for architecture: in the best aeronautical projects, you cannot move forward without an initial reference.

My architecture always and in any case comes from an overall vision. This initial image is what immediately appears in my first sketches; it seldom happens that I substantially alter this initial idea: the entire design develops from it. This does not rule out the possibility of the subsequent arrival of particulars that in any case come from another intuition that manages to work its way into the overall project. This has happened above all in my recent large projects, such as those prepared for Berlin[4], for example, which are based on an idea of how to reconstruct Berlin, although obviously the fact of operating in a given part of the city causes the often positive infiltration of various memories and fragments.

The ancients narrated that Minerva was born from the head of Jupiter already fully armed: the initial idea of my projects already contains the solution to many problems, not only of a functional or layout order, but also of a technological and constructive nature. Therefore although I certainly do not begin from the details, the general idea already contains them. For this reason, in fact, I usually have an excellent relationship with the figures delegated to focus on the specialized aspects, such as structural engineers and physical plant experts.

For example, in the project for the museum in Maastricht, Holland[5], I had developed a series of drawings for Alexander van Grevenstein, the director and a very active client, based on which my studio had developed the definitive drawings; when the latter were sent to the Dutch company hired for the engineering of the project, the technicians remarked that they had no work to do, since our drawings already contained all the information needed for the construction.

Of course in a work like the museum in Maastricht it is necessary to also intervene in the later phases of the construction, with a series of continuous observations that are absolutely crucial passages. As the years have gone by I have become more careful, but this is due to autobiographical factors, by way of carry-overs or references.

Nevertheless, today I can still boast about the fact that I have never had to check on the work directly at the construction site: the first drawings for the Gruppo Finanziario Tessile[6] that I showed to Marco Rivetti, the CEO who constituted the client, represented exactly the GFT that now exists in Turin – not a single brick was changed.

Also the project for the tower in Mexico City[7], though there were difficulties due to the present crisis in Mexico, was translated into drawings by a Dutch company exactly as it was born on paper, in local black volcanic stone, the kind used in Mexico by the Jesuits, with an arrangement of windows that is identical to the one seen in the study sketches.

Architecture and drawing

I am absolutely certain about the link between architecture and its expression, not only the graphic formulation directly connected to the architecture, but also the literary and even filmic or photographic expression, which are forms connected to the use of all the media technique makes available to us today. After all, this was always true for the architects of antiquity; I do not believe that good graphic or literary quality comes at the expense of the quality and knowledge of the means of construction. Of course, we have to also consider what it means today to talk about the means of construction and to evaluate the profound revolution that continues to advance in this field. Over the years, in fact, the experiences change.

I believe that even today it is very important for an architect to know how to draw: this aspect was not fundamental only in the golden age of the Renaissance, a period in which architects were generally also great painters, or vice versa. Drawing is and always will be a very important, indispensable form of knowledge of the real. I remember my first contacts with life drawing at the Politecnico di Milano: though they were disastrous, I made an effort to understand the potential of the media, the meaning of signs, the value of drawing. This discourse is not just an exclusive factor; it is instead based on a relationship of a statistical nature: many great architects were also great draftsmen, or even great painters.

Just think about Muthesius, Asplund, Berlage, who also kept painting up to a certain age, or Adolf Loos, who by temperament was perhaps more a painter and a writer than an architect. It is clear that the importance of this component remained very strong, all the way to the Modern Movement. For example, an architect like Mies van der Rohe, who opened the way for technology, setting new conditions for architecture, made drawings – just consider those for the

Alexanderplatz[8] – that for their beauty and richness of meaning can be counted among the world's most important works of art. Training is undoubtedly of great value in this field. Though in any case this does not negate the validity of other types of education: Alberti, for example, had a rigorous literary background, yet he can be recognized as one of the greatest architects in Italy, or even in the world.

I do not believe – and this is one of the problems we come across in architectural schools – that a direct line exists between education in the fine arts and architectural training, although the teaching of the academies and the *Beaux-Arts* schools of painting has undoubtedly had much influence on our discipline.

Drawing is the immediate method of expression of what is thought; the same discourse probably applies to music and literature, though architecture requires more time and a set of skills and collaborations for its making that is more complex with respect to the work done, for example, by a poet.

The value of drawing as the expression of an idea that already exists in the mind of the architect is strong even for those architects who in a provocative way claim that they are pleased to not know how to draw, or in any case to not know how to do it well: Rogers himself, in his sketches – some of which I think are very handsome – transmitted something of his intelligence and his poetic spirit that went well beyond the assessment of the graphic gesture.

The rational principle of architecture

Many students of all nationalities, from Japan to Malaysia to the United States, often ask me what it means to design all over the world in different contexts and situations.

I believe the concept of *transmissibility* it is very important in architecture, also for the goals of the discipline, or namely the necessity to create, by constructing, basic principles that are easily perceptible and reproducible. It is then on the basis of these foundations that the individual personality of every architect can develop.

When a rational principle of architecture has been established, it can be transmitted even if during the course of that transmission it inevitably undergoes a change: for example, the architecture of Palladio is based on elementary principles that are easy to encode, but already the Palladio of the villas in the Veneto is not the Palladio of Venice; so the 18th-century villas in the Veneto are no longer the previous Palladio, and likewise for all of Russia, England, France, Louisiana, where valid forms of Palladian architecture have been developed, which are no longer Palladio. Nevertheless, in his case a principle of architecture was established, which proved to be very valid and has produced much.

This is not intended as a defense against the attacks made at times against so-called "Rossian"[9] projects, because I am convinced of the fact that an architect can develop an individual language and personality precisely after having learnt the basic principle of the architecture.

The great Jesuit architecture, for example, has influenced many designers. I firmly believe in the importance of examples for the spread of architecture: once the rational principle of the architecture has been established, it survives for a long time through its potentialities of development.

Another example is the *Beaux-Arts* architecture of Paris, which transported to the United States created Broadway, transforming and acting as a model in the great American cities: because if you are on Broadway you can certainly not say you are in Paris, although the influence behind the place is clearly Parisian.

Narrating architecture "from the inside"

I believe it is very important – a concept that also recurs in Baudelaire, in the great critics and the French poets – for the artist to be someone capable of narrating himself. Very beautiful texts exist, supporting this aspect: among them I can mention precisely the most anomalous one, that of Pontormo, who in his autobiography, almost without talking about painting, manages to outline an overview of great value of Florentine painting. Also Vasari, who was a figure closer in terms of role, a historian, demonstrated this ability to speak "from the inside."

Naturally there also exists a criticism that is more "literary," which among other things has contributed much to architecture, such as Ruskin, Proust himself, or like the invention of romantic architecture, aspects that reflect on a craft of ideas that do not belong to the craft itself. Unfortunately today there are no more Baudelaires, and not even any more Ruskins. In Italy we have had one very outstanding example, that of Tafuri, who represented the architecture of this last generation not precisely from the inside, but with a very high level of literary and human interpretation, experiencing all of its vicissitudes.

Rogers, for example, is the person who disrupted the provincial seclusion of the Milanese world of the Polytechnic in those years, and with *Casabella-Continuità* he opened a very important window to the world. Rogers, I remember, evoked distant examples, as it is easy for us to do today: he spoke of New York as if it was Milan or Parma, Tokyo or Beijing. At the time there was truly an insurmountably closed situation, not just for practical questions of transportation or social issues, but precisely due to a closure of a cultural nature. Rogers was the first to open things up, to import the culture of modern architecture into Italy in a truly new way. Although there were other figures before him, I think more than the others he was the one who experienced things firsthand: he taught in Europe, America, Argentina. He had a truly variegated background: Trieste, Judaism, England.

Today, unfortunately, we are going through a moment of serious decline, a phenomenon that goes beyond architectural criticism. Previously the magazines like *Casabella*, or also the magazines against *Casabella*, were cultural magazines, who battled to defend their own ideas. I receive them all today, but unfortunately I do not even open one of them, because their only purpose is to fill up tables almost exclusively with advertising. At times they ask me to publish a project: they may do a very good job of it, but there is no longer any perceptible viewpoint, and I think this aspect is very negative, above all for young people and university students. The propaedeutic aspects and didactic impact implied by this type of publication are absolutely negative. I usually recommend only about twenty books to my students, along with the subscription to one magazine.

The decadence seems to me to have also spread into other international contexts, because by now certain types of publications simply exploit scandalous topics: no one develops a true analysis of architecture. Recently I saw an entire issue of Der Spiegel on Berlin, which completely resembled the gossip pages of our newspapers, more than the magazine I know and admire.

Architecture from expertise to specialization

When I enrolled at the Polytechnic in 1949, the two-year program in architecture was practically equal to that of engineering – we had professors like Masotti, Finzi, Chiolini[10] – and for me the great discovery of architecture came precisely in this period of teaching close to that of engineering, which also attracted me greatly.

Since then I have always had an interest in construction with an aspect of engineering, more than that of an architectural character. But my Milanese education ranges from Rogers to Gardella. In those years, we should recall, Franco Albini was also setting the tone. Though I have a memory of Franco Albini as a very courteous person, I have never felt much affinity or passion for his way of making architecture. I even feel a need to disagree on certain things: above all when the projects reach a certain scale and certain dimensions, I think Albini's method loses its validity.

Today things are moving increasingly towards a formulation of the project marked by a high degree of specialization.

When an airport is built, for example, one relies on an American company to supply the bridges, a German company to do the assembly, and so on, the architect becomes a figure comparable to that of the film director, who has to be well versed in everything: the nature of the comedy, the rules of acting, the use of lights. Without the lighting engineer, the director can do nothing. I believe that architecture today calls for directors capable of governing it, because it is impossible to manage an entire airport, or the two blocks I am building in Berlin[11] which constitute a piece of the city. Projects of this type represent great experiences for an architect: in situations like these, it is not easy to decide if the person who does the electrical conduits or the architect is more important, because both of them are absolutely indispensable.

When I designed the Linate airport[12], which is not even one of the biggest in Europe, I would never have been able to work without a team of specialists. The architect cannot afford, in such situations, to have control over everything, also because it would be absurd to overlook the high quality of today's technology. And today it is necessary to make correct use of technology.

The forms of expertise inside my studio, in the case of projects of great complexity and large dimensions, are very strong: for example, to supervise the projects in Holland there is a Dutch architect who has an ongoing relationship with the projects in progress, although I too, in this context, have direct ties and relationships which I pursue and cultivate. In other cases, as in Berlin, another type and another quality of work is habitual, so we have had to produce whole packages of drawings of details. Therefore for certain aspects – such as the fact of not monitoring the worksite – I am accused of traditionalism, while for others I am instead judged as being one of the most advanced.

An attitude such as mine is very widespread and extensively applied in the more developed countries. In America, for example, there is an increasing tendency towards this type of figure that is capable of coordinating the work: an architect like Philip Johnson – a master, in my view – is able to control projects of great complexity and size.

The old dream of the technological architects of the 1960s who went down to the smallest details, studying them, has no meaning for me: I have always refused – and this is why I have had problems with the architects' association to which I belong – to design a window frame when there are factories and designers specialized in designing and producing window frames, who also do it very well. For me it is absurd that today, to obtain approval of a project, it is necessary to make drawings of this type.

I believe, as I have always sustained, that no relationship exists that goes "from the spoon to the city." My success as a designer is the result of sporadic, personal episodes: I am a friend and neighbor of Alessi[13], who at a certain point asked me to design a coffeepot, and after that – also discovering autobiographical suggestions, where the form of the coffeepot evokes the world of domes – these designs were born that have entered the production process and then had wider development. While I reject the phrase "from the spoon to the city" from an ideological standpoint, because it is pure ideological decline, I instead think that the crafts process is an important thing for an architect, more closely connected to his work.

The greater the specialization, the more force the general idea must have, because at certain levels if you stop to look at the handle on a window you are lost. In a provocative way, I say that I do not go to the worksite as long as the project is not finished, but for me this means that I believe in the primacy of the project with respect to the worksite. The worksite is a machine that is gradually improving, deploying a production process that is increasingly precise, which in any case has to be at the service of the project. I must confess that I have never seen the Vassivière project[14] at its site, as is also true of other things: but I did spend time in Vassivière, for a few days, five months prior to doing the design. It is much more important to enter, understand, experience the place, before the construction, than to spend time on the worksite itself, which is supervised by specialized people when the project has already been very well defined.

What is important is not to let oneself by influenced by this world, but to know it in order to be able to control it, at least as far as it is possible to do so.

Milan, 28 June 1995 – Studio Rossi

Notes

1. The studies of Aldo Rossi, born in Milan in 1931, and the poetics of his works of architecture have their roots in the history and tradition, especially of Lombardy. Rossi studied in Como, in Lecco and at the Department of Architecture of the Politecnico di Milano. While still a student, he seemed to be more interested in research conducted outside the school, rather than the specific activities of the university: in 1955 he was invited by Ernesto Nathan Rogers to work with *Casabella-Continuità* on the editorial staff, a position that continued until the magazine was closed in 1964; during the same years, he worked for Ignazio Gardella, and later also with Marco Zanuso. This was the context of his cultural background, much more than the Politecnico di Milano, where he took a degree in 1959 with a project for a cultural center and a theater in Milan, under the supervision of Prof. Piero Portaluppi.

2. At the Department of Architecture of the Politecnico di Milano, ever since the period prior to World War II, the cultural orientation of architectural design was dictated by Prof. Piero Portaluppi (Milan, 1888-1967), dean of the Department from 1939 to 1945 and 1948 to 1963, and chair of the courses of Architectural Composition I and II. Parallel to the discipline of architectural design, the teaching in Urban Planning was guided by Eng. Luigi Dodi, a Milanese urbanist and chair of Urbanism I (4th year) from 1939 to 1955 – succeeded by Prof. Enrico Griffini – and later of Urbanism II (5th year). Ernesto Nathan Rogers began his teaching career in the Department of Architecture of the Politecnico di Milano as a lecturer in Stylistic and Constructive Characters of Monuments – from 1952 to 1962 – and later in Elements of Composition, becoming a full professor only in 1964. One clear demonstration of Aldo Rossi's tense relationship with the institution of the Polytechnic is the "revolt" in which he took part, in 1954, in a group with a number of classmates and future Milanese professionals, including Guido Canella.

3. From the early 1960s Rossi demonstrates a very fertile talent for design. His activity involves intense production of projects aimed at refining a theory of architecture based on autonomy and transmission of the discipline. His activities as a theorist, designer and teacher converge around these issues.

Until the beginning of the 1980s, most of his projects remained on paper, until the last decade of his life, in which he completed a dense sequence of constructed works. After the publication of *L'architettura della città*, in 1966, Rossi began collaborations with a number of figures on the Italian scene, mostly from Milan.

The constructed works of the 1970s are few in number but significant: the residential unit of the Monte Amiata complex at the Gallaratese district in Milan, starting in 1969, in which Rossi completed the complex designed by Carlo Aymonino (1967-72); the new cemetery of Modena, with Gianni Braghieri, resulting from victory in a competition in 1971; the city hall of Muggiò and the elementary school at Fagnano Olona, both in 1972; the school at Broni, in 1979. Rossi's phase of intense production seems to start with the winning competition project for the reconstruction of Teatro Carlo Felice in Genoa (1983), designed in collaboration with Ignazio Gardella and Fabio Reinhart.

Observing a list of the works of Aldo Rossi, it becomes clear that the projects and constructions increase in number starting in 1985, while the range of contexts expands from Europe to also include the Middle East and projects overseas: from the United States to South American and Japan.

From that year forward the completed works form an intense sequence, addressing multiple typological themes: the "CentroTorri" shopping center in Parma (1985-88), the "Casa Aurora" office building for GFT in Turin, completed in 1987, the residential building at La Villette in Paris (1986-92), the residential unit of Vialba on the outskirts of Milan (1985-91), the "Il Palazzo" hotel in Fukuoka, Japan (1987), the contemporary art center of Clermont-Ferrand, Vassivière (1988), a complex of single-family houses in Pennsylvania (1988), the renovation and expansion of Hotel Duca in Milan (1988), the "Cesare Cattaneo" university institute at Castellanza (1990).

4. The first half of the 1980s was an important period of Aldo Rossi's career, especially in relation to the projects and constructed works for Berlin: the bond with the German city, a factor of great influence and stimulus for the personality and background of the architect, found its first expression in the works for the IBA: the "Südliche Friedrichstadt" project in 1981, and a residential building at the Tiergarten, in 1984. These works both already contain many of the characteristics of Rossi's projects for Berlin, based on careful analysis of German architecture, from Schinkel to Mies, Behrens to the rationalist Siedlungen, focusing on the typology of the brick building featuring a regular pattern of windows and marked by simple features like the corner column and the tower volume. The connection with Berlin continued in the project for the Deutsches Historisches Museum (1988), the competition for Potsdammerplatz (1990), and the project for a building on Friedrichstrasse (1991).

5. The new headquarters of the Bonnefantenmuseum of Maastricht, designed in 1990 (with Umberto Barbieri, Giovanni Da Pozzo and Marc Kocher), was opened in 1994. For Rossi this project was a chance to continue his research on the theme of the museum, which was of great interest to him. Dutch tradition, classical forms, personal impressions, fragments of seagoing memory merge in a project of simple functional effectiveness and elementary forms. A foyer with a cylindrical form topped by a dome, a long staircase, geometric blocks paced by the rhythm of the windows and buttresses, all made even more orderly by the materials: brick, in different cladding formats, regular cut stone for the base, and modular geometric metal parts.

6. The office building designed by Aldo Rossi for Gruppo Finanziario Tessile was the result of a long process involving the demolition and reconstruction of "Casa Aurora" (from 1971 to 1987), the previous headquarters of the group, located in a suburban area of Turin whose character was set by the industrial growth of the late 1800s.

Placed at the corner between a secondary street and a larger artery, the office building designed by Aldo Rossi (1984-87, with G. Braghieri, G. Ciocca, F. Marchesotti, M. Scheurer, L. Uva) is composed of two perpendicular volumes with porticos on the ground level, introduced by two towers that constitute the extremities, converging on a third tower, an element of connection, placed diagonally with respect to the two volumes. The corner element juxtaposes a wall without openings, but by a single portal with two columns of a giant order, with the enclosure featuring regular windows of the two wings.

7. This is the "Proyecto Alameda," one of the last projects by Aldo Rossi – dated 1994 – involving the construction – not yet in progress – of a large office tower in Mexico City. Given the risk of earthquakes in Mexico, that project has been "tested" by a Dutch company specialized in structural calculations.

8. The drawings mentioned refer to the project presented by Ludwig Mies van der Rohe in the competition for the Alexanderplatz in Berlin in 1928.

9. Regarding this positive attitude regarding those who have adopted a "Rossi-like" language, we can include – as the sole quotation from the many writings of Aldo Rossi – some phrases that seem to be particularly significant: "There exist, in architecture as in other techniques, results that are passed down and belong to architecture; a copy exists of what is more personal, but if it is done by the finest architects it is a proof of affection and an authentic testament. In any case, in spite of the critics, I take a positive and affectionate view of any imitation of what they might call my architecture, and I believe I have nothing more to say on this topic. I have nothing more to say because it is uncontrollable, so to speak: the phenomenon of transmission of thought, of what we call experience, of the same world of forms, is not connected to a program or a fashion, perhaps not even to a school" (A. Rossi, *Autobiografia scientifica,* Pratiche Editrice, Parma 1990, p. 105).

10. In the years in which Rossi began to study at the Polytechnic, among the teachers at the Department of Engineering Giuseppina Masotti taught Descriptive Geometry starting in

1933, Bruno Finzi was the professor of Rational Mechanics from 1946, Paolo Chiolini taught Architectural Composition from 1949, and taught alongside Giovanni Muzio in the area of Architecture and Architectural Composition of the Department of Engineering.

11. The most recent projects for Berlin include an office building on Lansberger Allee and a residential-office block on Schützenstrasse, both dated 1992. Of these two worksites, the first to be initiated (June 1995) was the one on Schützenstrasse, a project calling for the parallel reconstruction and renovation of several historical buildings and the making of other constructions completely inside a single block.

12. In the project for the expansion of the international airport of Milano Linate (with M. Brandolisio, G. Da Pozzo, M. Kocher and G. Vercelloni, designed in 1991 and still under construction), Rossi approaches the theme of the "gateway to the city," restoring ancient roots to this typology in continuous change and evolution that is normally scarcely considered. The glass surfaces geometrically paced by a colonnade of brick pillars are interrupted only by the towers of the entrances and the metal bridges for the transport of luggage.

13. Halfway through the 1980s Rossi begins to design products for the company Alessi, an erudite client that encourages a stimulating relationship, not just in the sector of industrial design. Besides a series of objects for the kitchen and the home, Rossi has created architectural projects for the Alessi family, including a tower in the garden of the villa on Lake Orta (1986, never built) and the renovation of the villa at Suna (Verbania, 1989).

14. This is the center for contemporary art of Clermont-Ferrand (Vassivière, France, 1988, with S. Fera and X. Fabre), a building created on a small island at the center of an artificial lake, in a flourishing natural zone. Hence the reference to the typology of the large beacon, a favorite archetype of Rossi, which returns often in his sketches, his works of architecture, installations and objects. From the large conical tower in stone and brick containing the sculpture collection, the oblong volume of the museum extends towards the lake, containing spaces for exhibitions, education and services.

Guido Canella

Architecture of dissent

Contextualization of the theme: the specificity of the Italian postwar scene

I belong to a generation trained in architecture in the period after World War II. I enrolled in the Department of Architecture in Milan in 1950, in a period marked by the widespread popularity of the International Style. So it should come as no surprise that for us the urgent necessity arose for rethinking, conducted through a comparison between what the Modern Movement had pursued and meant in the 1920s and 1930s, and what it was pursuing and meaning in the postwar period[1].

The dean of the Department of Architecture in Milan was still Piero Portaluppi, with a group of teachers who prior to the war had resisted rationalist radicalism, urging a hybrid modernism, between Art Deco and Novecento. The sole exception was Ambrogio Annoni[2], more erudite and farsighted, who in his teaching of Stylistic Characteristics in Architecture had realized that the discriminating factor between modern and non-modern was not a matter of mere appearances, but a way of understanding, sensing and experiencing the design process. Unfortunately I did not have Annoni as a teacher; but I did have Ernesto Rogers, who took his place on the faculty[3]. While at school Rogers' lectures were able to directly convey the poetic experiences of the masters of the Modern Movement, it was above all in the books, and establishing comparisons of structure in the prewar cultural climate, that we became aware of how architectural Rationalism was ideologically tied to a Taylorist and Fordian vision of the growth of the city, since one of its fundamental ideological components – I am referring above all to Gropius and the Bauhaus experience – arose from a poetics of architecture that by then considered the industrial process as hegemonous, not only in the production of consumer goods but also, in perspective, in the reproduction of the city.

This interpretation of the history of the Modern Movement led to our reference, though perhaps only as traveling companions, to certain positions of Marxist culture, which was spread in Italy by the Communist Party, reflecting on what had happened in the countries with socialist regimes: the optimization of the development process based not exclusively on profit but also on effective needs, extensive prefabrication, the expression of architecture as the representation of values aimed at equal freedom and dignity of all citizens, thus extraneous to the notion of efficiency of the capitalist world, where the emblematic status of technique actually covered up exploitation and speculation.

Precisely in those years, we were faced by the event of reconstruction, with a series of connected problems and contradictions, where the building sector was concerned, with the continuation of crafts practices on the worksite and in construction techniques: the takeoff of the building sector in Italy had been welcomed above all as an opportunity for employment, with which the Piano Fanfani attempted to provide a response also in terms of voter consensus.

From these premises of an aesthetic, but even more so structural character (through which the growth of technique was stimulated by profit), we became convinced of the need for a critical reassessment of the Modern Movement, taken as an ideological position driven by the desire for a new cognitive engagement with the recent history of the European city.

It was at this point that the first travels for study and observation began: in my case to Holland, to try to understand the differences, for example, between the achievements of the architects of the Amsterdam school and the developments by Oud in Rotterdam; or to Germany, to compare how organically connected to the city were the projects of Fritz Schumacher in Hamburg, as opposed to the projects by Bruno Taut for Berlin.

From that point on, from that commitment to contextual investigation, in our statements and our work there emerged not exactly an underestimation of technical reasoning, but undoubtedly a prevalence of the *typological-figurative* aspect over the strictly *constructive* one, to the extent that the question of construction remained, for us, primarily subject to structural, insertional, representative and figurative obligations in the idea of the city.

Furthermore, it should be pointed out that in Italy, regarding this attitude of contextual interpretation of architectural phenomena, there was the convergence of certain masters with backgrounds in Rationalism. We can mention, for example, the essay on urban planning in European cities by Giuseppe Samonà[4] and the debate between Ernesto Nathan Rogers and Reyner Banham regarding the "Italian retreat" from the Modern Movement[5].

Not that in other countries there were no situations marked by comparable contradictions: in Germany in those years there was a sort of American "colonization" of the reconstruction, dictated perhaps by the aim of erasing the recent past in the International Style; in England, also emerging exhausted from the war, the Labour government, through the London County Council, shifted the problem of reconstruction to a larger, prevalently urbanist scale, returning to the theme of Greater London and the New Towns already approached by the

Rationalists of the MARS Plan and the Abercrombie Plan of 1943[6].

In Italy the structural and cultural rebound happened in a singular way, due to multiple reasons: the extreme, ancestral north-south dichotomy; the particular structure of the country's settlement (after all, it is known as the land of *a hundred cities*); and even our innate talent for transformation. These factors also contributed to place us in the ranks of the countries that may not have been winners, but were at least "less losers" (just consider the cinema of Neorealismo, with its way of bringing the causes and problems of our underdevelopment to international attention and aid).

Francesco Tentori was the first, in an international conference of young leftist architects held in Rome in 1954, to advance the very timely idea of the survival of a particular, utterly Italian interpretation of the Modern Movement in the postwar era.

The *Modulor* of Le Corbusier came just a couple of years after the *Manuale dell'architetto* published in 1946 and assembled by Mario Ridolfi and some of his young colleagues, while the war was still in progress[7]. But there is a major "philosophical" gap between the two texts, even a condition of opposition, in the way of understanding and approaching the problems opened up by postwar reconstruction. This was certainly due to an objective situation, but also to a sort of realistic or "neo-realist" wisdom which in Italy, more than elsewhere, made it possible to "loosen" a deterministic relationship between *economics of construction* and *design,* in the sense that case by case the problems reappeared in different ways, demanding a more flexible interpretation of phenomena. In other words, the modules of reproduction and spread of the constructed artifact were scarcely impacted by a national production structure that was not at all coordinated in the housing sector.

Usually the companies – most of which still relied on still autarkic types and techniques – supervisors who were to some extent of exceptional quality (the carpenters, for example), while otherwise they employed workers arriving from the countryside; therefore, even before Fiat, it was the construction industry that attracted the work force from the south.

Another factor of that period which made it impossible to compare to the present situation had to do with the aims and modes of transmission of professional knowledge, as pursued in the architecture schools.

In 1950, in the first year at the Department of Architecture of the Politecnico di Milano, if memory serves there were about 120 students enrolled. The first years included a two-year course in Elements of Construction: the first year was taught by Libero Guarneri, the second by Enrico Griffini[8]; both approached the topic in a meticulous, analytical and catalogic way, in any case completely separate from the teachings of the other courses and from any overview of the worksite itself.

Already this first contact with the practical aspect can convey the approach to design the school set out to impose, through instrumental and separate types of knowledge. In fact, parallel to the course in Elements of Construction, there were the courses of Surveying of Monuments and Drawing from Life, so one reached a synthesis of design only in the third year, with the course in Elements of Composition, officially chaired by the Dean Piero Portaluppi, but actually taught by his assistant Giordano Forti[9].

In the Department of Architecture in those years the sector of composition, where the application of design was approached, was marked by ephemeral, arbitrary themes and motives, without any logic; and this was true not only from the viewpoint of linguistic results, but also from that of the way they were arrived at. In particular, the practice of the *ex-tempore* – seen as useful gymnastics whose educational merit we will not discuss here – caused the sort of approach to design that wound up influencing all the subsequent experiences in the compositional area.

Parallel to the "modern" of the courses in Composition and Furnishings, where Gio Ponti[10] was teaching – a modern encouraged in a conventional guise, with some concessions to the bizarre – there was the grim course in Layout Characteristics of Buildings, taught by Antonio Cassi Ramelli, where typological particularity was mnemonically imprinted, as if it were a functional state established once and for all.

In short, belatedly and anachronistically, we were going through a phase of transition from traditionalism to modernism, where the "modern" acted as an external complex, not yet assimilated, with respect to the arithmetic gradualism practiced in the polytechnic education, after the downfall of the technical and stylistic consistency that had at least made the academic training of the previous century logical and unitary, from the classicism of Durand to the neo-medievalism of Camillo Boito. So I believe it takes some nerve to build a myth, as people often do today, around the professional training bestowed by the Polytechnic in those years, where the sole advantage was the fact that there were not so many students.

In my view, Italian architecture schools have never taught "construction," seen in the truly operative, positive and relative sense of the term, of a mentality, an obligatory "philosophy" of design, that extends to the dimension of the territory as engineering of the city, avoiding the misunderstanding of an "in itself" of technology. Something of the sort may perhaps have happened at the Department of Engineering of the Politecnico di Milano, where Giovanni Muzio taught in exile, an outstanding personality as an architect-builder[11]. Something of the sort may perhaps have happened in Rome, had Mario Ridolfi taught there, instead of never being allowed to do so. But as far as I know, at least, it has never happened in architecture schools.

Paradoxically, we might suppose that the technological shortcomings of those years had an active influence, as a reaction, on the pursuit of a new poetics, obliging us to look elsewhere for scientific rigor: better a direct relationship with the sciences than a badly misunderstood relationship with technology. Having graduated from classical high school, I had but mediocre results in scientific subjects, which did not stimulate me to apply myself; the same was true during the first years of the Polytechnic, until in the third year the course in Rational Mechanics opened up the fascination of the technical-scientific world for me; so much so that I then completed the exams in Science of Constructions and Technique of Constructions with excellent results.

What I am saying serves to underline the fact that in the itinerary of training, on the one hand, the usefulness and even the indispensable nature of *technical knowledge* cannot be denied; but on the other hand, if they are reduced to notions learned by rote, they can be counter-productive and harmful to the essence and the role of architectural design.

Architecture today in Italy

Coming from a family with generations of engineers and architects, I did not intend to continue the tradition[12]; then, fortunately, I decided not to abandon the vocation: in fact, there is no greater fortune than to have a passion for your own job. Yet for architecture the present times are times of discomfort, due principally to the awareness of how an increasingly widespread mass-media subculture has come to the fore, in contrast with the potential of enrichment of architecture's functional value and meaning in historical centers and suburbs. Therefore architecture has become a scapegoat for the spread of ignorance regarding the authentic factors of the environment, so that administrators and urbanists, after decades of misdeeds, have managed to camouflage themselves in greenery, in standards and in the voids (till when?) of the so-called "abandoned areas." But isn't the disfigured visage of our cities the result of their prospecting, their building regulations, their master plans? Nevertheless, what gets put on trial is architecture, especially when it is of high quality. And this cannot help but make us sorrowful.

Italian architecture, for a period that has perhaps not yet come to an end, has attempted to reassert itself in the historical environment that surrounds it, though coming up against the low level of information of a public opinion that has done its utmost to deprive it of the right to exist.

Unlike what has generally happened in other nations – think Germany, Holland, or even another Latin country like Spain – in Italy modern architecture has never managed to take off as a *builder of cities*. And this is not the fault of the architects (as can be seen in an important series of works), but of those who have held power and responsibility in determining the image of the city, making it reflect their own interests and tastes, claiming that they are managing, expanding and even conserving it through fragmentary and fiduciary assignments, thus removing the design from the hands of those who would effectively have had the proper expertise.

We must admit that elsewhere this kind of debacle has not been reached. Perhaps the process of construction of the urban organism has happened through individual works of architecture that are qualitatively inferior to ours, but it has taken place with a wholeness that unfortunately cannot be found in our country. And to think that the public function of collective interest has, by tradition, played a decisive role in the landscape of the Italian city.

The relationship with construction: technology

For those accustomed to proceeding from an envisioned stimulus, *the passage from the idea to the construction* is undoubtedly a concatenation that is hard to reasonably explain; and it is not without its dangers, when it is not yet sustained by experience, when typological-figurative intuition has to be combined with technological reasoning, which is not always tamed with knowledge sufficient to achieve what is desired.

In our initiation into technique, as I have said, there was a lot of self-teaching; so much so that with self-irony we can boast of having the "privilege" of being among the few architects who have restored one of their own works: the City Hall of Segrate[13], where the fair-face concrete had visibly deteriorated. Those were years in which – passionately following the rationalist teachings –*beton brut* was considered an eternal material, like stone, with all the consequences such a misconception could wind up transmitting to architecture. And to think that in our activity we have almost always been able to rely on engineers with great experience, much more expert than us, for the supervision of the work. Self-critically, I have to acknowledge the fact that there were also errors directly committed by us: again at Segrate, for example, I remember the large U-glass expanse facing south, with its easily imaginable impact on the climate in the offices behind it.

I have never had a chance to investigate the technical training provided in other countries. Once, however, after a conference at the Architectural Association of London, I was shown the works of the students, and I was able to observe that – all things considered – their training in this field was even worse than ours, since it was sacrificed in favor of a perceptive-expressive approach that ran the risk of burgeoning into virtuoso graphic effects.

Acting as an advisor in the preparation of degree thesis projects, I rely on the structural observations of colleagues in that field with whom I am familiar.

If by paradox I were to have to take an exam in this area, I think I would probably fail. In fact, as the years pass the architect who does not pay particular attention to structural calculations has to proceed by means of intuition. Nevertheless, when designing I take comfort in the realization that my configuration and dimensioning of structures and layouts, though intuitive, remains within tolerable margins of approximation. And I believe that this "virtue" comes from experience, more than from the legacy of an engineering mentality.

From drawing to architecture: the method

I like freehand drawing; but I believe that between the phase of envisioning and that of building there is a difference similar to the one that exists between the work of the screenwriter and that of the director.

In my case, therefore, the itinerary of architecture does not happen through a procedure of *deduction,* but through what I would define as *experimentation:* trial and error. The project starts in the studio, on a drafting table: it is tested in the various phases and scales of the drawings and models: but the work of architecture, in its final configuration, is developed only in contact with the reality of the worksite.

Beyond the design, it is also a great satisfaction to observe how the construction emerges before your eyes, also through decisions that become necessary along the way. In fact, architecture takes form on the worksite. Every time I have been able to reach the construction of a project, it was precisely in this phase that I experienced extraordinary emotions and tensions.

The practical verification of the materials or the specification of construction details in the implementation phase, precisely from the viewpoint of the narrative, takes on a decisive role for the rhythm, similar to the results of the decisions made by a director on the set.

Architecture cannot be locked up in the two dimensions of the drawing. Even transpositions comparable to certain allusive images of painting, certain figures suspended in metaphysical time, change into something else when translated into architecture.

Architecture is always a work of lived experience, a livable situation. I cannot think of a work of architecture without at the same time imagining what will happen inside it, and around it. This is why I suffer greatly from the failure to implement a project, which unfortunate happens (even in most cases).

I have never wanted to take responsibility for the supervision of the construction, because on the worksite I prefer to have a relationship as a critical counterpart of those in charge. And in fact the designer, even when hired for the function of so-called *artistic consulting,* is merely "tolerated" on the worksite.

Therefore every time the need for a modification during the progress of the work arises, I am gripped by the doubt that the ultimate goal is to raise costs; and often, perhaps for lack of specific expertise, I am not able to reply to that doubt. Nevertheless, in the design a mechanism is triggered, which we might define as the "survival of the work," which leads him to seek other creative solutions, as consistent as possible from the architectural standpoint.

Also because, were we to have to find a logic in the procedural path that governs a public work, we would have to venture into a field in which the design is often left at the margins. This is a phenomenon – perhaps not only in building – of complex bureaucracy not always free of vested interests, which by now has become tragically pathological.

In this sense, the path of the new headquarters of the Istituto Superiore "Bodoni" in Parma[14], commissioned by the provincial government, may be indicative: a project carefully conceived and designed, in its delicate relationship with the surrounding historical context, is entrusted for its implementation to the contractor that won the bidding on the basis of that project: but right from the start of the work, requests for variations are advanced, based on motives that are often incomprehensible for the designers, yet the supervisors of the construction (a functionary of the province, in this case), seems to approve. As a result the construction drags on for years, also because the funding has been depleted. The designers appeal to the administration, explaining their dissent regarding the variations imposed by the worksite supervisors and the contractor, but to no avail.

So designers often find themselves faced by decisions that have been made, without allowing them to intervene. Even when even a small margin of intervention remains, the instinct of the survival of the work kicks in, as I was saying, calling for the creativity of the designer so that at least some degree of integrity will not be lost.

I do not believe in a spontaneous process, so to speak, a self-implementation of the construction; namely technological reasoning that is capable of being directly translated into architecture. In the design and the implementation, a logical-constructive process that tends toward simplification is combined with a logical-representative process that fatally leans towards complication. Precisely in the particular combination of these two logics – one tending to be objective, the other to be subjective – lies any approach to the project, any singular poetic construct.

Even if we were to schematically outline the application to the project in two phases – the first one planimetric, two-dimensional in nature, of adaptation to the site and study of the layout arrangement, the second three-dimensional, of the organization of space – these would still be two phases that intersect and interact simultaneously in a dialectical way inside a single imaginative world.

I have always thought that *collective architecture* should be seen in opposition to *domestic architecture;* that it should not be produced as an extension of an intimate comfort, but pedagogically induce the "trauma" of reflection on the very essence of behavior in public. A school, a theater, a town hall, a building destined for collective use, should not limit itself to providing a service in the best possible way, but should also stimulate a desire for knowledge, making the people it serves engage in thought.

Luckily I have come across some administrators in the areas around Milan who share in this conviction, agreeing that the public building to be constructed should not have to reproduce in miniature the model of the center, simplified and conventionally indicated, but should appear as independently new, offering inside it the landscape of a microcosm capable of interfering with the residential standardization of the periphery, precisely because its purpose is to serve the community. The indispensable unity of the public building thus opens up two landscapes, two narrative plots of architecture: external and internal.

It is also possible that this conception is based on autobiographical factors, because I arrived in Milan at the age of six, coming from a very protected childhood and from a different landscape, so the Stazione Centrale and the nearby complex of the Salesians of Sant'Agostino[15] were undoubtedly traumatic for me; not in a negative sense, however, but as grand castles inside which it became possible to find and to know, by condensation, everything that pulsated outside the walls of the home, i.e. the complexity of the metropolis.

The elements of design

The use every architect makes of design tools is always connected and in tune with the role and the virtual specificity he assigns to architecture. Something like what happens to the writer, who is generally inspired by a general idea (for example, in the case of Manzoni, the plague in Milan in the 1600s); from there, the story moves outward, assigning roles and attitudes to characters to express the depth and authenticity of the narrative construction in all its detailed shadings.

Describing my design path towards architecture, I have insisted on putting an accent on the impact of *times and generations.*

The family environment in which I was brought up had a strong influence, and I developed an interest in literature, painting and music early on; an interest that tempered the engineering tradition of my father, by immediately seeking the construction of the design plot, the functional hierarchy, its rhythm, the characterization of the main and secondary figures, the tones to bring out and those to suppress.

Unlike the generations that came before us, impacted first by Fascism and then by the war (with the exception of Ernesto Rogers, who had read and traveled extensively), in the path of acculturation our generation had the benefit of regular schooling, in spite of the general crisis of certainties in the wake of the disaster of the war. During all the previous years technique had exerted the charm and faith in an irreversible progress on the generation of our mentors, which perhaps only the atom bomb was able to break down; while for us it was a trauma experienced in political terms, which influenced our interest, by analogy, in the techniques of representation employed in literature, painting and cinema.

On the possibility of reducing the project to properties of simplification and reproducibility with basic geometry, and to its symbolic meanings, I can simply observe the fact that in the extraordinary singular character of public functions it is possible to pursue everything that cannot be found in the repetitive ordinary character of the field of housing.

Nevertheless, there are various ways of applying this intention of transgression. With respect to certain past and recent gestural and formalist fashions, for example, the research of Konstantin Mel'nikov[16] stands out (not by chance one of my favorite architects, who years ago I failed to manage to bring to Italy due to false bureaucratic obstacles), whose "machinist" figuration is the result of a typological engineering that gets beyond functionalist mechanics, organizing it in the symbolic explosion of the *unexpected* and thus granting it that majestic "magic" that public architecture has unleashed in the past (from the Acropolis to the great cathedrals, to Campidoglio) and which, in my view, it should always unleash.

So my relationship with the technique of use of materials happens without myths and without prejudice, without anything pre-set or of a deductive nature. In the first building I constructed, a two-family house at Lentate sul Seveso[17], a town between Milan and Como, the cladding was in exposed brick, with the insertion of prefabricated concrete balconies. In the next passage, of scale and image, to the public building in Segrate, the infill was done with specially designed cylindrical parts, prefabricated in concrete and left exposed to make the facade texture. To be honest, at first the project called for smooth walls, but when the model was made the necessity arose, precisely from a figurative standpoint, to give the walls the vibrant effect of drapery. In the case of the Civic Center of Pieve Emanuele[18], the exposed brick cladding, to adhere to the cylindrical surface of the vertical access towers, was combined with steel and glass in the horizontal infill facing north, and with the giant order of the large prefabricated concrete parts that form the gymnasium.

So in every project, on the basis of experience and with the limits of my technical know-how, case by case I try to make the choice of material and details congruent with the figurative idea that guides the design. In fact, I consider the design of a detail not as the solution to a problem on its own, but as an accident (not a mishap) to be overcome as an obligatory passage, indispensable for the course of the architectural idea.

I think the famous sentence where van der Rohe idealizes the role of the detail – often misunderstood and taken too literally – should be taken as a rhetorical provocation, almost as if to screen the authentic value of immutable completeness achieved by his architecture. While even the devaluation of the detail, all the way to its rough simplification, can at times be useful and appropriate for the purposes of figuration.

Certain visitors, and even some colleagues, are astonished by the roughness of some of the finishes in a house I built on Lago Maggiore[19]. But a house remains a house, so since I am not a lover of embellishments and, in general, of soft domestic comfort, I like to think that at least where the finishes are concerned it does not look like the house of an architect-decorator.

At this point, since they have been mentioned, let's compare the nearly opposite procedures of two of the greatest figures of Italian modern architecture: Franco Albini and Mario Ridolfi, respectively exponents of expressionism and purism.

From the moment of its conception the architecture of Ridolfi[20] seems to grow, already specified, inhabited and humanized by skillful handiwork, unlike that of Albini, the result of laborious experimentation gradually honed to abstraction. We could find another extreme example in the poetics of Carlo Scarpa, who in my view redeems decoration, giving rise in architecture to a sort of "utopia of inhabitability" (while I think the "Scarpa-like" efforts of those who set out to reduce the magic into terms of decorative utility are just pathetic). Instead, the concept of purist rarefaction that can be attributed to the work of Albini does not mean that it gives up on making itself inhabitable, but that by concentrating on the transparency of the technical-functional device, it takes on an autonomy that abstractly takes into account the presence man and the city, offering itself as a speaking organism on a par with the environment, without getting involved in their physical character and history.

Generally, I believe the secret of architectural quality cannot be surmised by following the grain of the wood. And yet, as happens in things artistic, in the design of Albini and of Scarpa, the configuration of the detail, of a resting point or a simple interlock, can on its own reach that degree of exaltation, of extra-corporeal transfiguration, that authoritatively sanctions the exception to the rule. I have been told that the famous "tensile bookcase" I had a chance to admire in Albini's house collapsed one day, losing the balance of forces that kept it erect. Well, in my view, paradoxically, the earthbound surrender of that collapse only further enhances the structural evanescence of the most sublime piece of furniture designed by Albini.

One case seems significant, above all others: that of the Torre Velasca by BBPR, where the "Milanese quality" seems to be pursued and achieved right from the basic idea that guided the project: the *trunk* of the offices topped by the *cube* of the residences. So much so that it would be hard to make a choice in the series of successive versions: from the transparent ones in steel and glass to the masonry with borders alongside the casements, as it was made in the end. The alternation of the solutions, so radical as to shift beyond any technological premises (in which the "existing environmental features" of Rogers must have had a decisive role), takes on exemplary value in the Torre Velasca precisely because of the constant of the idea of embodying the *genius loci* of the city in height, ideologically and allegorically.

In conclusion: if it is true that in the Wagnerian melodrama words and music form an inseparable dramaturgic mixture, it is also true that in Verdi's opera the music, though composed for a libretto, is what sustains and advances the dramatic plot. After all, wasn't it Ruskin who suggested the hypothesis of adapting new poetic texts to the music of opera?

The same could be said for the great work of public architecture, which cannot develop by sticking to a preconceived technological understanding, but has in any case to be sustained and advanced by a solemn figurative intent whose aim is the composition of the city.

Milan, 4 March 1993 – Studio Canella

Notes

1. Canella's public debut, after training in Milan during the years in which Rogers played an extremely important role, dates back to the second half of the 1950s: two of his writings – the paper read in the name of a group of students/architects at the *Debate on tradition in architecture* organized by the MSA of Milan in 1955 and the essay published in *Casabella-Continuità* in 1957 on the *bourgeois epic of the School of Amsterdam* – immediately reveal an attitude at once critical and unwavering in relation to the legacy of the Modern Movement.

2. Ambrogio Annoni (1882-1954) taught at the Polytechnic from 1914 to 1951. Piero Portaluppi, a disciple of Annoni, became dean of the Department of Architecture in Milan in 1939, succeeding Gaetano Moretti, the first to hold the position in 1934.

3. A great influence in the background of Guido Canella was the figure of Ernesto N. Rogers, for whom his student once spoke of a profound "devotion." After having met Rogers already before enrolling at the Polytechnic, Canella established professional ties with him in the context of the university: attending his course in Stylistic Characteristics of Monuments – in which Canella wrote a paper titled *Characteristics of Milanese romantic architecture, from Carlo Amati to the Torre Velasca* in which he described how eclectic architecture had been able to interpret the problematic transformations of Lombard society in the period of the first industrialization, from the viewpoint of typological invention and commemorative image – and becoming his assistant after graduation; even prior to taking his degree, in 1957 had also begun a long collaboration with *Casabella-Continuità*, after which he officially entered the staff in 1962.

4. G. Samonà, *L'urbanistica e l'avvenire della città,* Laterza, Bari 1959.

5. The argument dates back to 1957: in response to Reyner Banham's article *Neoliberty: The Italian Retreat from Modern Architecture,* published in 1959 in no. 747 of *The Architectural Review*, Rogers responded that same year with the editorial "L'evoluzione dell'architettura, risposta al custode dei frigidaires" in *Casabella* no. 228. The debate had vast repercussions, and continued with various contributions in architecture magazines by well known Italian critics, including Bruno Zevi and Paolo Portoghesi.

6. The group of British architects M.A.R.S. (Modem Architectural Research Group) was founded in London in 1933 to prepare a plan for the reconstruction of the city. Patrick Abercrombie (1879-1975) was the British urbanist who prepared the plan for the reconstruction after World War II of the metropolitan area of London, as well as master plans for many British cities.

7. Le Corbusier completed the studies for the *Modulor* – begun in 1942 – in 1948, and then published them in the volume *Le Modulor* dated 1950.

The publishing project of the *Manuale dell'architetto,* developed based on the intention of providing a publication for updating on technical and scientific innovations in Italy, was based on an American model. The "cultural father" of the operation was Mario Ridolfi, who had already approached the theme of the unification and standardization of construction, and prepared the first version of the *Manuale* – which would be periodically updated – under the aegis of the C.N.R. and with the collaboration of young professionals and some already renowned technicians, including Pier Luigi Nervi and Luigi Piccinato.

8. Enrico Griffini (Venice 1887 – Milan 1952) was a fundamental figure in the process of establishment of the teaching of technology inside the Department of Architecture of the Politecnico di Milano. After the publication of a profoundly "modern" text on the approach to the project and the question of innovation in the construction sector – *Costruzione razionale della casa,* Hoepli, Milano 1932, a text that was to become a basic element in the training of many generations of architects – in 1939 he was awarded the chair of the two-year program of Elements of Construction, which he retained until his death. For many years Griffini was assisted in his teaching by Libero Guarnieri (Cremona 1916 – Sanremo 1962), who starting in 1952 continued his work as a lecturer in Elements of Construction II. The two-year program of Elements of Construction set up by Griffini approached technological systems and materials in

the first phase, and the application of those studies for the design of housing and its groupings in residential typologies in the second. On these topics and more generally on the process of disciplinary constitution of technology of architecture, for which in this contribution Canella touches on important episodes and personalities, see F. Schiaffonati, "Cultura e insegnamento della tecnologia edilizia", in the anthology *Il Politecnico di Milano nella storia italiana (1914-1963)*, Quaderni of the *Rivista milanese di economia* no. 17, 1989, vol. II, pp. 657-658, and L. Crespi, F. Schiaffonati, *L'invenzione della tecnologia,* Alinea, Firenze 1990.

9. Giordano Forti (Milan 1910-78) began his academic career as an assistant in Elements of Construction in 1936, then in Composition starting in 1945, the course in which he became a lecturer in 1954. With Gio Ponti and Piero Portaluppi he designed the new facility of the Department of Architecture of the Politecnico di Milano (1953-63).

10. The teaching activities of Gio Ponti (Milan 1891-1979) took place entirely in the course on Architecture of Interiors, Furnishings and Decoration I and II, across a long time span from 1936 to 1962.

11. Giovanni Muzio (Milan 1893-1982), a professor in the Department of Architecture from the mid-1930s, was appointed full professor of Architecture in 1951 at the Department of Engineering, where he taught until the end of his academic career in 1968.

12. Guido Canella was born in 1931 in Bucharest to an Italian family – his father, a hydraulic engineer, was of Venetian origin – with many generations of engineers, architects and painters. During his childhood in Milan, Canella met Michele Achilli with whom, together with Daniele Brigidini, encountered at the Polytechnic, he collaborated for many years. The professional partnership of the three began before their graduation – in 1959 – and was destined to last in time.

13. After the years of formation, the city hall of Segrate (Milan 1963-66) and the service center for the INCIS village at Pieve Emanuele (Milan 1968-82) represent the first important works by Canella.

The new city hall of Segrate (with M. Achilli, D. Brigidini and L. Lazzari; Eng. G. Cozzaglio and Eng. B. Giovanardi), a sculptural and complex building located between the old settlement of Segrate and the new zone of expansion, offers itself to the context as a place of gathering, combining the administrative functions of the offices with public and cultural, health care and civic services.

The organism presents itself as an arrangement of planes and volumes developed around a central core of technical services: a cylindrical volume contains the library, with the book storage facility below and a space for exhibitions above, open to the surrounding countryside; in a trapezoidal volume, a service hall is placed between an archive below and the council chamber above; a fan-shaped part contains financial offices with welfare office below it, served from the outside, and representative offices above (mayor, aldermen, secretaries). A rectangular volume facing east contains services for the public, with storerooms, heating plant and a garage below, and technical offices above. Entrance is along ramps that wrap around the building.

The vertical and horizontal load-bearing structure is in fair-face reinforced concrete, with slabs in brick and reinforced concrete poured in place, and semicylindrical infill panels prefabricated in natural concrete. The continuous walls feature variable compositions of prefabricated parts. The technical and rotation office have a facade in U-glass parts, with windows that can be opened placed behind the columns.

14. The Centro scolastico secondario superiore "G.B. Bodoni" (with P. Bonaretti, asst. Okpanum; Eng. F. De Miranda) was inserted in a fragmentary zone between the outskirts and the historical center of Parma. In this project the provincial government was both the client and the supervisor of the construction, through its technical division: the initial project development commissioned in 1985 to Guido Canella was not only for the school, but also for a large project including several areas – which were never built – for recreation, as a supplement to the scholastic activities.

In terms of type, Canella defined the school organism in an open "nave" arrangement so that the facility would become an intermediary connection with the *community* and the *context*. The large school building with its forcefully unified, symmetrical layout is composed of a central volume of monumental size to contain spaces for sports and recreation, flanked by two lower wings for the classrooms and services. At the moment the building has been only partially completed, after a long hiatus caused by lack of funding.

15. The buildings mentioned are the Stazione Centrale in Milan (1912-1931) designed by Ulisse Stacchini, and the Chiesa e Casa dei Salesiani on Via Tonale (Cecilio Artesani, 1894-1920).

16. Konstantin Stepanovich Mel'nikov (Moscow 1890-1974) was one of the great protagonists of Soviet architecture in the 1920s, and of Constructivism.

17. At the start of his career, following experiments conducted on the small scale of exhibit design and furnishings, as well as participation in a series of important competitions, Canella had the chance to apply his conceptual approach to the creation of houses at Sesto Calende (Varese) and the single-family house in Lentate sul Seveso (Milan 1961-63, with M. Achilli and D. Brigidini).

The latter is a grouping of towers clad in exposed brick, organized in the plan according to a typological scheme – a crosswise volume with a portico on the ground floor and two emerging wings – that explicitly reformulates the villa typology.

18. From 1968 to 1982 Guido Canella was commissioned to design a long series of services for a district of 8000 inhabitants for government employees, including an elementary school, a daycare center, a shopping center, a parish complex and a multipurpose building.

All the projects have the primary objective of regenerating a particularly deteriorated situation; the overall project began with the construction of the piazza for the INCIS village, launching the typological pursuit of integration and functional consolidation developed later.

The civic center with town hall, middle school and sports field at Pieve Emanuele (Milan 1971-78, with M. Achilli and D. Brigidini, asst. G. Fiorese; Eng. G. Binelli) is composed of the grouping of the municipal offices with the two wings of the secondary school: the result is a complex of variegated volumes placed at different heights around a core for various functions (cultural, recreational, sporting). The possibility of alternation of scholastic and youth activities with cultural initiatives, entertainment and sports for adults, inside the various spaces, ensured full-time use of the structures, leading to remarkable savings in terms of facility management.

The architectural, administrative and scholastic complex aims to create multiple opportunities for leisure time thanks to the relationship of interpenetration of the various volumes, and the external link to the surrounding countryside – through a ramp for pedestrians and bicycles that rises from ground level across other floors to a raised trapezoidal piazza. The matrix of the whole project is the gigantic glazed architrave-volume, resting on two circular towers in exposed brick: the horizontal volume contains the civic library and is placed above the offices, while the towers contain vertical connections leading to the access to the library. Besides the library, the cultural and recreational services contained in this part of the complex include an auditorium for 500 viewers, and a gymnasium inserted in a multi-sport facility for 600 spectators, also serving the school.

19. This is a house for a family of six, built near Meina (Novara) in the early 1970s (1973-76; Eng. A. Valenti). The two-story building with a semicircular layout, placed symmetrically around a central staircase, faces the lake with a rectangular front hollowed at ground level by two exedras that generate a sheltered path at the perimeter.

20. Mario Ridolfi (1904-84), a Roman architect and urbanist, represents a fundamental reference point in the interpretation of the Modern Movement and in the architecture of Neo-Realism in the Roman context, above all in several residential projects.

Vittoriano Viganò

Architecture of experience

Experience in architecture

I believe architecture is an experience in which we engage in the name of an intention. In this sense, it is not possible to "be in architecture" but only to strive towards architecture (*Vers un architecture* is the title chosen by Le Corbusier for his finest book).

The question is not a trivial one, because it does not permit space for certain and immutable premises, but instead offers only hypotheses to nurture and realize along the process and in its outcome, where the latter is no less experimental than the process itself.

The concept of experience is reflected in the moment in which we investigate the basis of needs and the resulting methods to satisfy them through the tools of design, and to an equal extent in the moment of implementation.

A clear phenomenon of solidarity exists between theory and practice. Inside the term *experience,* then, we can reduce these two worlds to one unit: one helps the other in a sort of pendulum-like interaction. Two worlds, both endless. There is no theoretical aspect that concludes in a theory, no practical aspect that concludes in a finished work: I prefer to think about a theory that becomes, and a work of architecture that becomes more finished the more it is open to interaction, and therefore to triggering infinite processes in time, not just in space: inside and outside itself.

Making and narrating

In the age of information the term "to make" curiously loses presence, while the term "to inform" gains more and more space: what is transferred takes on more importance than what is done, the importance of a *communicating* fact. One can be present, speaking or *communicating,* even prior to *making,* unlike what happened in the historical city which was informative in the same moment in which the communal assembly came into being, the house, the palace, the fountain, the statue by Cellini or Michelangelo.

In the present state of the art we see a remarkable phenomenon of general doubling, as if to attempt to determine two great truths: that of he who *makes*, well or badly, and that of he who *speaks*, well or badly.

Those who lean towards making are as if overwhelmed by the world of verbal imagery, so they feel an increasingly pressing need for simplification, to also know in keeping with practice. This is because information, commentary, critique are always complex and increasingly intricate: it may be that he who *makes* has an interest in availing himself of this availability, but at the same time has an interest in putting it aside, to avoid being overshadowed. I think it was Picasso who said: "To make things you also have to be a bit dumb."

Those who are in charge of the great dimension of words and their instant spread possess reality but run the risk of getting inebriated, of getting drunk on this new discipline: a drunkenness that can become troublesome. A "harassment" that in this case is manifested with an excess of words, a surplus that does not always correspond to that concept of *laboratory* so much in vogue today, also in Italian architecture schools. A term to which people attempt to make an also tangible, material need correspond, that of having a discipline – architecture – that without the pencil, without the tool, without the direct relationship, struggles to become a living entity: and architecture is, and must be, a living entity.

There is also the fear that in the long run a surplus of information runs the risk of being a machine towards potentates or trends, with the resulting institution of closed areas, rather than a pure and generous contribution of generalized and stimulating culture.

Architecture has to be *theoretical* because it possesses its own recognizable and recognized theoretical substrate: architecture has to be *operative* because it has its own entire operative substrate. Architecture has to experience itself in its fullness, avoiding becoming a mere tool of information, if it does not want to grant to others – whoever they may be – the impossible substitution of its essence: globality.

Architect and training

A school of mass enrollment and above all a program of five years are scarcely enough to approach such a complex, humanistic and scientific-technological discipline as architecture. This is why I do not believe that we can demand everything from the school alone.

In my activity as a teacher[1] I have worked so that in the school the student will have an "impact at the same level" as architecture: to make the approach to architecture imply zeroing out any preconceived ideas, to reveal and to understand what a problem is, what a critical culture is, what a process is. To put into being a state of necessity and sufficiency in a methodological sense, means that the expressive exercise can become legitimate precisely in the imaginary that with this approach we have put ourselves in a condition to be able to induce.

All young people bring with them the forceful amazement of self-discovery inside an endeavor – in this case that of architecture – that has been chosen, and towards which they transfer all their innocence, their immense curiosity, intelligence, their inhibitions and victories over them, the destruction of all the false models previously unchallenged, their very identification as it takes form in the process between method and expression, reason and possible reality.

It is an impact that has to happen at all costs, and it has to happen inside the school: on any scale, in any way, using the tools considered most suitable for the occasion: if you want to reach a given objective through techniques, go ahead and do so, as long as you have an "impact on the level," deeply and genuinely the level of architecture.

The school can certainly not supply everything. Architecture school ought to be the place in which to make contact with the meaning and ceiling of architecture, getting to know them as much as possible: the deeper investigations will happen gradually, over time, through an everyday, continuous process of starting over again. I think it should not be said that "we become doctors of architecture, and then we will learn, over time, to be architects"; it would be much more reassuring if architecture were already touched in that context – that of the school and with ourselves – to then learn, in a successive phase, indeed, to *profess* it.

When we are young our capacity for learning is at its height, and generally the virtual capacity for expression is too. Learning does not happen through the figure of the professor, but through the work of teaching of the entire system: you are taught by your companions, the competition, the collective discussion, the climate in which you operate. The school, unlike what is generally presumed, does not constitute the phase of true learning: rather it remains the only, ultimate, true opportunity, socially conveyed and contextual, of the foundation of one's own identity through lofty thinking in architecture. If one is immersed in the profession without having first gotten to know architecture in its true disinterested, scientific and poetic basis, the flight towards the outside and the future starts from a very low point, and the young person runs the risk of being rapidly devoured by the banality of the context.

Rogers and Albini

Two masters, two worlds. Ernesto N. Rogers was a figure of great complexity, culturally more political than experimental, and more critical than material in expressive terms.

Certainly a didactic example, a master of maieutics, but also intangible and exclusive, as are true intellectuals. Therefore I prefer to allow his vast overall output of writings to speak for itself.

Of the two, Franco Albini was undoubtedly the one who influenced my design most, especially in relation to two or three points I feel are essential in making architecture.

Albini was an architect of dissent; I too believe I am an architect of dissent. Albini was a great admirer of rigor; I consider myself an architect with a moralistic temperament.

Albini made such significant works, taken to such refined, extreme detail – his furnishings, his museums, his residences, his particulars – so charged with technical value yet also with poetry, that no one else, like him, could be seen as a complete master, simultaneously classical and ready to propose new things. Those who have studied him, who have interpreted him, have come away with many things: I do not know how much of him I have managed to transfer into my design logic, but I certainly have imagined him, investigated and loved his work.

I feel Albini as a figure, as if at my fingertips. Analyzing my work, were I to have to find architectural points or episodes in which this figure of Albini comes more to the surface than in others, I would first have to make an operative distinction: for the *exteriors* I do not think I can identify recognizable points of contact between our productions, because Albini had a capacity for historical recovery and architectural refinement I have not known how to seek.

Where the *interiors* are concerned, on the other hand, I believe certain similarities can be recognized: not so much of a linguistic-formal nature – each of us has his own – but in the shared pleasure of making the internal space rise, point by point, detail upon detail, material upon material, to reach a composed and perhaps poetically plausible whole.

Episodes like the Arteluce store[2] – I remember he liked it very much – unconsciously recoup experiences of his, I think, though of another nature and quite another genre: among them all, I think the designs for museums were a great lesson for me. In 1968 I designed a "house in the historical center of Milan"[3] where I was ably to develop certain refinements which I think come from the experience of Albini, though obviously re-experienced by me: this is also because, I must admit, I have never been capable of copying. Among all the various references utilized, in fact, I always willingly mention Franco Albini, because more than others he was instructive, and useful in terms of authenticity.

"A middle generation"

I belong to a generation of architects recently defined by Guido Canella as being in the "middle."[4] When Canella speaks of a "middle generation" I think he does so with poorly disguised guile, identifying two specific moments of our century, or of the movement that has crossed it, in the founding moment of the masters and the moment of theoretical reflection he feels has been enacted by his generation, while in the "middle" he places those who by birth do not have his age and do not, to clarify, have the age of Terragni, Pollini, Gardella, and so on. This is typically shrewd, in the style of Canella; a very nice portrait that reveals all its subtlety and, in part, all its amiable but astute treachery.

I don't know, in the long term, who will be *before, after* or *in between:* the extent to which Canella and his contemporaries will be *in the middle* with respect to the next generations will be up to him to observe. Already today, I know that when something happens for which he feels "beaten" by a younger competitor, he traces the causes back to a presumed question of generation. So has his generation also become "middle"?

I believe our generation – I am thinking for example of Giancarlo De Carlo, Achille Castiglioni, Vico Magistretti, Paolo Chessa, Marco Zanuso[5] and others, to stay within our Lombard area, and within one generation – has done quite well in picking up the thread of events, history, the times. I believe, that is, that our task, our role, which could also be *in the middle* – all relay races have their subdivisions – has been carried out with a certain authenticity, adequately passing the baton to those who have come after us. A legacy we have in any case attempted to enhance, enriching fields of investigation those before us perhaps did not investigate or genuinely, globally experience.

Our generation has its own identity, I believe, its own recognizable evolution: an evolution in which we have been the actors with an innovative attention, of method and technical, expressive application, which I am not sure can be considered equally permanent and verifiable in the generation to follow. I believe that some of us leave a culturally plausible sign through tangibility. While it is true that great events have happened, if it is true that the *modern* has given way to the *post-modern, purism* to *eclecticism, avant-garde* to *academism,* this does not detract from the fact that on the plane of cultural necessities and values the picture – for those in the middle – is open and gratifying, especially when many myths return and the values of a clear, solid period – the one crossed by "those in the middle" – are establishing a profile as non-deceptive references.

It is not too risky to assert that the generation of which I am a part – to return to the discourse on *theory* and *practice* addressed earlier – is perhaps the one that more than others has mixed the two factors both in teaching and in the profession, in interaction.

Those who legitimize this pungent definition of the *middle* legitimize the fact that surely the great culture of the Italian Modern Movement and that of the generation that immediately followed it – which can be considered my generation – with the exception of a few great interpreters like Giuseppe Pagano, in part, and Edoardo Persico, in another part, who went deeper into the theoretical field, has been mainly of an expressive nature. Giuseppe Terragni is a champion of expressive prowess, envied and admired the world over.

There is no doubt that the entire Italian Modern Movement has had a function of experience of the great theories of the Modern born in Europe, also far from here: we have absorbed them with the ability and attitude that belong to us, we have understood them and returned them in a "finished" state, leaving the role of theorizing up to a few. There has also been a kind of criticism – see Bruno Zevi, see Giulio Carlo Argan – that has moved in parallel, also in tune: we have not had a critic "against." There has been an attunement, a theorization we might define as systematic, certainly not as alternative. The crisis emerges when the first signs of theoretical deepening appear, which explodes in alternative behaviors, also from an expressive standpoint. Signals that can be perceived in Paolo Portoghesi when he promotes the Post-Modern and becomes its incisive spokesman, or in Aldo Rossi when he theorizes an independence and didactic dimension of architecture that has Pre-Modern characteristics, reducing the overall and virtual framework to a game of risk of formal materials.

There is little doubt that this latter generation has experienced *theoretical curiosity* more closely that ours. This is probably due to the fact that the major processes were in motion and therefore reaching their consummation: to assert that we have also further consumed the heritage set up by the colleagues who came before us corresponds to an effective datum. Just as it is objective to state that it was not easy to pursue this work of erosion of a material we were collectively enriching, "digging" abundantly into it. Back then, perhaps it seemed easier and more productive to latch onto challenges of a more general character than to re-foundations, which would also be of a more general character.

Whether the academic proposal of Rossi or the Post-Modern proposal of Portoghesi are arterial blood, or necessary blood, or blood in perspective, is a matter for the examination of things. I, like others, have kept faith with a critical and expressive formulation closely tied to *my* roots, roots I have felt it was not useful to sever. I have preferred, at least, to stay on the path and when possible to reiterate the intentions of my research more clearly in things.

Nervi and Terragni

Nervi and Terragni: two great parents. In Nervi, I was fascinated by the *mode* of his reinforced concrete, the plasticity expressed through this material, the poetics of its forms: these are items that constituted a fixed point in my never concluded process of formation. Before my eyes, I can see all the elegance and spatial character of the stadium of Florence, the hangars of Orbetello, his fantastic vaults, his buttresses in the sporting facilities in Rome[6].

I have attempted to understand and to extract the enormous architectural potential that was there inside these great ideas of construction, besides the remarkable technical skill of their making: his works constituted outstanding models of constructive intelligence, and always will, establishing a rightful relationship with the great tradition of construction of architecture. The dome of Brunelleschi in Florence, the Pantheon in Rome, are great constructed experiences and equally necessary and poetic precisely in their typological and structural essence. For me, Nervi's works should be seen alongside such episodes. But I would like to specify something: I think it can be said that Pier Luigi Nervi, the more he was able to "play the engineer," the more due to his magical destiny he made structures and structural space, then the more he became a vehicle of exceptional original ideas and entered the realm of architecture. I don't think he achieved the same levels when he set out to "play the architect": he had remarkable difficulties in performing that task, and even made mistakes in the choice of colleagues when he had to collaborate with others.

I have always wondered, with regret, why I never had the chance to do a work with Pier Luigi Nervi. I am certain, in fact, that I could have been an aware counterpart for his contribution, fervent in my effort to exalt it. I felt that I could coherently interpret his intuitions and therefore answer the questions his idea might have raised on all scales. I had the precise sensation of being able to act as his right arm, knowing that Nervi fully understood the spatial aspects of the structure, its germinating force, and that it would be marvelous to share in their meaning and stimuli. I have an enormous debt to him for the comprehension of this specific – and, I repeat, not architectural – perfection of the large constructed artifact.

Giuseppe Terragni, on the other hand, made me see and understand, I would say, when I went looking for testimony and references in architecture, his own "correctness" fully achieved, from the whole to the detail, perfectly interpreted and combined.

His was an architecture full of ideas, in the process from the function to the construction and the form; a rule-breaking architecture, but never abandoned, always taken back to measure, logic, correct use of materials, even to cultured and creative simplicity when he wanted to operate in an elementary and economical way with tools that were all spatial. The building of the kindergarten of Sant'Elia[7] is a work of art that reaches absolute levels with "nothing": it is a work of art on a par with a fresco by Paolo Uccello or a gold-ground panel. I believe his premature death was a loss hard to evaluate for an architecture that at the time was heading towards major choices and significant breakthroughs. In fact, I think that if he had been able to continue his path, Terragni would have simply developed and enlarged the main lines of the Modern Movement he himself had already followed and configured. In any case, his presence would have been fundamental in the recent years of doubt, disturbance and retro eclecticism.

Architecture, a heteronomous discipline

With respect to other arts that are substantially abstract rather than materially useful, architecture is subject to this inhibition that at the same time also grants its own dynamic specificity. An "inhibition" if the nature of the conditioning is of a low level, if the request and the commission are not "strong crutches" in their own right; a "dynamic specificity" if the conditioning is in the problematic between contextual reality and design culture. A conditioning that is at the same time suffering and hope.

I believe, in this sense, that architecture is not an *autonomous* discipline, but one that is *heteronomous*. Architecture cannot stand back to rediscover its terms of subsistence in itself, its form and its history. From its history architecture can certain rediscover all the guarantees of measure, value, methodological intelligence: but it cannot, however, in my view, exempt itself from the necessity of continuous reformulation of the problem, the continuous rediscovery of a pertinent method, point after point. It cannot exempt itself from the joy of "getting its hands dirty" in the contingent, the real, from suffering in difficulties, because in all probability this is how architecture manages to authentically grasp and experience the truths that can potentially take form to envision a *new* condition for our habitat.

To design by honoring the philosophy of technique

Technology is a fundamental factor of *making architecture*. As such, it simultaneously takes part in all the values every factor can always possess, and all the limits to which each of its factors may be subject; at the same time, however, it partakes of all the privileges, all the contributions of which it can become the object in an overall framework.

Techniques, be they inherent to the factors of functionality, production processes, construction, language, take part in that concept of *relative connection* or *mutual necessity* through which everything hovers, between intentionality and circular interaction of its terms.

If architecture is an applied art – and that is the case – technology is its constituent factor, extending to a role of a semantic nature.

Personally, I find that every time technology stimulates potential new applications, new methodologies, a new configuration, it becomes extremely interesting. And I feel pleasure in honoring it. It should be clear that when an architect honors technology he is not being an engineer, but he *honors the philosophy of technique,* playing that much more complex role, of its recovery in the culture and thus in the global essence of architecture.

On materials and other elements

Materials are an inalienable condition for construction. Each of them bears its own prerogatives, which have to be discovered, recovered in technique and form, from the very first day...

I have used many, in construction, furnishings, objects. I think I have never betrayed, at least not in my intentions, the characteristics and meaning that can be reflected in the work, case by case, thanks to its material identity. I recognize that I have also brought some contribution of method every time I have found a novel condition of application for a new material somehow still without a destiny. In the explosive or rather heroic manner of the 1950s.

In that decade I experimented with reinforced concrete, in the "La Scala" house on Lake Garda and the Istituto Marchiondi in Milan[8]. I took all the historical overtones of that mixture of aggregates and binders as far as I could, a material that had been so unprecedented from its advent in France to the experiences of Perret and Le Corbusier, from the great structures of Maillart, Nervi, Morandi, Zorzi[9], to the elements of prefabrication. A material of great scope; but there was the curiosity to adapt all of its technical as well as plastic, figural potential to the themes of civil construction.

Then, in the 1970s and 1980s, I tried working with iron, to grasp its "measure," its "energy" and "form." I remember the Mollificio Bresciano and the Department of Architecture in Milan[10]: I believe the material changed, but not the characters of the space.

I have also worked with brick, wood, glass, and other materials. In 1960, for example, a company from Brianza launched an intriguing type of felt that had not yet found its purpose: I offered it – using it in an unusual way, vertically, horizontally and in the details – the chance to set the image of the Cinema Cavour[11]: it was a success for both of us.

When nylon appeared, I imagined – in the early 1950s at the Milan Triennale[12] – a big suspended aviary. It was an unusual but captivating thing: we might say that that white, eternal net encountered itself and that it lives on due to the particular typological, figurative and environmental situation granted to it by an experimental design.

It is undoubtedly true that every material leads to its own method, its own form. However, I believe it is also true that the formal structure each of us bears within us constitutes, so to speak, a point of expectation and verification. What I mean is that I do not believe there is a doubling with the variation of the means... There is a doubling of specificity, but not of form. Every experience that investigates the material component is a linguistic enrichment, but to no less an extent it is a heightening of methodological consistency. The example of Mies can suffice on its own.

Architecture and detail

We all know, with Mies, that God is in the details. In other words, I believe this also means that even a particle of architecture will probably contain the same density as the whole. The problem is to decide where and how – case by case – the detail and the whole begin and end. Scarpa did not sacrifice a single material detail: but his details were always produced by the whole and aimed at the whole. Le Corbusier left the details implicit, instead of cultivating them: they were, so to speak, sketched out. A piece "honed" by Albini, after all, has the value of a whole environment or language.

Architecture can make its contribution by offering itself in the form of a thousand harmonious details or – with another, antithetical effectiveness – it can retreat into the essential, dominant theme, leaving those who live there the possibility of inducing all the sub-measures of use and space, in a creative, experimental way.

I believe I do possess one small aptitude: that of knowing when to stop. I am fully aware of the fact that making architecture, or simply inhabitable spaces, we have a violent impact on the counterpart and his or her existence. We can be despotic, just as we can also be great stimulators of cognitive satisfaction. This is the essence of the project and of those, like us, who have to design for others. It is a relationship of risk, but also a responsibility we cannot avoid. Probably you cannot make architecture without being yourself and being didactic to the same extent. This belongs to the Modern Movement, and not at all to the Post-Modern. In any case, I feel I am a carrier of a certain experience on the meaning and possible modes and places of habitation, so I cannot act purely as the servant of a counterpart who almost always has less legitimacy of expression on this subject.

Only if the client – to indulge in a paradox – was, for example, Franco Albini, would I be willing to take part in that kind of submission. The truth of the matter is that he would take care not to subjugate me, fully aware that it would make me useless. When I manage to get a grip on and to formalize certain fixed points of my approach, I would also like to know when to stop; I am conscious of the fact that it is necessary to leave a field I would define as plastic still open, related to the time of adaptation of use, to its constantly possible variations, to the time of design growth which a solid, responsible but open project can induce. The experience of the project is an experience of growth, for everyone.

The detail can be a part, but also the whole. There are situations in which certain choices of detail are essential, others in which a margin exists, a tolerance where the detail can become irrelevant, once the main factors are in place. Architecture is methodologically full of gaps to be filled – space can be a bridged gap – which in any case are never anonymous, but provocative.

Milan, 14 December 1994 – Studio Viganò

Notes

1. After taking a degree in 1944 at the Department of Architecture of the Politecnico di Milano, parallel to his design research Vittoriano Viganò also focused on teaching, acting first as an assistant and then as a lecturer at the same school. In 1979 he was assigned the chair in the course on Interior Architecture and Furnishings; at the same time, he widened his teaching range as a full professor of Architectural Composition. At the Politecnico di Milano he worked with the Department of Architectural Design – in which he took part in many research initiatives, including the project for the environmental organization of the university campus at Bovisa, 1989-90 – and from 1988 he was dean of the department.

2. Trained under the dual influence of the Lombard tradition and the international avant-garde, Viganò began his career with a series of experiments on "minor" themes such as interior, galleries and exhibitions. After projects for art galleries across the 1950s, the Arteluce store at Via Spiga 23 in Milan (1961-62) was a fundamental step in Viganò's spatial research in the field of interior architecture. The store was designed in terms of the indoor-outdoor relationship, where the shop window became the main vehicle: rejecting alignment with the street, the glass was set back under a portico and broken up by a modular geometric shape that offered a foretaste of the spatial complexity inside. The display space was organized on five levels including semi-basements and upper levels, in a game of partitions and perspective views laid out around the main feature of an elliptical staircase.

3. The house in Milan, in the historical center, in 1968-71, represents a significant episode in the output of Vittoriano Viganò in terms of research on and definition of the relationship with the context, a theme already investigated in other projects focusing on the issue of domestic space. The project involved the spatial rearrangement of the ground floor of a building in Milan with a neoclassical layout, whose original character had been erased by subsequent interventions. Viganò's project reorganized the spaces and, above all, the relationships between them in keeping with an ordering principle based on the axis of connection between street, portico, courtyard and garden. The internal spaces – entrance, living area and dining room – and the external setting are combined in a single spatial movement superimposed in a non-traumatic way on the irregular shape of the building, thanks to the refined play of vertical and horizontal surfaces, transparent features and level shifts, made even more varied by the chromatic contrast between white plaster and very dark felt alternating in the cladding of the surfaces and in certain furnishings.

4. The term "middle generation" had been introduced by Guido Canella in his essay *Il nero e il rosso* contained in the catalogue of the exhibition "A come Architettura" organized in honor of Vittoriano Viganò and held at the Department of Architecture of the Politecnico di Milano in May 1991.

5. Giancarlo De Carlo was born in Genoa in 1919; Marco Zanuso, Achille Castiglioni and Vico Magistretti, all from Milan, were born respectively in 1916, 1918 and 1920; Paolo Chessa, also Milanese, was a classmate of the same age as Viganò.

6. Pier Luigi Nervi (1891-1979): Florence Municipal Stadium, 1930-32; Aircraft hangar in Orbetello, 1939-41; Palazzetto dello Sport, Rome, 1956-57.

7. Giuseppe Terragni (1904-43): Asilo Sant'Elia in Como, 1936-37.

8. In the second half of the 1950s Viganò designed two works that gained visibility on an international level: the new headquarters of O.P. Istituti Riuniti Marchiondi Spagliardi e Protezione dei fanciulli, and the "La Scala" house.

Istituto Marchiondi at Milan-Baggio (1953-57) represents a fundamental threshold in the creative path of the architect: the building – still one of his best-known works – was categorized by Reyner Banham, together with the church of the Madonna dei Poveri by Figini & Pollini, also at Baggio, under the heading of international "brutalism" – or more precisely the "new brutalism" – due to its expressive vigor and the display of concrete in its humblest form. This label was challenged and disavowed by the designers at some length, but it was hard to erase. From the outset Viganò's research was oriented towards modulations of internal space and external composition regulated by the structural skeleton, displayed and enlarged in its predominant role. The trabeations, pillars and volumes of Istituto Marchiondi, totally in raw fair-face concrete, represent a personal interpretation of the Modern Movement, and more specifically of the legacy of Mies and Le Corbusier.

The house for the artist André Bloc at Portese on Lake Garda (1956-58) is built on a steep slope descending towards the lake, and connected to the shore by a very long staircase. The large living area, thanks to two reinforced concrete slabs placed on the iron pillars, takes on a character of suspension and fluidity with respect to the surrounding space, in a design attitude that makes the natural environment an active force in the definition of the domestic space.

9. Robert Maillart (a Swiss engineer, 1872-1940), Pier Luigi Nervi (an Italian engineer, 1891-1979) and Riccardo Morandi (an Italian structural engineer and university professor, 1902-89) represent some of the most significant figures in the field of experimentation on the technical-expressive potentialities of reinforced concrete in relation to the achievement of maximum synthesis between formal investigation and the structural value of this construction technique. The engineer S. Zorzi was a collaborator in various projects of importance for their structural content designed by BBPR and by Luigi Moretti towards the end of the 1960s.

10. Across his entire career the design research of Viganò investigated different construction techniques, experimenting with the forceful plastic accentuation of reinforced concrete, and also with the expressive impact of steel. The Mollificio Bresciano at San Felice del Benaco (Brescia 1968-81) and the plan of expansion and refurbishing of the headquarters of the Department of Architecture of the Politecnico di Milano (1974-85) represent two salient episodes of the design research on the expressive potential of metal structures. The Mollificio stands out mainly for the three-dimensional and multiple modular grilles that add rhythm to the volumes of the industrial building, also in relation to the natural characteristics of the surrounding setting.

The expansion of the Department of Architecture features a dense network of black metal pillars that form a contrast with the glass surfaces of the infill, in a complex arrangement of levels, connections, open spaces, exposed conduits and physical plant systems.

11. The project for Cinema Cavour on Piazza Cavour in Milan dates back to 1963.

12. From the postwar period to the end of the 1970s Vittoriano Viganò worked in various guises and with different tasks for the Milan Triennale exhibitions. At the 10th Milan Triennale in 1954, Viganò designed and installed an "Aviary with a Tensile Structure" in Parco Sempione, a provocative metal structure with a conical form made with steel cables and nylon screens.

Vico Magistretti

Architecture
of reality

An attitude: architecture, method, "reality"
It is no simple matter to talk about and describe a method when you live it from the inside: the same is true of what we have defined as a cultural attitude, with respect to architecture and even more specifically to architectural design.

The first instinctive consideration that comes to me in relation to these aspects is on the parallel of *music-architecture,* and in particular on the significant influence the latter receives, unlike the others, in the impact with the world we define – to simplify the concept – as "material", "real."

I believe, I am convinced, that everything is conditioned: music itself, in fact, receives influences from literature, for example, or from history. But one of the particular characteristics of architecture, and one of its main nourishments, is the concept of reality: architecture and as a result everything the architect is, along with his fascinating activity, always and in any case have to come to grips with a reality.

Everything I have tried to accomplish in these years as an architect has always been characterized by the fact of never pursuing a "concession," or a compromise with *reality*; instead, I have always tried to grasp *reality* as an integral, compositional, landscape-related part of architecture.

If I think about a work of architecture in the mountains, for example, I know I will have to take certain climate conditions into account, given environmental situations; if I build in Japan – which I have done, in effect – I build in a way that is indubitably different from what I would do in Turin.

This conditioning is the *conditioning of reality.* And reality is the primary nourishment of architecture.

The house at Arenzano, which I built in 1956[1], for example, was forcefully influenced by a constraint, which then became a design criterion, represented by the existence of a very small lot: that is why I created a real garden on the roof.

It might seem absurd or almost a paradox, but in definitive terms things that could be seen as constraints or limitations, in the house at Arenzano, instead become a way of gaining awareness, in the interpretation of the reality that surrounded me: the slate, the shutters...

I took part at the last CIAM congress in Otterloo in 1959, when the CIAM was then dissolved. I remember very well that on that occasion I was scolded by other colleagues taking part in the congress – though they saw me as a good architect – for being guilty of using old elements and tools, such as those shutters.

Ernesto Rogers – who was one of my teachers – wrote a beautiful article in *Casabella* about the house at Arenzano[2].

Apart from this – without mentioning the case of Parma, which I think is successful, representing a typical example of conditioning that is not so much environmental as based on a specific productive reality that one could not and should not have failed to take into account[3] – from reality I try to derive all my choices in making architecture, basing them on it: whether I succeed, or if I only succeed in certain episodes, is another type of discussion, which unfortunately is not always controllable.

When, for example, I made the round core for the physical plant systems in the work in Parma, the primary aim was to propose an element that would be a center of gravity: a decision made after a long encounter with all the representatives of the bank and the technical/collaborators of Austin – the contractor that handled all the engineering of the building – to understand if the criterion proposed could have its validity, not so much on an aesthetic level, which at the moment interested me less, as on a functional plane.

So it is a crosscheck of a correct adaptation to a reality that should always be considered in every instant, every phase of the project: the multidirectional testing of reality, which is an indispensable phase of making architecture. Dialogue has always been important, both in architecture and in design[4].

One has to constantly adapt to reality: it is absolutely useless to make one more "little piece" that stands up only by magic, obliging the contractors or builders to perform acrobatic feats in an attempt to assemble a piece of wood, or to support an overhang: it is simply and uselessly foolish to deny the great contribution that reality always offers, in my view, to those who design and those who build.

The force of gravity – not a marginal consideration – is another fundamental part of reality: so when you make and conceive of something you cannot get away from the characteristics – also the physical ones – of the real.

There are engineers who with their ability manage to keep a skyscraper standing by supporting it with two cables; nevertheless, to achieve that result you would have to make a foundation that reaches from here to Bressanone! Today almost anything is possible, but precisely for this reason one should avoid childish and unjustifiable positions, being careful to steer clear of such a line of operation.

My procedural and design approach is to always and in any case come to terms with a conditioning that is never negative, because the interaction with reality is, in any case, a positive influence.

Limitations like building regulations or a particular standard are never a valid excuse for a qualitatively questionable result, especially on the part of figures actively operating in architecture: this is not making architecture, it is compromising oneself, like an incompetent, with reality. It is precisely becoming to terms with reality, instead, that one creates the uniqueness of the architectural act.

For example, in 1965 I designed a building on Via del Conservatorio in Milan[5]: the form and the volumetric design of the work were the result of a Detail Plan – another tool created by human stupidity – whose stipulations, rules and limits meant that you had to deduce the layout from these constraints, which determined the project grid in advance. The result is a work of architecture that in my view is not bad, if you consider the fact that it was design more than thirty years ago, and even today has its meaning inside the fabric of the city.

I too would have had to justify my architectural choices as obliged by the Detail Plan: instead, I interpreted the plan as a starting point from which to try to come to terms with its dictates.

In any way, in any form, we have to come to grips with reality, in the field of architecture and in that of product design – whether in the study of the structure of a building or the structure of a chair – never putting ourselves in the position of having to justify a defect or a given detail through motives of a functional or structural character: it would be a declaration of failure, of an erroneous design approach.

Vico Magistretti: production

I have spoken of "reality," a concept and a gauge I feel is indispensable. Obviously reality, taken as context, place, micro-environment, should not be seen exclusively as an entity charged with metaphorical meanings, or connected with existing contextual factors: reality is also the sum of existing factors and material, socio-economic and productive values that are not always taken into sufficient consideration.

I have had the good fortune to be one of the leading exponents of modern architecture – even without knowing it – and later a privileged witness of that very particular event that goes by the name of Italian design, which has basically been the space-time encounter between those who *created,* those who *designed* and those who *produced.*

This encounter did not arise through the initiative of some "creative" professional, who as often happens turned to industry to propose the production of a ladder, a chair or a glass; it was rather the opposite, or in any case a common effort in keeping with the principle of collaboration, whose reality has always been particularly emphasized by the manufacturers themselves.

This continuous conversation, this exchange of ideas that I still have today with the world of industrial production, has never been and is still not a matter of conflict, but instead a positive dialogue of proposal; also because I do not have much admiration for those who design only for museums.

I believe one should design for people: by this I do not mean only for "production," but I am a son of the Bauhaus, and the Bauhaus had its own logic and theory – though it was not carried out with complete success – which was that of drawing, designing and producing for large numbers, given the fact that behind us we have a long, deeply rooted tradition of industrial civilization.

Shifting the discourse to the present society and canons of life, today we should not continue to think only about *big numbers*, though I do not have the ability to design a single object: I always and in any case need the help of production and its logic.

For me it is absolutely useless to design a chair like the one by Duchamp, with a nail in the middle of the seat; though there are undoubtedly museums willing to purchase it, and – why not – even people as well, this basically means excluding oneself from the market. You can only indulge in such an operation once, because immediately after it the industry will turn its back on you.

This discourse does not set out to feed a compromise that taken to extremes would lead to the revival of a "fake Baroque" chair.

I design and I will always design behaving as I did in the past, paying close attention to envision the desires of people in advance, their effective needs.

I also believe that this type of "attitude" can be called *adaptation to reality*, in a positive sense.

I do not have regrets about any of the objects I have designed, including the ugly ones or those that have turned out to be mistakes: I have never reached the point of saying, "if only they had allowed me to do as I suggested." Never.

Probably I would have dropped the project, though this has only happened very rarely in my life. I remember, for example, that years ago I had to design a hotel for an American corporation in the center of Milan: after a short period of work with them, I understood that we belonged to two different cultures. I was not interested in what they wanted to do, and in any case I wasn't interested in doing it in Milan: they repeatedly asked me to remain and to continue working for them, with the obvious result that what emerged was a cultural hybrid it would probably have been better not to make.

In my professional life there has only been this one episode of true lack of comprehension, from which I learned that the final result of a work of architecture comes from a combined fusion of intentions between all the players in the development process: economic, productive and above all cultural interests.

So it is not a question of *purity* or of not wanting to take part in compromise: it is instead an inability to do certain jobs where the paths are completely divided.

In other episodes of my activity and in the relationship I have with production in general, not one single object by me exists that is the result of a compromise: at most, I repeat, I have made ugly objects, but never squalidly "negotiated" things.

Otherwise, in the design sector very good results have been achieved, in my view, reaching the point of having a quantity of things I would not do again in the same way that amounts to just five, maybe ten percent of my entire personal output.

Another significant parameter of good results and an important confirmation of the adaptation to reality of one's work is to see, as in my case, objects designed over thirty years ago that are still in production today. I think that 80% of my objects are still in the catalogues; and this is a sizeable number, also because in their ranks I believe only five or ten percent could be improved by rethinking.

Also in design, or above all in design, the ultimate goal should not be to produce masterpieces, but simply to work. After all, one always operates in a state of "necessity": you produce because there is a need for a certain object, not because one morning you woke up with the abstract thought of creating a chair. There is no basis for that sort of approach, in my view.

To work in production also means making mistakes, because it is only through experience that you can achieve valid results; experience also means making mistakes.

Vico Magistretti: the elements of design

If designing means experiencing reality, all the elements that contribute to the process represent indispensable means through which to pursue architecture.

For me technology is a tool, just like a hammer is a tool: this is why I never get excited about a technology, and above all I do not think technology on its own can ensure that you make a contemporary object. The contemporary object comes from correct and appropriate use of the tools you have available, the first of which is the brain. Technology doesn't matter at all to me, or almost. The real technology is the brain.

Geometry is a very important variable, of which I am very fond. Geometry is a bit like the *consecutio temporum* in Latin: it is something that makes you stay inside reality, that gives a sense of reality, and provides a tool with which to measure reality. I have made extensive use of it. In this period, for example, I am designing an object for Cassina that is almost exclusively based on geometry. The attraction and the use I make of it are above all conceptual in nature. Certain movements in space are always regulated by geometry, making it a true key of interpretation of reality: in design, therefore, I rely extensively on its regulating capacity and its principles.

"God is in the details": what Mies said is very true, but it is also true that a work of architecture or an object can never be resolved through detail. Only after the development of the concept does it become a natural, almost automatic operation to refine things on the scale of the detail. It is the coherent quality of the design, never a decorative problem, that allows you to approach the detail in a correct way. For this reason my process of ideation and design never moves from the particular to the general: I always, in any case, start from drawings on a large scale, to then progressively address the single problems.

Furthermore, I love materials very much, their choice, their reasoned use, but again in this case I do not have a fetishistic approach. I can make architecture in aluminium, wood or brick: I think my work has never demonstrated preconceptions or preferences in the choice of materials. Any material can be used, as long as you have in-depth knowledge of its semantic and physical-mechanical characteristics. In this regard, I am not interested in elaborate materials: for example, in the case of a piece of furniture, instead of precious damask I would be infinitely more willing to use burlap. This choice is more connected to the conceptual value than to the simple formal value.

The project of architecture, as of design, has to be a conceptual design, i.e. it has to express concepts. From a stylistic-formal standpoint there will be those who are good at it and those who are not; those who appeal to people's taste and those who don't; it is in any case the conceptual aspect and its profound meaning that interests me most, both in my projects and in those of others.

Vico Magistretti: the architectural project, and its management

Designing today, or in any case architectural design in the traditional sense, due to the greater complexity implied by an infinite series of variables inside it, requires the architect to have a capacity of adaptation to the system of development and that of delivery, a system in a state of constant evolution and change.

The creative process has to take many things into account, since it cannot limit itself to just some of them, discarding the others. For this reason my drawings and sketches are small, above all in the case of large projects, in order to be able to oversee them as a whole. It is a mental mechanism that also prompts me to number the sequences of sketches, to understand the genesis of the project itself and be able to interpret it better.

I like to concentrate and devote effort to the concept of the project, its deeper contents. I chose to be an architect, not a captain of industry: this is why, in terms of structure, I have a very small studio. I do not agree with studios containing 30 or 40 people, except in certain particular cases like that of Renzo Piano, with whom I have a very good relationship, who inherited his father's talent for entrepreneurial pursuits. Other studios with numerous staff that would seem to have a very innovative approach to the project seem to turn out a product that is not suited to the times, and performance that is in any case insufficient with respect to what can be supplied in a very sophisticated and complete way by a company whose basic objective is to deliver specific services.

I have on a number of occasions experienced collaboration with an engineering company: Austin, a company with which I have established an excellent working relationship[6]. I provide them with the conceptual criterion of ideas, while they develop the project in all its parts. In many cases – as in that of the Centro Servizi "Cavagnari" in Parma – I also propose design details, delving into questions that a service company, by nature, cannot completely approach, above all when the choices are particularly delicate and can have a decisive influence on the architecture. I intervene in a decisive way in the initial phase – that of the conception of the project – and then I let them develop the theme, while perhaps I come back into play, for example, in the questions of details or physical plant systems.

Being an architect also means knowing the science of construction, knowing that a pillar cannot measure 20x12 but has to be about 40x50, or in any case having an awareness of proportions and the relationship of stresses and dimensioning of a structure, though without having to make the calculations.

The "Cavagnari": an example of an attitude

The entire project for Centro Cavagnari in Parma, done for the Cassa di Risparmio[7], is based on the arrangement of the physical plant systems, which in this case represent the most important and complex factor, something like 3000 or 4000 square meters of space: this inescapable datum formed the starting point for the design and its evolution. The division of tasks between the architect and the engineering firm in a project like this, with its high level of physical plant and technology, implies very close collaboration between the parties involved.

By now I have consolidated this method and I continue to test it and hone it through practice: it is suited to the present times, and the characteristics of the requests. Once the project has been "packaged" and all the choices have been made, I have observed that the basic idea I had in my imagination is conserved and even reinforced, also with respect to the operations of graphic translation. This phenomenon was also apparent during the construction, and it is fundamental for the translation of ideas into architecture.

The control of the path to implementation happened by means of my visits to the worksite, which though I never my decisions on the spot, are very useful to see if the drawings have been correctly interpreted. In the case of Parma, the drawings were translated with expertise, since the Austin firm operates at a very high professional level.

The scenario in which the project unfolded and took form involved my counterparts on the "material" side, namely Austin, and an important economic-productive reality, represented by the Cassa di Risparmio, the client: the synergy between the architect and these figures is not just important: it is indispensable. Operating in contextual conditions that are the result of the sum of different geographical, climatic, cultural and social factors, through the active and pro-active collaboration of all the parties involved – contractor, client and designer – means also acting jointly on typological-formal choices, also involving construction technologies.

There is a significant phrase of a great treatise writer of the past which states: "The father of the work is the architect, the client the mother." I found an excellent client. My contacts at the Cassa di Risparmio di Parma – like those at the Cassa di Risparmio di Bologna, for which I did a similar job – were extremely cooperative, and proved to have an estimable cultural level. This is demonstrated by the restoration of the headquarters of the bank, in the historical center of Parma.

Following a conversation with them and the collaboration that began with an absolutely preliminary phase of the project, very useful aspects and themes emerged, from which to create a work whose validity is also a result of this attunement.

The formal and "aesthetic" choices come as a consequence: I used the materials I always use, the simplest of all. I was in Parma, so it seemed right to use bricks; I used copper, which is a material I love, because I adore materials that change. Materials should age, showing their history; an immutable material, that always looks new, even if it existed, would leave me completely indifferent.

Material, if it is correctly used, will last well, which is why it is proper for it to age. I would never restore the facades of the buildings in Venice: they are moments that pass and will never be repeated, moments you have to be lucky to catch.

Form and material, form and technology: in the Cavagnari they are the outcome of intertwining choices, inside the project and outside it, and therefore hard to distinguish from one another. The external factors, after all, are never really external; they are instead closely linked to an interpretation of reality, the most objective one possible: this interests me more than stylistic values taken as a variable in their own right, or as an element of evaluation independent of the whole.

The parts of the project form a whole and cannot be kept far apart from each other. In the creative act, especially that of the architect, we should remember that we are applying a synthetic procedure, to reach an extremely refined analysis of the project. To investigate and understand factors like that of dimensioning, its functioning, and the relationships that regulate it, are indispensable operations to conceive of an abstraction in a realistic way.

The abstraction is the synthesis, that is; a synthesis that takes all the previous factors of analysis into account.

The synthetic process can never be separated – at least in my case – from the simultaneous consideration of form and function.

In the design of an object, when I have investigated the function this object has to "serve" I no longer need to raise the issue of enhancing or transforming it by force, to modify its appearance according to a formalist logic, since the characteristics already stem from reasoning that has intervened during the process of genesis of the project, prior to the definition of the idea.

The Cavagnari is precisely the result of this methodological and cultural approach, whose basic philosophy lies in the essential simplicity of the choices. The construction elements used for its implementation confirm this.

In Italy, by tradition, we have the habit of reutilizing tools and parts "from the catalogue." Nevertheless, I often try to use the most common things, even in cases such as that of Parma: this is why I like brick. I try to use this material in ways that are perfectly in tune with a reality and a tradition of construction, because it is useless to try to make bricks – or any other material – perform acrobatic feats that their nature will not allow them to do. Moreover, also on a visual level the use of a "usual" material like brick is always a positive factor, because it conveys an image that ages extremely well, and this is a very important aspect, but works of architecture inevitably have to age.

For the components, I follow the same logic: when I make a choice it is as if I were choosing a car. I never design components like window frames, because I would never consider carrying out an operation other people have already done for me. When I have understood the characteristics certain components should have – for example, in the case of a window frame the form it should have, the size, whether it should be mounted flush or not – I know I can rely on what is in production.

I am not capable of having an approach like that of Renzo Piano, probably because I find it hard to go along with certain passages of method.

It is important for an architect to make good use of catalogue items, because in my view it is rather questionable to decide to create molds, dies or mechanical equipment – which by nature are envisioned and conceived by industrial culture, for large numbers – for limited production, perhaps limited to just one architectural episode.

To make a casting of a detail makes sense only if that detail is repeated

150,000 times, to amortize the costs, not 15 times, because in that case it becomes an autonomous object, a "sculpture," and I am not interested in making a sculpture 15 times that provides nothing more for my architecture than what it already has.

This discourse, in my view, is also valid in cases of works such as those of Norman Foster, my friend and in my opinion a very good architect: if we take his bank in Hong Kong[9] and eliminate some of the tubes, with a sizeable number of structures attached on top, which are very complicated and frightfully expensive, the building will be equally beautiful, because it has a valid spatial arrangement.

In Parma, as in all other situations, I chose the same universal criterion: the building is the result of dialogue and the choice of simple methods and parts. The advantages of this attitude extend beyond the phases of design and construction: later the aesthetic-functional maintenance of the building is undoubtedly easier, thanks to the simplicity and coherence of certain choices (on this topic, I would like to underline one strong point of the client for the Cavagnari: I have never seen one of my works kept in such extraordinarily perfect condition. The division of the Cassa di Risparmio responsible for maintenance has demonstrated and continues to demonstrate an approach that unfortunately is "not Italian").

The positive outcome of the Cavagnari project is not independent of the context in which it grew: a context, in this sense, that is not metaphorical but real, i.e. economic-productive and above all cultural. Parma is a city in which one works in optimal conditions: the contact with people is very direct, and their participation in the life and problems of the city is active and constant. Unfortunately cities like Milan are lost by now: until they do not solve problems like that of circulation and automotive traffic, it makes no sense to discuss matters for this city.

Architectural quality does not just sprout up like a weed: there is little doubt, however, that in cities of medium size it has a better chance. In Parma I believe we have achieved architectural quality.

Milan, 5 March 1993 – Studio Magistretti

Notes

1. Milanese, with a father who was an architect, Vico Magistretti was born in 1920. From the start of his career he has divided his activity between architectural design and product design. In the 1950s, working mainly on architecture, he gained acclaim with several projects such as the office building on Corso Europa in Milan and Villa Arosio at Arenzano (GE). The latter, built in 1956-57 for a friend in a residential and tourism zone of the Pineta di Arenzano, is a volume on several levels that follows the height contours of the very small lot. Inside, this arrangement takes the form of a subdivision of spaces on three main floors, according to functional groupings – kitchen-dining, living area, bedrooms. Outside, the flat roofs at different levels are utilized as terraces and gardens, accessed from various points. The attempt at symbiosis with the natural environment is the most characteristic feature of the design.

2. Magistretti is part of the so-called "middle generation," between that of the "Modern masters" active in the 1930s and 1940s, and the one born after the teaching of those masters, which launched its own research beyond the modern, developing various less unified, more separate but no less stimulating languages.

After studying at the "Champ Universitaire Italien" in Lausanne, he took a degree in 1945 in Milan, where he took classes taught by Rogers, the mentor to whom he often declared a "great debt of gratitude." It was Rogers, in 1959, who published the project of the Arosio house in *Casabella* no. 234.

Villa Arosio was presented together with the Torre Velasca and the dining hall of Olivetti in Ivrea at the last CIAM congress, held in Otterlo, Holland in 1959: the building by Magistretti was forcefully criticized by the supporters of Modernist *orthodoxy* due to certain characteristics, such as the fusion of the modern approach with elements of traditional architecture, and the attempt to establish a dialogue with the surrounding setting.

Rogers wrote as follows: "For me this house is the work of an authentic artist capable of renewal without self-denial. Magistretti thus evolves from his functionalist background, which he never rejects, widening and deepening its range. It is a proof of consistency, of confidence but also modesty, which many young architects do not show that they possess, which precisely for this reason makes him one of the strongest personalities among those who have extensively operated in the postwar period with well-deserved success. Here we find confirmation of his ability as a composer, who knows how to give meaning to every theme with an appropriate style; not a matter of eclecticism, but with methodological rigor. In the new Centro Residenziale Punta San Martino di Arenzano, which embodies a conscious urban and architectural orientation, among those built to date this work is the one most in tune with the existing contextual factors, without vernacular or 'modernistic' indulgence, but recovering the truest values and originality of the culture" (in *Casabella* no. 234, 1959).

3. Magistretti refers to the project for the services center of the Cassa di Risparmio di Parma, which he discusses in greater depth in the last part of the dialogue.

4. Magistretti's activity, as in the case of many other Italian designers, is closely connected to the field of product design; but in his case, the contribution to the industrial design sector has been very decisive and consistent, above all in the field of furniture design. Many of his objects have won prizes and are included in the collections of various museums, becoming part of the international design history. Also for him, the start of his career came in the sector of exhibit design and furnishings. The first objects designed by Magistretti were created for specific situations, for his works of architecture, without the involvement of industrial production. Only after 1960, the years in which he met Cesare Cassina, did Magistretti begin to work for serial production, stimulated by his rationalist background. Many of his pieces were produced by Azucena, then a small company founded by architects in 1949, already oriented towards the surpassing of the paradigms of the Modern Movement in the furnishings sector as well.

5. The architectural output of Magistretti, across his career, reveals a great ability to shape

volumetric groupings in such a way as to bring out the value of the site, in which they are inserted with the expressive force of their image, thanks to precise use of materials and composition. In the many works built in Milan for the residential sector – the Torre al Parco on Via Revere (1956), the house and cinema on Via San Gregorio (1958), the building on Via Leopardi (1959-61), the apartment tower on Piazza Aquileia (1961-63), one of the first concrete towers built in Milan, a small apartment building on Corso di Porta Romana (1965), one of the first to feature the mini-apartment typology, the building on Via Conservatorio (1966), the building for offices and apartments on Via San Marco (1972) – the volumetric interlocks of his works of architecture are inserted in the Milan cityscape, becoming an integral part of it.

6. Austin Italia S.p.a. is one of the leading engineering firms operating in our country – founded in 1966 as an affiliate of the American Austin Company – and it specializes above all in projects for the industrial sector and the advanced service industries. The firm relies on an operative method – the "Austin method" – that sets out to supply full-cycle engineering service, offering clients "turnkey" solutions and taking responsibility for the entire organization of the process, from the initial idea to the finished work, passing through the phases of design, purchasing, supervision and organization of the worksite. This method can be applied with good results thanks to the possibility of operating through the overlapping of design and purchasing activities with those of construction, permitting sizeable savings in terms of costs and timing with respect to traditional methods, where the various activities take place in a sequential, linear and therefore accumulative way. Furthermore, Austin applies a particular procedure of subdivision of contracts and suppliers in such a way as to operate to a large extent with local companies, usually forced to operate as subcontractors. Since 1985, when the company became entirely Italian, the relationship between Vico Magistretti and the engineering firm was consolidated through an ongoing relationship of consultancy – the architect was also part of the board of directors – above all in the area of projects of large size requiring a high level of image. In the 1980s Magistretti and Austin worked on complex service facilities, such as the two banking technocenters built in Parma (1985) and Bologna (1986), and the office building of Barilla built in Parma in 1990.

7. Cassa di Risparmio di Parma – a banking institute founded in 1860 – faced with the need for expansion, appointed a special consulting commission in 1980 composed of managers and functionaries of the bank, with the aim of developing the basic indications for the construction of a new service center. The structure located in a suburban zone of Parma was set aside to contain data processing facilities and their related offices, as well as technical divisions, storerooms and archives, and services structures including a retail banking facility, a dining hall and an auditorium. The need for a highly qualified building in technical terms led to the decision to assign the design and implementation of the project to an external company specialized in such initiatives: Austin. Given the focus on high architectural quality, as in previous situations Austin turned to an internationally acclaimed Italian designer – Vico Magistretti – for the development of the architectural project.

8. The main volumes of the Cavagnari are those of the high-security data processing center, the warehouse, the dining hall and the auditorium, the retail branch and above all the technological plant, necessarily located in a very visible position and containing all the physical plant systems.

This element thus became the characteristic feature of the service center at the level of its image: a large curved volume where one portion of the circumference is the core around which to organize all the other buildings; as the design put it: "a group of satellites in circular orbit around the central ring of the physical plant systems for the supply of energy." The desire clearly expressed by the client not to have a large office building developed vertically, and the request for luminous offices that would be spacious and flexible, filled with natural light, led to the idea of three buildings with square footprints for the offices and the data processing center, with a portico open on the ground floor and a characteristic intersecting pitched roof.

9. The skyscraper for the Hong Kong & Shanghai Banking Corporation in Hong Kong was

designed by Foster Associates – the English architecture firm founded in 1967 by Norman Foster – as the result of an invitational competition held in 1979. The building, whose image is based on an exposed load-bearing structure with enormous reticular steel beams, became a symbol of new technological invention and the art of engineering when it was completed in 1986.

Vittorio Gregotti

Gradual architecture

Attitude and method

The social, cultural and economic context is now impacted by a series of substantial changes, with clear repercussions not only for the formal results of architecture, the result of a "cerebral" operation, but also for the methodological questions of making architecture, its organization and the structures of provision of the project.

I do not have a deductive concept of architecture: there is no initial idea from which to be able to deduce everything. Instead, there is an idea that because it is initial has to be approximate, still general. This process, in the best of cases, represents a great enrichment, because with the approach of specific questions the facts begin to reveal themselves in a less general way; things become gradually less cloudy and increasingly precise, as the architectural problems to be solved start to present themselves. This is a factor that is even more evident in very large projects.

The project has to proceed by augmentation, not deduction: one begins, then, case by case, to establish differences and identities in constant growth, never decreasing. Those who work on architecture from the inside start to make distinctions, to discern exceptions, to set the elements that will progressively "specify" the project, making it architecturally more identified. From the outset values like the context – a theme on which I've been working for a lifetime – history, memory and tradition represent design elements of primary confrontation, inescapable, from which all projects come to life.

In our studio[1] this methodological praxis of progressive definition is experienced in everyday operation. At present the large works on an urban scale we are developing, in particular the one for Strasbourg or the work done in Lisbon[2], have both developed gradually through the executive phase of the architecture, that is when one has to define, even in formal terms, the individual parts of the project.

It is a work that is configured in a "cascade", continuously and progressively increasing. The possible detail cannot be imagined working on very large scales:

you can and should study it in the moment in which you come across it, and specific problems begin to arise such as choices of materials and construction techniques, not just from an expressive standpoint but also in terms of economics and performance.

One begins with a very general problematic, that can also be the big sign made on the territory, to then reach the smaller details, through progressive definition. I am certain that this is a sufficiently widespread rule, though in some cases the progress of this "way of designing" is not so expectedly linear.

One useful example is the episode of the University of Palermo[3], the project that more than all the others has allowed me to come to grips with the large scale: that experience is a confirmation of the fact that today, above all in works of a certain size, the quality of the designer, and obviously of the builder, lies above all in the ability to adapt to transformations and the continual modifications demanded by a series of factors that cannot be completely foreseen in the design phase.

The work began as a university appointment: in those years, in fact, I went to teach at the University of Palermo together with Gino Pollini – I began in 1968, he arrived one year later[4] – and in our position as university professors we developed the first rough project.

I was very lucky to be able to work with Pollini, an extraordinary person. In operative terms, he focused more on the details than on the whole, because that was his temperament and his way of thinking about architecture, while in any case making a truly significant contribution to the design operation.

The project was prepared in 1969 on behalf of the University, and was then discussed with all the professors and the persons responsible, after which it was poi approved. After approval, though a long time passed due to various differences, above all between the municipal government and the university, it was no longer possible to make modifications.

Once the disagreements had been resolved, construction began at the end of the 1970s – ten years after the design – with all the difficulties caused by having to stay inside an already existing scheme[5]; luckily for us, that scheme turned out to be quite durable, in the sense that we had identified with sufficient clarity both the basic arrangement and the structure, thus allowing the project to survive the successive formulations. The fact of having to alter many of the layouts, especially the interiors – the professors who were to use the spaces had changed, and with them the needs changed too – did not invalidate the typological-functional premises of the project, which through a regular grid and a very clear reticular structure in any case stood up to the negative effects of the big time gap between the design and the construction.

This was, and continues to be, a very long effort that has seen the collaboration of a good worksite supervisor – a local professional – and an engineer, with whom I had also worked previously, who deserves credit among other things for having had the "resistance" to stick with what had become an interminable operation. To follow the progress firsthand, one of the collaborators in my Milan studio went to Palermo and stayed there for two years, with the task of organizing the set-up of the worksite.

Unfortunately the making of the finishes and details is still incomplete, and continues in a very slow way, in step with the issuing of financing[6].

In spite of the trials, I am relatively pleased with the fact that the project is standing up to the critical distance – which is also a cultural distance – and to the *temporal shift* between design and implementation; I am obviously very anxious to see the facility in function, also because architecture is architecture only when it works, when it lives, with people, students inside it, even when as in this case unforeseen furnishings and equipment are introduced, or details are added stemming for the shared use of the structure.

After the experience in Palermo, with the aim of safeguarding the architectural idea in its most extensive possibilities, when we have had the opportunity to do so we follow all the project phases, excluding the structural calculations and the physical plant design, for which we work with other firms. We try to act as the direct guarantors of the project. This operation is not always possible, but when it is we take responsibility for the project, also indicating who can do the physical plant, who can be the structural engineer or the figure with the expertise required for that job: always in such a way that the main choices are submitted to us for our evaluation.

For example, the Belém Cultural Center in Portugal[7] is a work that as a whole we have been able to control very well, all the way to its completion, also due to the fact that I had a local colleague with whom I have signed the project[8], who played the role of project director perfectly, with the result that the work was done very well and correctly, both for the external masonry and for the interiors, which presented a certain complexity.

The center was built very rapidly if we consider the fact that from the moment when we won the competition to the moment of the inauguration of the complex just four years passed: design and implementation in such a limited time span is miraculous for a country that we consider, erroneously, to be almost in the "Third World." The implementation was organized very well, while from time to time having to solve the conflicts and obstacles that normally arise.

In my view, the work is extremely interesting, also because we have been able to eliminate the idea of making a big building, a great macro-structure, and have instead create a sort of "urban micro-structure" where everything is broken down into small parts, into "fragments" marked by the presence of something like the small streets that are typical of the reality of Lisbon.

Designing for the public sector in Italy and Europe

The work in Lisbon was commissioned by the government: in the first phase we were lucky to have a very intelligent and erudite Minister of Culture as our main counterpart, who enabled us to work at our best; those conditions changed in the second part of the operation, when the Minister of Culture changed and we found ourselves having more difficulties with the new one.

In the perspective of the relationship between an architect and the representative of the client it is indispensable to make a fundamental distinction, between a public client and a private client. And this relationship has to be seen in different terms if it is in Italy or outside the country, because the contexts are very different from this standpoint, especially in the relations with public agencies.

Although many of the factors that intervene in the path of the project are connected with the economic vicissitudes of individual situations, and are therefore not subject to generalization, the relationship with the public sector goes through many different situations, if we compare what happens in Italy with what happens in other European countries.

In the latter, usually, the design process and the exchange of expertise take place with a type of client who knows very precisely what they want. Often the initial contact with the designers is the result of a competition: on the basis of an initial selection, considering qualifications and requirements, invitations are extended that cover a precise time span, with a general program of reference.

The architect or architecture firm that wins the competition is contacted to formulate a true contract for architecture that establishes all the elements of the project, defining them with great precision in terms of program, timing and costs.

This first phase represents a very delicate moment of great difficulty in the conducting of the project, because the task is to make all the aspects of a contractual nature coincide with the more specifically qualitative factors.

In any case, it is a moment of certainties: through this type of operation one approaches discussions useful for the transformation of what until then has been the configuration of a simple idea, given form in a series of representations from which the architecture will emerge.

The production of the definitive design starts from this precise moment, which abroad – more than in Italy – already represents a form of absolute prediction of the work to be built, studied at a very advanced scale of detail, though during the process changes or small modifications may take place.

This means that in many European countries, in general, the responsibilities of the designer are decidedly wider than in Italy, where they begin and end with the project itself, and where once the design phase has been concluded, the construction is entrusted to other figures who assume responsibility for the supervision of the work – the public authorities – and its management.

In other countries this delicate phase is generally assigned to the architect, to a single figure that represents someone who has a say in all matters, assisting the client also in the moment of the choice of those involved in the implementation. The degree of responsibility is very high – and in fact architects usually protect themselves with specific insurance policies to cover the risk – though there is little doubt that this method represents a significant step towards complete control of the designed work.

So these are two different "attitudes" that have repercussions on the work of architecture. Very often in Italy choices and decisions are marked by a high degree of vagueness that in spite of the specificities of the individual administrations never permit a clear definition of the object of the commission and the types of performance it has to provide. For example, it is like going to a dealership and generically saying "I want a car," when instead it is necessary to specify what type of car, the size of the engine, the price range, the required characteristics. In Italy, the public sector generally says only "I want a car": in practice, what is lacking is a program.

This results in an ambiguous and seldom productive situation: to make up for the lack of a program, much of the work is done by the architect, who therefore has to make important and crucial decisions, although once the project has been developed he will lost responsibility for and control of the implementation phase, which more than others has a great impact on the successful completion of the work.

Going back to the project for Palermo, we should not forget that the work proceeds inside a reality – that of Sicily – that has very different inner logic and problematic issues than European countries like Sweden or Germany, where there is maximum control and everything works perfectly; so taking these aspects into account, as a whole, I can say I am fully satisfied with the results.

In other contexts the approach to the problems of design and implementation are very precise and correct: in Europe, where the project is concerned, there is generally a high sense of respect – also involving costs – dictated by the awareness that one never works alone, but within a delicate and important system of relationships.

In France, for example – but this also applies to German or England – in the design phase one interacts with a type of client represented by a series of professionals, always well-trained and competent, flanked by "control departments" that report directly to the state or are personally selected by the client, and have the job of intervening to resolve any possible controversies arising from the work performed. This is to emphasize that the range of people involved in the project is very large, much larger than it is in Italy.

I can mention two extreme cases. One of the most painful episodes of my life, undoubtedly, has been the experience of the Zen district in Palermo[9]. After the competition and the resulting definitive project for the preparation of a model, we were completely excluded from any phase of implementation and decision making. Though the project was quite accurately followed, in practice this exclusion led to the failure to build many of the envisioned structures, leading to a lack of all the main services. The biggest problem was the absolute lack of control over the execution, which culminated in a disconcerting invasion of the district on the part of many people even before the construction was finished. No one checked on the correspondence between the analysis we had conducted, regarding among other things the social competition of the inhabitants, and the real use of the structures[10]. It is discouraging to see the impossibility of intervention, when the envisioned situation was based on quite different premises.

An episode symmetrical to the story in Palermo, but with completely opposite results, was the work on a stadium we conducted a few years ago for the city of Nimes, in France[11]. Immediately after winning the competition, we drew up the contracts that would establish the costs, timing – 12 months for the complete preparation of the project, 14 months for the construction of the entire complex – and responsibilities for the operation, which would be left entirely up to us. A responsibility, also in relation to small discrepancies with respect to the stipulations of the contract – we went over the budget available by about 3% of the overall value, for which we had to pay a small penalty – that in any case guaranteed the kind of quality control and extreme precision of execution that only this type of management can provide.

I think the example of Nimes is particularly significant, but I could cite many other places and situations in Europe where this type of approach is taken to architecture: to work with these premises and in compliance with the schedules and budgets has always led to a high level of precision and an overall implementation of good quality.

Client, designer and contractor

Projects like the one for Palermo and that of Lisbon have very different paths and, above all, fates, depending to a great extent on the different modes of behavior of the public sector counterparts. Design for private clients, and its implementation, constitute an area of a different nature. Again in this case, the project development can follow very different paths, since the relationship with private clients is enriched by ulterior, different parameters, making it more complicated, flexible and linked to personal relationships, with effects that are also of a psychological character.

To have great freedom in relation to the client is at times an indispensable factor, not just for a positive outcome, but also for the achievement of works of architecture that with respect to the times can take on an innovative position.

The building for the employees of the Bossi company[12], for example, is a work of which I am particularly fond, apart from its virtues and its shortcomings: it was a job that made us discover and articulate all the themes that have then be discussed for twenty years. Those of the local historical tradition, of the relationship with the context, of architectural identity: an operation made possible by the stated unity of intentions on the part of all the figures in the triad of the designer, the client and the contractor.

The building, forty years after its construction, is in excellent condition: it is a sort of manifesto in which we outlined the type of positive critique we began to formulate with respect to the Modern Movement, which is why I believe that work was, and still is, quite significant.

It is a project of very limited size for a client that gave me an advantage, since he was my brother: so I did not have big problems with the client, in terms of knowledge of his needs or a level of cultural understanding. I remember that he took an active part in the series of discussions from which the project developed, helping to contribute to the idea of renewal.

To prepare small projects developed in close contact with the client is like making a project to measure. The house I built at Oleggio[13] also represents a case in which the client is a person I know well, and have known for a long time: and industrialist in the brick business, who asked me to design a house for him in a very beautiful place in terms of the natural setting; no obstacles ever arose, and in fact this was another episode marked by a direct, very precise and positive relationship.

From the symbolic-representative viewpoint, unlike what usually happens in workers' housing, this investigation of the theme of the single-family house, though shifted towards a certain type of research that can also be seen in the formal results – expressed in the elimination of the external facades and the creation of an introverted volume – has a less programmatic value, not taking on those meanings of *change* which the apartment building, or housing for workers, possesses by nature. The choice, use and interpretation of the typology constitute, in every situation, a fundamental element to be challenged, to avoid passively accepting and indiscriminately applying a sort of range of models inherited from the past.

In such situations the fundamental question, which becomes an extremely positive and fertile premise, is to attempt to activate a culturally possible relationship with the client. The task is to consolidate the fact that he has decided to come to you, because he wants exactly the things you know how to do, through a series of necessary discussions conducted on a terrain of possible shared understandings.

In this regard, there are understandings that come *a priori* and others that materialize along the way: it has also happened, in some cases, that I have not accepted a job, or have decided not to continue in a professional relationship, precisely due to questions of incompatibility of views. Logically, even when the incompatibility arises along the path of the design, certain variations also arise that may often be seen as episodes of improvement: requests and exceptions, therefore, that make it possible to better organize the project, in a more detailed, positive way.

In certain cases these variations become particularly problematic: as in the headquarters of AMPS in Parma[14], a very complex project to develop and oversee, due to the fact that during the work the client underwent many internal transformations and reorganizations, of both a structural and a personal order, with obvious repercussions on the decisions to be made and their timing.

The control of the project was very problematic, because these reorganizations during the process triggered new needs, with the resulting necessity to develop new variants, though they were plausible and justifiable changes: the program was unfortunately modified countless times, though in the end the overall arrangement has remained almost completely as it had been initially envisioned. The project was implemented in an accurate way, so the design did not suffer too much from the "additions" it had become necessary to make.

When the architect is called into play by a construction company the situation is more complicated, because the figure of the developer coincides with that of the builder as well as that of the client, so one part of the triad is missing. When the client is also the builder, a series of problems may arise, including grave ones.

I have only found myself working for a contractor once, though in that case I was called in to do a project for the public sector. The contractor – ENEA, a government agency[15] – turned out to be particularly intelligent and expert, which is why the results of the collaboration were positive: together, we solved a series of practical problems, also of a complex nature, like those regarding the company's equipment. A good work of architecture is also the result of a good interpretation of the structural and material potentialities of the apparatus that makes the work.

There are companies that are capable of developing specific technologies better than others: awareness of this factor is an extremely interesting element, important to avoid misunderstandings in the execution.

When, however, the *real estate speculator* – without giving that term a negative spin – is the same for both the land and the building, and also coincides with the role of the client, major difficulties may arise because the architect finds himself completely in the hands of this figure; I do not have any particular experience in this type of situation, because I built few things in the period of widespread development in the 1960s and 1970s.

Vittorio Gregotti

Another experience of great interest I am currently involved in is the episode of the Bicocca district[16], although recently the scenario regarding the long-term works has become even more complicated.

After having won the competition in 1986, we prepared an initial development and then began with a second phase: from this hypothesis the work has taken off and evolved, obviously with transformations, though the timing for the completion involves a very long span.

There are clients who have a certain cultural foundation, a certain respect for what you are and what you do, with whom there is always a way to reach a cultural understanding, though in certain cases they may have to force the issue since the interests in play are very large. So faced with certain necessities and needs, any type of question can be resolved, and everyone winds up being on the same side. But unfortunately this is not always the case.

Obviously the only real assessment comes at the end of any experience. For now, in the case of the Bicocca project, the first works we are constructing belong to the ideological and design direction traced from the outset, which has not undergone particular transformations, apart from several well-known issues regarding a change of the future users of the buildings or a change of purpose of the university departments previously planned: instead of CNR there is ENEA, and the Department of Environmental Sciences will be replaced by that of Analysis of Materials. These changes have an impact almost exclusively on the building typologies, which become more feasible.

Gregotti Associati

When designing it is very important to always hold the elements involved together and to be constantly aware of all the passages of the process, developing them and intersecting them.

This is why I tend to demand nothing, or in any case to demand as little as possible. Gregotti Associati[17] has excellent collaborators – moreover, they have chosen us, we did not choose them – who constitute our good fortune. Many of the people in the studio have been here for many years: this is a very strange aspect, for me, because in my day you worked for one or two years in a studio, before moving on to another.

Some of our people have been here for five, eight, even ten years: many were students who after studying with me came to work in our studio; there are also about ten foreigners, from different countries: usually they are people who have come here to work for a few months, or as interns, in agreements with foreign universities; sometimes they remain, or after some time they return to their countries. This is the emphasize that the people who work with me in the studio go through a long period of training, so we can all quickly understand each other.

Gradual architecture

Everything can be done through discussion: and this is even more valid in the case of architectural projects.

Due to my background, I am used to working by discussing things with others, and this operation raises no difficulties for me. Through group discussion you can make ideas gradually grow.

Recently we conducted an interesting experiment with some of the studio staff and external people: we participated in a competition, and won it, for a city of 150,000 inhabitants in the Ukraine, towards the Black Sea[18]. We brought together a group of people we know quite well – specialists with different backgrounds, sociologists, economists, transportation experts – organizing a series of encounters, something like "seminars" held here in the studio together with some of my collaborators who had already started to work on the project. The discussions we had were initially of a general character, on the "city," its meaning, because being able to design an urban nucleus from scratch nowadays is a very rare opportunity, especially in Europe, a reality where for some years now many of us have preached just the opposite, namely that we should focus on the transformation of what already exists.

As the discussion progressed some of us took written and sketched notes: after the first sessions we began to individually bring our drawings for collective discussion. Thanks to these continuous, shared and egalitarian reviews, in a few encounters we already had a rough design inside which each of the specialists could go to work, following the main plot. The experts thus brought us further information, which we in turn transformed.

This experience was meaningful because it confirmed how the working method based on discussion is an indispensable practice, which above all in the first phase of the design process can provide extremely positive results.

Past the initial phase, the project is generally assigned to a specific group, a small team of people who take charge of it. For certain projects – in the case of Lisbon, for example – we have created a true separate studio where three or four people worked, with whom I was in constant contact, joining them periodically for days at a time to work only on that project: this type of practice, a sort of full immersion, brings excellent results because it allows you to be isolated and to concentrate exclusively on a single project, proceeding rapidly with its development.

It is also important for the timing not to go beyond a certain limit, so as not to lose the *tension of the project*. Its production has to be dense, short, concentrated, because this leads to better quality, since the internal logic is always more stringent. This also happened in the project for Lutzowstrasse in Berlin[19], developed in our studio in Milan but then carried out at the site by a young collaborator who previously worked with Ungers, spent several years in my studio, and now works as an independent architect in Berlin.

For a period of about four months, we opened a small local studio where three people worked, monitoring the worksite step by step. The job was quite complicated, so it required their constant presence; furthermore, it went through many difficulties, almost exclusively of an economic character, due to problems of implementation: very strict, penalizing standards, a very low budget, practically comparable to those of INA Casa. Managing to complete the work was a truly difficult task.

Although as a whole it stands up well and also functions well – I have returned to the place recently – I am saddened by the fact that we designed a different building, because a project had been prepared for the other facade as well, with the insertion, at the back, of a plaza: these elements were never built[20] but would have been fundamental for the relationship with such a dense, significant context. It is a place enhanced by a series of eclectic villas, by the *Bauhaus Archiv* and, a bit further on, the work by Mies: so it is an important position, which fully justified the plaza we designed.

The question of method

The question of method, while it has a rather wide overall validity, nevertheless may admit transgressions, reversals of direction, particular cases.

Were we to reactivate a parallel, the one with Franco Albini, in spite of a personal approach that leads to a path that is the opposite of mine, he too had an overall vision of the project, which should not be overlooked.

It obviously depends on the episodes: for example, the Museum of the Treasure of San Lorenzo is a case in which the general idea was very precise, based on the meaning of the *tholos* with the circles, then carefully developed through a series of details.

It is in any case true that he always had an idea independent of the fragment: for him, the detail was an autonomous element, self-contained, a factor that embodies the force of his details.

This aspect came from the fact that he had conducted lengthy research on the detail and the small dimension, so in this sense he had a great ability in managing the assembly: Albini put the elements together, all in a row, and managed to make them work.

I believe, in any case, without taking anything away from his superlative gifts as an architect, that today the problem of design management and its extension into an unlimited series of facets would cause problems for a professional approach like that of Franco Albini. The greatest effort he made from this standpoint is the Rinascente in Rome, where the exercise on the relationship between the detail and the whole, the particular and the general, is taken to the largest dimension and the greatest tension possible. Nevertheless, I believe that today he would not be the person best suited to an overall reiteration of the project. Albini has always been on the side of the minority, experiencing opposition firsthand: I don't think he would enjoy playing that role today, just as in his time he did not enjoy being in the company of the majority of the protagonists of the debate.

I have always had a certain leaning towards a type of design capable of shaping a "strong" recognizable "sign," where the general has more importance than the particular, where the main thrust of the research is aimed at recognizability and identity. Obviously this discourse too should be filtered to remove generalizations, and kept within certain limits.

Nevertheless, detail and materials are perhaps the most decisive elements among all those that contribute to the making of a good work of architecture. When you work on large-scale projects it is very easy to lose sight of the detailing: so it is important to *cultivate* it, so one should always have a *testing ground*, a small project on which to continue the exercise, down to a greater depth. In my professional activity I always try to move forward with a work on the small scale, because it is a productive and value way to stay in touch with the idea of the detail.

When I built something, it is hard for me to be satisfied with the general idea. And I am not satisfied when it works, but the detailing does not: in this sense, I am perhaps a bit too much an architect, and too little an urbanist.

Milan, 5 July 1993 – Studio Gregotti

Notes

1. The design activity of Vittorio Gregotti, born in Novara in 1927, begins halfway through the 1950s: together with Aldo Rossi and Giorgio Grassi, he is one of the best-known students of Ernesto N. Rogers, with whom he worked as a university assistant and on the editorial staff of *Casabella-Continuità*, as well as in the studio BBPR precisely in the years in which the Milan-based group was designing the Torre Velasca. In 1953, one year after his degree, Gregotti opened a studio in Novara in partnership with two university classmates, Lodovico Meneghetti and Giotto Stoppino. The firm Architetti Associati (Gregotti, Meneghetti and Stoppino) moved to Milan at the start of the 1960s; in 1974 *Gregotti Associati* was founded in Milan, with many partners and collaborators, focusing on a more "managerial" dimension of design, while conserving – as Gregotti himself sustains – the artisan quality implied by a production structure similar to a "workshop."

2. Among the recent works of Gregotti Associati, the "Etoile" project for Strasbourg (1991), with the aim of interconnecting the historical center and the southern districts of the city, covers an area of 200,000 square meters; the Belém Cultural Center, opened in 1992 in Lisbon, has a constructed area of 110,000 square meters.

3. The engagement of Vittorio Gregotti in the architectural debate has also extended to teaching, starting in 1968, the year of his appointment as a professor in Palermo. The start of his teaching activity coincides with the design of a series of large projects for university facilities: the Universities of Palermo (1969), of Florence (1971), and of Cosenza (1973), developed through the work of different groups.

The project of the Departments of Biology, Chemistry and Physics at the University of Palermo, in the Parco d'Orleans area to the north of the historical center, covers not just the departments – for a total of 235,000 square meters – but also a complex of buildings for general services and student lodgings, as well as spaces of connection such as parking areas and plazas, organized around the axis of the existing Viale delle Scienze and developed in a series of enclosures placed on three levels, extending over a slight slope of the terrain.

4. Gino Pollini (1903-1991), after a period of university teaching in Milan, transferred to Palermo in 1969. The commission for the new departments of the University was assigned that same year to him and Vittorio Gregotti – respectively the directors of the Department of Architecture and the Institute of Composition and Institute of Elements of Architecture – together with Giuseppe Caronia, director of the Institute of Urbanism.

5. The structural grid of the project was defined by a system of total prefabrication in prestressed concrete with a module of 7.2 x 7.2 meters.

6. Since Gregotti and Pollini prepared the volumetric plan and the definitive project (1969-70), 25 years have passed and the work has still not been completed due to a series of circumstances that have caused delays in the construction. The project had to wait ten years before it could begin in 1979. The "rustic" part was completed very quickly: in 1981, over a span of two years, it was already finished, reaching its present level. The finishing and installation of the physical plant systems, on the other hand, have been impacted by major problem, also in relation to the large time gap between design and implementation, and the intervening changes in regulations. Of the three departments, only one is currently functioning, while the other two are still without physical plant systems.

7. The Belém Cultural Center in Lisbon (1988-94) is divided into three parts, which can also be defined as *modules* due to their individual recognizability in the larger organism: the Convention Center, now the headquarters of the EEC; the Exhibition Center, with a museum on four levels, spaces for temporary exhibitions and a specialized library: the Theater Center, with an opera house and concert hall (1500 seats), another theater with 400 seats and connected services.

The complex, entirely clad in local stone, has the appearance of a compact block from which the fly tower rises over the stage of the auditorium. The main facade on *Praça do Imperio*, the street also faced by the impressive building of the Jeronimos Monastery, is regulated by a symmetrical composition and features two access ramps parallel to the front, along with a portal that leads to a longitudinal pedestrian walkway.

Terraces and roof gardens are placed over the base composed of parking facilities, as an important mediation with respect to the surrounding landscape.

The building is the result of an international invitational competition held in 1988. Construction began at the end of 1989. On January 1st, 1992, an initial part was opened, while the work inside the theater and the completion of the roof gardens came in December 1992; the theater was opened at the start of 1993. These three modules will soon be joined by a hotel and a commercial building with cinemas.

8. The architect Manuel Salgado, whom Vittorio Gregotti met in Portugal in the period after the revolution.

9. In Palermo, after the episode of the university, Gregotti began an equally extensive project for an IACP complex for 20,000 inhabitants located on the continuation of a historic traffic artery of the city. The project for the ZEN (Zona Espansione Nord) development, prepared in collaboration with Franco Purini for a competition held in 1970, is based on the grouping of cubical blocks in a compact geometric scheme, in line with the tradition of the Modern Movement. This severe geometry, associated with the use of prefabricated structures and elementary volumes, is at the origin of the urban models of great impact found in Gregotti's output starting at the end of the 1960s. The Zen complex is organized with 18 residential *insulae* – the typological unit of the settlement – placed on three different levels attached by towers at the ends, and supported by a collective services center.

10. The Gregotti-Purini project, winner of the competition, has gone through a difficult process of implementation and has never been definitively completed. In fact, it was "destroyed without ever being finished," as the designer regretfully emphasizes. In practice, those who had obtained the right to a home there through registration with a public agency did not become the inhabitants of the district, but instead rented the houses to third parties. No type of identification or control exists, to the extent that these occupants do not pay rent; they overcrowd the spaces, renting them to other inhabitants; there are no hygienic services, and at times the apartments are even without an electrical system.

11. The name Gregotti Associati, in the second half of the 1980s, has been associated with several outstanding examples of design of sports facilities, especially stadiums. Of five projects designed, three have been built: the Olympic Stadium of Barcelona, the Football and Rugby Stadium of Nimes (1986), and the refurbishing of the Stadium of Genoa (1986); two others are still on paper, for the cities of La Spezia and Rome. In the case of Nimes, Gregotti Associati won the competition in 1986 and developed the definitive design in 1987. The stadium, with a rectangular footprint, is topped by four buildings with a height of 13 meters containing service spaces and supplementary functions, such as the box offices and the gymnasiums.

12. The residential nucleus for the employees of Bossi S.p.a. of Cameri (Novara), dated 1956, was one of the first projects done by Architetti Associati (Gregotti, Meneghetti and Stoppino). The work had characteristics of composition, technology and materials that went against the trend at the time, above all in the sector of low-cost housing, a field dominated by Rationalist architecture; the design was thus a rightful part of the approach of "orthodoxy of heterodoxy" and critique of the modern tradition that was emerging in those years. The complex composed of three duplex houses is organized in plan with juxtaposed rectangular volumes, staggered in a symmetrical way with respect to a central axis. The living areas feature small bow windows that emerge on the outside from the masonry texture in exposed sanded brick, alternating with parts in prefabricated concrete. The work was published in 1958 in *Casabella-Continuità* (no. 19), with an essay by Aldo Rossi titled "Il passato e il presente nella nuova architettura" (Past and present in the new architecture), which underlined the correspondence between functional choices and continuity with the local past, in a totally new moment in history.

13. The Beldì house at Oleggio (Novara, 1977-83) is a single-family dwelling placed at the crest of a small hill. The typology is formulated in an attempt at inward reversal around a central courtyard. The building, with a symmetrical geometric layout, appears as a rectangular block

topped on the outside by buttresses and open to the courtyard, towards which the pitch of the roof extends downward. An iron and glass gallery cuts through the house and the courtyard, extending beyond the perimeter of the building.

14. The AMPS headquarters in Parma is configured as a system of independent buildings unified by choices of a typological character – low, regular constructions – and a material character – external cladding in exposed brick, roofs and finishes in galvanized sheet metal. The system is made up of: offices, a courtyard building with a square plan on two levels; the laboratories and workshops, also with a square plan, topped by a large metal roof that forms a semi-sheltered space; the CRAL (workers' recreation center), extended lengthwise; the garage for light vehicles, with a square plan and a series of large portals; the general warehouse, a complex structure that gathers together and organizes all of the company's storage needs, both inside and outside; the two crosswise volumes of the heating plant and the garages for trucks.

After the preliminary project (1985-1986) and the first version of the definitive design (1987), developed by Studio Gregotti in the facility in Venice, the project was completely revised, in 1989, following changes in the requirements of the company.

The effective start of construction came in June 1989, and the work was completed in May 1992. Studio Gregotti was supported by an engineering firm that worked on the physical plant systems, structures, estimative metric computation and technical specifications, leaving the entire architectural design including artistic direction during construction up to the studio.

15. In 1985 at Casaccia (Rome), Gregotti designed a reliability testing and data processing research lab for the Ente Nazionale delle Energie Alternative. The building is an austere, compact volume based on the module of the prefabricated panels in gray concrete with deep openings. It is organized on a quadrangular plan crossed by a glass corridor that divides two large halls for mechanical and technical testing, faced by the balconies of the laboratories and offices.

16. The international invitational competition for the transformation of the Pirelli area at Bicocca (Milan, 1986-88) concerned the construction of an advanced technology complex in that zone to the north of the city. The winning project developed by Gregotti Associati called for large blocks of edification (one for collective hospitality, residential and commercial functions; one for offices, corporate services and residences; and another for university facilities with spaces for research and offices), connected by a sequence of public spaces and routes.

17. The Gregotti Associati group, which presently oversees a structure in which over 40 people are employed, was founded by five partners (Pierluigi Cerri, Vittorio Gregotti, Hiromichi Matsui, Pierluigi Nicolin, Bruno Viganò) and two collaborators (Spartaco Azzola and Raffaello Cecchi). After the departure from the group of Nicolin, Viganò and Matsui, since 1981 Augusto Cagnardi joined the firm, with Gregotti and Cerri, constituting the present Gregotti Associati. Cerri works mostly on graphic design and interiors; Cagnardi comes from a background in territorial planning and the study of transport systems. With an increasing quantity of work, the number of collaborators has grown, leading in 1980 to the opening of a studio in Venice, and in 1987 to the expansion of the studio in Milan.

18. The project for a city of 150,000 inhabitants on the Black Sea (1993) identifies the elements necessary for the creation of a settlement principle in its approach to the conditions and characteristics of the site.

19. The residential block on Lutzowstrasse in Berlin, designed in 1984 for the IBA by Gregotti Associati (with Walter Arno Noebel, Michele Reginaldi, Peter Salomon), is a building destined to connect and unite the fronts of four parallel wings of row houses previously built. The unity of the volume is interrupted by two symmetrical portals stemming from the differentiation between the metal grille structure and the clinker cladding of the remaining part of the construction. The project called for the construction of another volume that would group the other extremities of the wings, and would have faced onto a public space.

20. The implementation of the project stopped, because the IBA decided not to continue. After this, the IBA itself interrupted its activity, leaving the project in a mutilated state.

Enrico Mantero

Architecture of the essential.
Giuseppe Terragni

Still a timely lesson
When one makes what we might call a "diachronic" interpretation of developments, there is obviously the need to pay close attention to contextualizing the people, stories and events in their proper temporal dimension. At the same time, this exercise becomes interesting if we compare it to present situations, attempting – based on the elements available to us – to catapult the object of research into a contemporary setting. Designing 60 years ago certainly did not mean finding oneself faced by the advantages and disadvantages of the present: the techniques, materials, technologies and economic or ideal forces in play were completely different.

The interest – and here the concept of "cultural attitude" returns to timeliness – lies in trying to understand Giuseppe Terragni as a designer in the present: to see what methodologically transmissible teaching can be drawn from his work, with respect to this theme. It would be interesting to understand if a type of approach like that of Terragni would guarantee the possibility of keeping faith with its semantic and linguistic variables, and to what point his architecture would survive from the viewpoint of feasibility, or would change with the modification of the attitude.

The fundamental question lies, in part, in the intelligence of the figure: though this aspect of forceful "change" was not experienced by Terragni – unlike his contemporaries who had the good fortune to survive the war, also because some were a few years younger[1] – it is easy to assert, on the basis of his lesson, that Terragni took an indirect part in that change, through his message.

He was not able to experience the phase of major postwar reconstruction and the building boom, a privilege enjoyed by many of the figures we consider most important: like Franco Albini, Mario Ridolfi, or the BBPR group, or Gio Ponti, to name a few.

In effect, the latter had the possibility to consciously evolve in their "design gesture," not so much as a consequence of what had been done in their youth during the Rationalist period – in the 1930s and 1940s – but by taking new cultural questions as a new foundation for their architecture: in this sense, the work of Asnago & Vender[2] is of interest.

In definitive terms, then, we cannot separate someone like Ridolfi, his work, his attitude, from Neo-Realism; we cannot separate Albini from a proactive regard for certain Lombard architecture, or certain questions related to existing environmental factors. In this context and scenario, the figure of Ernesto Rogers stands out. For figures like BBPR or Portaluppi, there was instead the task/privilege of building the Casa degli Sposi ("house for young newlyweds") at the Milan Triennale[3] and then of inventing the Torre Velasca, which has a character almost similar to Filarete.

Getting back to Terragni, I think he too would have found the reasons and stimuli to take part in debates and cultural movements that sustained and shared the contents of architecture, as in the case of Neo-Realism, or as in certain questions of relative contextualized value, i.e. the historical reasoning of design. History and design, a bond that exists in the works of Terragni, though in an abstract, transfigured way, in an intelligent mediation between *history of the city, typology* and *project*. He would undoubtedly have joined in, or at least entered the fray, perhaps also making use of brick, which he had never done, in the name of this new research that was coming into play.

This would not have been because the clientele or other factors indicated, though unconsciously, new visions of architectural composition and above all of its physical-technological result, but because for everyone – above all Ponti and all those who in Rationalism had had the possibility of making many projects and constructions – in the passage from Fascism to the Republic there was a clear demise of the obstinacy dictated by the fact that under Fascism Rationalist architecture had to triumph, to become the architecture of the State.

This fundamental historical enemy was lacking, and a question instead opened up about democracy, about a more direct bond between architecture, literature, poetry and cinema, or between architecture and painting, a bond that had been very strong at the time of abstract art, of the Rationalists[4]; although the figures of Guttuso are present in Neo-Realism, this bond is fundamental for architecture, based more on literary criticism, on cinema.

When I wrote *Il Razionalismo italiano*[5], I remember that I cited the fact that in *Rocco and His Brothers* the most dramatic scenes were shot on the Ponte della Ghisolfa, while the home of Rocco and his brothers was located in the buildings on Viale Argonne by Franco Albini[6]; I have always associated this cultural moment with two or three images of this type, and the images of the film *Obsession* by Luchino Visconti.

I would like to emphasize that these can only be conjectures, because Terragni did not have the benefit of experiencing this second chapter of Rationalism, of a "new Rationalism": I think, in any case, that he would not have been isolated, because having all the required technical and cultural capacities, he too would have taken part in the nascent democracy.

This was true of people of his same stature, such as Franco Albini, for example, who although he was not as Michelangelesque as Terragni, and less characterized by an "artistic" ability – at least in the times of Rationalism – had also found an innovative path, not marked by the linear continuation of stylemes.

Giuseppe Terragni: the attitude of the *architect-sculptor*

The fact that the conclusion, in the work, was connected for Giuseppe Terragni to a vision of style and above all of compositional aspects, which mainly focused on a certain purism, even prior to a certain rationalism, seen in the sense of functioning and logic, meant that "making the project" and giving it character, all the way to its "physical" conclusions, were operations carried out in a sort of symbiosis that did not call for substantial differences between the *drawing* and the *project*, apart from changes that might be requested by the client.

Making this type of consideration, we have to take into account that fact that one of the primary objectives of Rationalist architecture was widespread scientification: principally the major investigation of the building type, which is one of the aspects that Terragni, like Le Corbusier and a bit like all his contemporaries, carried forward with great commitment. In the design of a kindergarten, for example, we can clearly see the research on a typology, also invented for the occasion; there is the modern updating of the pedagogical function, specific to the concept of the kindergarten[7].

Where the individual houses are concerned, there is the vision of architecture *en plein air*, along the lines of Le Corbusier. In the large public buildings, at the same time, an attitude emerges of strong ties to the tradition, which has prompted me to assert that in this aspect Terragni was a direct disciple of Michelangelo[8].

His way of designing large works, these great masses, considering all the design questions already so intrinsic to the positive preconception of the initial design, prompts us to observe that automatically, in Terragni's attitude, in line with the forceful operation of simplification effectively assumed by Rationalism, there is an identity and a simultaneity between *project* and *physical fact* that almost never led – apart from some small details – to a revision done by the designer or caused by reasons external to the initial design idea.

In this regard, we should recall that the architects of that generation, of which Terragni is perhaps one of most emblematic examples, urged and fought a true battle: on the one hand against the Futurists, and above all, on the other, against the exponents of eclecticism. Against the complication of the architectural design, that is, against having resort to styles, to the famous "neos"– neo-Romanesque, neo-Gothic – against Boito himself, in a certain way, since in any case they were in opposition to this series of principles, principles that had also – in certain expressions and figures – led to interesting results of architectural research; just consider Sommaruga, or Boito[9] himself.

Construction materials and techniques were greatly simplified, both structurally and in the use of finishes: the beam-pillar system, stucco, stone were all enhanced by new developments arriving above all from European Rationalism and the Modern Movement in general, represented by closures, window frames, glazings, materic paintings of the iron/window type.

In the course towards this ideal *purist* perspective, the "detail" and the attention paid to it were fundamental: it was one thing to be purists in the simplicity of the sketch, the essential approach of the drawing, and the linear order of theoretical intentions, and it was quite another to be purist as a whole, down to the last details.

This is probably the main platform of the architectural experience of Terragni, an experience we should remember was carried out independently, not by raiding the pantry for the leftovers of the Modern Movement.

The position of Terragni – also from a standpoint of *ideation-construction* – was very original if we consider the fact that at the same time he was paying attention to the works of Le Corbusier, or to those of the Constructivists, as well as others, without effectively regulating his activity on correspondences to these other developments[10]. His vision and way of making architecture are very personal and recognizable.

The Master Plan for Como[11], which was prepared with a team that included the outstanding figure of Bottoni, while not totally overlooking the theoretical premises of the Athens Charter, in any case found its deepest reasoning in urban history, which the Athens Charter, on the other hand, took as a given; in parallel, there was no formulation in that plan that was not strictly verified with respect to the specific nature of the city of Como, for which the plan was made.

This basic question, this general framing of the attitude of Giuseppe Terragni, is fundamental to understand his work, also from the viewpoint of the passage of his design idea from the immaterial, conventional state to the spatial, material state of the constructed work of architecture.

From another standpoint, we should take into account the fact that Terragni's work was carried out in the short time span of 15 years, which is why for him the battle on the front of architectural figures was more important than the demonstration, as Vitruvius said, of functionality, *utilitas,* strength, *firmitas,* and beauty, *venustas.* This Vitruvian triad is in any case intrinsic to the work of all the great masters: Terragni is no exception to the rule.

The fact that his "virtue" had such a rapid span of experimentation – given the quantity of projects he made in that period – should not lead us to exclude the existence of a "constructive" background that oversaw the execution of the work, its formal but also technological contents, the detailing, etc.: to the contrary, his production and working modes tend to reinforce this sensation.

It is not by chance that in Casa Rustici in Milan[12] the most beautiful drawings are those of details; the same can be said of Casa Giuliani Frigerio[13], here in Como.

In effect, we can observe an almost preset mode – not in a negative sense of the term – a directly consequential link between *cause* of the drawing, *reason* of the drawing and the *final effect,* all the way to studies of light and shadow, and of the whole, which was already part of the same immediacy. Probably in the design of a facade with ribbon windows, for example, the thickness of the sill was already implicit, along with the type of frame, the thicknesses of the two, their depth, the quality of the overhangs; for this reason, it is possible to assert that Terragni is like Michelangelo, because in effect there is a strong sculptural aspect in his projects.

Therefore, as for every sculptor, in the mind the detail is almost entirely envisioned in advance: in the very moment in which he conceives of the architectural work, as in a sculpture, the material is removed, honed until it reaches its essence.

From the idea to the implementation through the drawing

Reading and interpreting the drawings and documents connected with Terragni's design process it is possible to trace or at least attempt to identify a red thread in his way of making and envisioning architecture.

In the sense of a method that can be compared to the approach of a sculptor, the work embodies not just the essence of Terragni's formal response in architecture, but also a type of "modelistic" vision belonging to sculpture.

The design process, like that of sculpture, goes through an itinerary that descends from the general to the particular, through progressive "excavation" of the theme; for Terragni it was certainly not a question of "design," linked to deeper levels of certain hopes such as remaking, succeeding, expressing, which started from the detail: absolutely not.

The fact remains, in any case, that this aspect can be seen in the sketches – which are few in number – and in the definitive drawings of the most important projects that have not been lost, and which are perfect drawings, probably done by the studio, by collaborators, I would even say by geometers. They are perfect drawings in terms of execution, while those few detail sketches that exist – above all those of the Giuliani-Frigerio house which he had sent from Russia[14], with the impossibility therefore of sitting down at a drafting table, but with all the desire and force required to give the detail sketch its own truthfulness – are equal to the project, i.e. they are like corollaries, completely necessary appendices, final, for the success of the project from a semantic standpoint, of language, from the perspective of formal cleanliness.

A bit like saying: to be certain that you have to make an angel with blue eyes and blond hair, since this is the conclusive vision, you cannot help but make details that specify blond hair and blue eyes.

Terragni, perhaps also due to a question of generation, was a man closely connected with making; my father and Terragni were good friends, and having also done one or two jobs together, they were very close[15].

One aspect of that generation, above all that of my father – he was born in 1897, Terragni in 1904, so they were nearly one decade apart – was the fact that they were almost all men of the worksite. If not for other reasons, simply because this habit was still alive, and lasted more or less until the 1960s; as we know, in that decade and the one to follow architects almost avoided going to the worksite, seeing it as a debasing material aspect of the work.

Above all during the 1960s, due to the debate on professionalism that arose in that period, many had a certain hostility, a true hatred of the implementation, of the fact that the work then had to be made, and one had to go and see it made, because most of the protagonists of the debate were men "of paper," men of drawing.

This aspect represented a big problem, because for example Rogers himself – who was a man of the worksite, although the personal supervising visits were above all done by Banfi and then Peressutti, who was the keystone in terms of construction in the firm – in any case did build a number of works. If we have to attribute specific roles to the members of the BBPR group, it is well known that Rogers was more of a critic, Belgiojoso and Banfi were more operative, while Peressutti was the one who paid attention to implementation, who brought projects into reality.

To understand the difference of thinking and position that existed in us, also in the 1960s, just consider the fact that in continuity with the previous generation, if you will, because I came from an architectural family, during my fourth year of high school, at the age of 18, I was already supervising two worksites for INA Casa, one at Lomazzo and one down on the way to Lecco, and I drove the car my father had never driven. I had designed them myself, infatuated with the teachings of Ridolfi[16].

Normally, in any case, in that period there was a big gap between drawn reality and constructed reality. In Terragni's generation, on the other hand, things were held together by the fact that daily involvement with the worksite ensured the completion of the work, through modifications, adjustments, through the "sculptural continuity." One operated on the worksite as one made drawings. It is the great teaching this generation, and Giuseppe Terragni in particular, has left to us in methodological terms.

Enrico Mantero

Today, in fact, the ability of the architect – driven by other motivations that would have been unthinkable at that time – is to know how to live in real time with the variables and variations to which the project is subjected by the continuous actions of modification with which the architect-designer, to keep faith with his idea, has to cope: one of the specific places of this operation is the worksite. Even today, as then, perhaps more than then, the objectives have to be transmitted to the makers.

One very important thing must be held in account: the workmen available to Terragni and his contemporaries – like the master builders and contractors – were older and more solid, structured to build eclectic, neo-Romanesque, neo-Gothic houses, houses in the style of Sommaruga, with very complicated detailing, so that probably the bare mallet probably didn't exist, it wasn't called for.

This aspect also reflects one of the main reasons those architects were present at the worksite: it became a necessary practice to be certain that the implementation, even if the details had already been designed, would be done in line with the figurative and formal objectives, while it was taken for granted that it would be done properly, since there were no doubts about the quality of the workmen. Unlike what happens today, the workmen could even be too highly skilled, specialized and affected, oriented towards particular finishes and solutions of a 19th-century character.

We should also consider another thing: Terragni in particular – I don't know if the same thing happened for others, such as Ponti for example, who had lived through the first Rationalism (I call it "first" because I think that Rationalism also went forward in the postwar era) – always made use of very close collaboration with an outstanding expert on structures.

In Terragni's specific case it was the engineer Uslenghi[17], who constituted a constant presence of technical know-how during both design and implementation: he could reassure Terragni that a pillar measuring 30x30 cm could extend across two levels without bending. This fact, however, did not only grant Terragni the certainty of being able to design a slender pillar; it also meant the certainty that someone could calculate it, placing it beyond any doubt. In Uslenghi, Terragni had a formidable ideal sidekick, which whom he (probably) also studied the details, the attachment to the wall, the pillar, the slab, etc.

At the time, in any case, there were also different figures: Muzio[18], for example, though he was an engineer, was an architect in practice, as were the ancient architects, without wanting to abuse this comparison; like Leonardo, an engineer, painter and architect. There was still this coexistence of technique and art – a virtue that has been lost today – which was very clear in Muzio.

It was also clear in Sommaruga[19], and in the case of the younger, eclectic talents, such as my father: their university training, to become civil engineers, called for three years at Brera and two at the Polytechnic. This factor meant that they had an artistic, humanistic, literary side: my father's enormous library, starting in 1922, contained art books, literature, all the German magazines, everything that was published in the 1920s and 1930s; there was the ability to enclose these many facets of the *creative process,* of the *process of implementation* in their figure, in their identity.

Terragni was already different, as were all those of his generation: they relied for everything on the force of the drawing, while being aware – and this is the most important and transmissible element – that what was on the paper perhaps had no basis, and would have to undergo further testing; this is why they always worked with the support of valid engineers, who could understand these innovations.

Mucchi, for example, was an engineer and a partner of Bottoni[20]. This aspect of collaborations was passed down: probably Albini and others relied on colleagues who could provide some certainties. Intelligent technicians, in the sense that they flexibly attempted to solve the questions raised by someone like Franco Albini, like Gio Ponti, and so on.

For me the Pirelli skyscraper[21] remains a building of the same beauty as the Torre Velasca, although as students for partisanship we rooted for the Torre Velasca. The Nervi-Ponti relationship reveals a symbiosis, a complicity between structure and architecture. This symbiosis between the expressive value of the structure and what in any case was to be the ultimate seal from the viewpoint of language, colors, materials, form, has meant that many works until the 1970s have this identity, this coexistence of architecture and technology, where by technology I mean the structure and the materials in general, precisely in unison. Like a successful symphony, which if it is in C major is entirely in C major.

Terragni, technology and production

I think it can be said that if we make a proper interpretation of the term technology, in Terragni's work it corresponded or sustained a very high level of linguistic clarity and formal purity, practically as a basic assumption.

The great *battage* then was not only for the architects like Terragni, but also for the engineers: just consider Pier Luigi Nervi, the theme of the validity of the system of pillars, the structures in reinforced concrete, the foreshadowed vision of lightness, prior to Italo Calvino's writings in the *Six Memos.*

Within this set of objectives, in a period of continuing research, materials immediately had their part to play, as happens in a sort of orchestra. One example is Terragni's use of glass blocks: the way this material was deployed at the time was very different from what is done today. He placed it in epidermic and expressive continuity with the solid parts, with the pilasters, positioned for certain very precise functions: the same discourse also applies to the system of opening of the glass, inside the typology of the window frames.

If we consider, for example, the window frame of the ground floor of the Casa del Fascio[22], in a material to all extents noble and therefore also sophisticated from a typological standpoint, of the use of metals: this aspect, interpreted in its essence, has a derivation that is of a fully "pictorial" character.

The use of steel, as of bronze, or of the painted frame, had its roots directly in abstract painting and its expressive criteria, enhanced precisely by this chromatic effect that the detail added to the outstanding overall chromatic impact of the architecture of the building.

All this is to indicate that in Terragni's way of working we cannot overlook or separate the typological idea, the compositional idea of the facades – one example will suffice, that of the typological invention of the plan and the compositional invention of the elevation in the Casa del Fascio – from the "technology" in its true meaning, which reached the point of providing this ultimate seal, above all of a precisely compositional character, at times also chromatic, of pale and dark hues.

From the outset, in Terragni's technology there was a coexistence of the architectural ideation and the materials: that latter, above all, played a decisive role from the beginning, precisely because they had already been identified. As in an orchestra that has to play a given piece of music or a certain symphony, in the moment of composition the instruments are not already predetermined, since in any case that is part of the creative moment.

Logically, the range of materials or technological options available to an architect working in the 1930s was not comparable to that of today, but much more limited and controlled. Those too, however, were years of continuous discoveries and achievements in the construction sector, and in this sense the research could move in various different directions.

Given the type of documentation found in the studies on Terragni, this aspect can obviously not be approached with mathematical certainty. It is a fact, however, that the window frames, usually made with iron, were for windows produced by Ilva, and that a great contribution had been made in those years by Fidenza Vetraria through the production of glass blocks: undoubtedly, those of the time and in any case of Terragni were references to companies, more than to actual "catalogues." Companies that applied the most advanced technologies also to individual construction elements, such as the brick with which architects, and above all Terragni, conducted extensive experimentation.

To carry out this comparison with the present situation we can attempt to draw a parallel: again, in the field of window frames and finishes today we have a wide range of offerings, with the result that every object is completely different from the others.

Today, in definitive terms, we all have to debate our choices, because the range of possibilities is very wide; instead, the designers of that generation, in this sense, were not very Vitruvian, that is they did not have the problem of *firmitas*.

We all know that Rationalist architecture had the great limit of its lack of durability; the buildings of Terragni, in particular, could not escape this logic, but many other buildings as well, if we exclude certain things by Ponti or Muzio, were made with generally not very durable materials – stucco, small tiles – and the window frames certainly would not have complied with today's regulations. As a result, not only in Italy but also in Germany and Holland, the works of the Rationalist architects have gone through and are still going through major projects of restoration: in the case of Terragni we can consider the Asilo Sant'Elia[23], or in any case an infinity of other works that have been restored, often with varying results.

So if we want to deduce a basic philosophy regarding the technological aspect and to find a ranking of values, we can say that probably in Terragni, beyond the aspect of simultaneity between *architectural design* and *technological-component design*, there was also a profound logic of experimentation with materials, construction components like brick, glass blocks, or the base joint of window frames: all factors, in any case, that by virtue of the fact that they too contributed in a decisive way to the formal-expressive result, were "bent" to that result, apart from their exclusively technological characteristics; this meant that at times they were used in an improper way, or in an overly simplistic way.

"Technology," in Terragni, is in first place from the viewpoint of figurative objectives, but not as a repertoire of secure, acquired technology, as it was in the immediate postwar era, for the various authors like Albini, Ridolfi, Libera and others.

With the constitution, for example, of the *Manuale dell'architetto*[24], with the fact of having to contribute in an economical, social and lasting way to the reconstruction of the country, obviously the focus on certain technological solutions – the least costly possible but at the same time certainly not the most durable – led to the revolution of certain concepts and the utilization of new construction techniques.

Just consider, to name a couple, the abandonment in some cases of the flat roof, or the return to wooden window frames, seen in the works of the post-Rationalism of the 1950s and 1960s.

All told, the decay of some of the finest complexes of INA-Casa, as of some of the individual houses that were still being built at the time, is quite different from the degree of decay that has impacted the above-mentioned kindergarten of Sant'Elia, built in 1938 and already in need of restoration in the 1950s: in fact, an initial, poorly done restoration was attempted in 1960, followed by a more recent renovation overseen by Studio Terragni, done with technologies from the original era[25].

So the reason behind a change of vocabulary, of language and of a different interpretation of the role of technology in the postwar era was not a betrayal of old banners, but a need consciously accepted, taken to a catharsis also of a cultural nature: to establish relations with Neo-Realism, with a certain literature, with cinema, meant that this new architecture – apparently more "strapaese" – found its motivations on the one hand in the adoption of a new technology, and on the other by rooting itself in contemporary cultures, as in literature, cinema and the arts.

From this vantage point, the "change" was not based on a sort of impracticability or inadmissibility of *continuity* with Rationalism: it is sufficient to observe the finest works of Franco Albini, of Vittorio Gandolfi[26] or certain things by Gio Ponti. I think that in this perspective the Pirelli skyscraper constitutes the high point of this exemplification: I feel that this work, on a par with others, exists in profound continuity with Rationalism.

Physical plant systems, details and decorations

In Terragni design aspects like the physical plant systems and their relationship with the construction did not arise. The present-day problems of climate control or technological networks did not exist: the systems were still totally simple and traditional – heating was done with a coal-burning boiler, air conditioning did not exist, safety regulations were as they were – and were all inserted in the walls, because leaving them visible would have been considered almost shameful. Projecting Terragni into the present, it is easy to imagine that the linguistic cleanliness he pursued in his architecture would have been conserved with respect to the current technological complexity: he would have concealed everything that was not architecture in the classical sense of the term.

It is impossible to imagine that someone like Terragni would have been able to design something like the Beaubourg, where the display of the escalators and all the physical plant count as major factors in the expressive result: I don't think he would have adopted this technology bared in order to become a profound part of the language and the style, and I think he would in any case of hidden it away.

This attitude is fully in tune with the battle against decoration: like Adolf Loos when he speaks of *ornament* and *crime*. Nevertheless, if we carefully analyze their architecture, we see that the Rationalist architects were great decorators, because a rationalist window, or a curtain wall system, or a ribbon window, is a large decorative feature. Terragni was against traditional decoration, but he clearly followed a logic in which the contribution of the detail was to be interpreted as an element of decoration.

The process of reduction applied to the detail can be seen as a path towards easier implementation, towards simplification: nevertheless, the elimination of adornments, of complications, of hard-to-make details, called for the introduction of other very difficult tasks, because a curved wall of glass bocks is far from easy to build.

The rationalist choices, though driven by the hatred of ornament or decoration, were actually also dictated by the desire to simplify the work from the viewpoint of implementation, obviously with all the pertinent risks, because the builders and craftsmen of the time were probably oriented towards another type of work.

This capacity and desire for greater constructive simplification equaled those of Le Corbusier, who years later made a conscious choice, using fair-face concrete in the knowledge that those who would make it would probably do so with ease, and well, while suggesting more complex things it would be difficult to reach the right level of communication of the architectural thinking, which in any case did not depend on the richness of the materials.

There is a continuity to which an architect is clearly subject and faithful, even more in the case of strong affinities with Rationalism, or the greater intensity of his use of that language. So if Giuseppe Terragni had also lived in the successive period of history – in purely hypothetical terms, since he passed away in 1943 – the matrix of his profound though brief experience of the question of Rationalism would certainly have remained; we are not saying that he would have made a Casa del Fascio in brick, but that he would certainly have taken part in the also methodological and technological renewal, that of an "attitude," never denying everything that for him had been the foundation of his Rationalist existence.

Cernobbio, 13 February 1993 – Studio Mantero
Cernobbio, 10 December 1994 – Studio Mantero

Notes

In his long activity of research on Giuseppe Terragni, Enrico Mantero has taken part in and organized many national and international conferences, written essays and published, among other works, the books Il Razionalismo italiano *and* Giuseppe Terragni e la città del razionalismo italiano. *Gianni Mantero, Enrico's father, worked on projects in collaboration with Giuseppe Terragni in the 1930s.*

1. Giuseppe Terragni was born in Meda, between Milan and Como, in 1904, and died in Milan after having repatriated from Russia in 1943, when he was just 39 years old. The son of a construction contractor, he studied in Como and then enrolled at the Superior School of Architecture of the Politecnico di Milano, where he took a degree in 1926. In Milan Terragni got to know Pietro Lingeri, still a student at the Brera Academy, with whom he began a relationship of friendship and professional collaboration in various periods, extending from 1926 throughout his lifetime. This partnership had to do above all with competition projects and apartment buildings constructed in Milan. For his works in Como, Terragni was almost always joined by his brother Attilio and Luigi Zuccoli, his assistant in the studio he opened in Como in 1927.

2. Mario Asnago (1896-1981) and Claudio Vender (1904-87), architects trained in Milan active since the 1930s, represent a lineage of purism in the interpretation of the Rationalist lexicon, based on an abstract compositional approach and the use of elementary geometric forms. Their production, with its solid line of continuity, was made for private clientele in and around Milan, mostly in the areas of apartment buildings and office buildings.

3. The "*Casa del Sabato per gli sposi*" was installed in the park of the 5th Milan Triennale in 1933, with design by BBPR and Piero Portaluppi.

4. Giuseppe Terragni had a strong connection to the world of painting. He too was a painter, mostly in his youth, and during his career he frequented a circle of abstract painters that included artists like Mario Radice, Manlio Rho and Aldo Galli, who together with the architects Terragni, Lingeri, Luigi Vietti and Cesare Cattaneo were the protagonists of cultural life in Como. These figures balanced between the figurative and abstract currents had a strong influence on Terragni, not only in the choice of painters and sculptors for the decoration of his works, but also in terms of a more general compositional approach.

5. E. Mantero, *Il Razionalismo italiano,* Zanichelli, Bologna 1984.

6. The houses on Viale Argonne where Luchino Visconti shot part of the film *Rocco e i suoi fratelli* (1960) were those of the IFACP "Fabio Filzi" development by Franco Albini, Renato Camus and Giancarlo Palanti, built in 1935-38.

7. The project that was never built for a kindergarten in Como for 200 children, developed in 1931-32, represented Terragni's first approach to this typology, foreshadowing several themes of the Asilo Sant'Elia, built a few years later, such as the portico, the use of translucent diaphragms, the ramps, the strong indoor-outdoor relationship, and games of light.

8. The "Michelangelo-like" character of Terragni's way of making architecture has often been emphasized in critical writings. Still a student, the architect from Como made a trip to Rome, after which he produced a famous series of "Michelangelesque" sketches that already revealed his sensitivity to plastic forms, relationships of volume, contrasts between full and empty zones. Piero Bottoni described Terragni at age 21: "He studied Michelangelo in great depth, perhaps due to affinities of plastic and spatial sensibility. He sensed the big surfaces, the profiles and relief with the force of his own character; the drawings of the statuary had the perspective effects and power of Michelangelo; the figure was interpenetrated in the architecture, as by an architect" (quoted in B. Zevi, 1980). Terragni was attracted above all by the plasticity, the monumental scale. Another constant reference, in fact, was Antonio Sant'Elia, especially his production in the Futurist period, a source of inspiration above all for the many projects for monumental and commemorative works of architecture.

9. Like many architects of the Modern Movement, Terragni was trained and began his career by making reference to the classical vocabulary, without however engaging in the "revivals" of the architectural Novecento promoted by Camillo Boito and Giuseppe Sommaruga. The continuity with the example of Boito was instead in the desire to define a renewed language that would be the expression of a new national reality. Terragni makes reference, in fact, to "a tradition that is transformed on takes on new aspects" when in 1926, a few weeks away from his degree, he was one of the most active authors of the manifesto of Gruppo 7, with Luigi Figini, Guido Frette, Sebastiano Larco, Adalberto Libera, Gino Pollini and Carlo Enrico Rava.

The group took part in 1928 in the first "Esposizione di Architettura Razionale" in Rome, where Terragni showed projects for a pipe foundry and a gasworks, and presented his first project on a European level, that of the "Novocomum" apartment building in Como, under construction at the time: a project that impressed the public and critics for its mastery of the new modern language.

10. Throughout his training and the early years of his career Terragni focused on deepening his culture, above all striving to stay up to date on developments in other countries. Luigi Zuccoli has often recalled that Terragni was "driven by the desire to know about the architecture of the whole world," demonstrating particular admiration for Gropius, Le Corbusier and the Dutch architects.

11. During the CIAM congress that led to the Athens Charter, together with Piero Bottoni and a group known as CM8 Terragni presented a master plan for Como: the project was the winner of the competition for the Master Plan of Como in 1934, in which Terragni and Bottoni took part in collaboration with C. Cattaneo, L. Dodi, G. Giussani, P. Lingeri, M. Pucci, R. Uslenghi.

12. Casa Rustici, a luxury apartment block on Corso Sempione, was part of a series of five residential buildings designed with Pietro Lingeri in Milan halfway through the 1930s: the first was Casa Toniello (1933), full of references to Le Corbusier; this was followed by Casa Ghiringhelli, Casa Rustici – the most famous – Casa Lavezzari and Casa Rustici-Comolli (1934-35).

In the Rustici building the two designers, coming to terms with a lot with an irregular form, rejected the traditional U-shaped footprint in favor of a freer and more innovative layout that permitted better use of the space: a double linear arrangement formed by two parallel volumes, perpendicular to the street, defining an open courtyard towards the street, though bordered by a series of balconies that join the two ends of the blocks, with the result of an emptied, transparent facade to guarantee suitable lighting and ventilation for all the apartments. Construction began in 1933 but was not completed until 1935, a delay caused by problems that arose in the process of obtaining a building permit from the municipal government: due to its extremely new typology, the design was rejected nine times before finally gaining approval.

13. After the experience in Milan, Terragni returned to residential design at the end of his career: in 1939 he was commissioned to design the Giuliani-Frigerio apartments in Como, his last major project. The matrix of the building is a complex, detailed compositional scheme that regulates the altitude of the apartments – three per floor, placed on different levels – determining the figurative result, since the organization is reflected in the facades. From the first formulations, the complex has an almost square plan in which circulation takes place along the perimeter around a central core.

14. Drafted into military service at the start of World War II, Terragni was stationed in the Balkans in 1940, and then in Russia. The Giuliani-Frigerio building was completed by Luigi Zuccoli, his assistant, based on the preliminary drawings and the sketches Terragni sent from the military camps in Russia. Later Zuccoli completed the definitive drawings and supervised the worksite until the work was finished at the end of 1941. Repatriated to Italy at the start of 1943 due to a nervous breakdown, Terragni died that same year, in circumstances that have yet to be fully clarified.

15. Gianni Mantero worked for the first time with Terragni on the design of a lakeside vacation home for an artist at the 5th Milan Triennale in 1933.

16. Enrico Mantero took a degree in 1960, beginning his career in practice and in teaching, as the assistant of Ernesto Rogers in the course on Elements of Composition at the Department of Architecture in Milan, where since 1981 he held the chair in Architectural Composition.

17. Renato Uslenghi, an engineer, worked with Terragni on various projects, the most important of which was the Casa del Fascio in Como, for which Uslenghi did the calculations for the reinforced concrete structures – completely independent of the scheme of the perimeter walls and the internal subdivisions – on the basis of a general arrangement established in advance by Terragni.

18. Giovanni Muzio (1893-1982) was one of the most outstanding exponents of Novecento architecture.

19. Giuseppe Sommaruga (1867-1917), Milanese, a student of Boito, freely interpreted the Liberty style, putting a strong accent on plastic and sculptural decoration.

20. Gabriele Mucchi, with Mario Pucci, collaborated on many occasions with Piero Bottoni. Giuseppe Terragni and Pietro Lingeri, with the group of Bottoni, Mucchi, Pucci, prepared the project for the competition for the new Fiera Campionaria of Milan in 1938.

21. The Pirelli skyscraper was designed by Gio Ponti (architect and designer, 1891-1979) and Pier Luigi Nervi (engineer, 1891-1979) in the second half of the 1950s (1955-58). The building, with a height of 120 meters, symbol of the new potential of engineering, is a volume with tapered ends built around a structural core in reinforced concrete.

22. In 1928 Terragni joined the Partito Nazionale Fascista, with the enthusiasm that would then guide him in the design of the Casa del Fascio in Como, the symbol of the Italian contribution to Modernism; he began work on its definitive version in 1932. The building, a cubical volume organized by means of a modular grid, has four levels and is oriented in an optimal way thanks to the contribution of a specialist, Prof. Neufert. It has a large sheltered central space faced by the circulation routes, meeting rooms and offices. The spaces, functions and orientations are reflected in the facades, different in their contents and forms. The sense of compactness but at the same time of transparency, in keeping with Mussolini's statement that "Fascism is a glass house into which everyone can look," grant a unified character to the whole composition in keeping with a design procedure that references Le Corbusier, generating the architectural volumes from hollowed or cut cubes, working by subtraction and an effect of stratification of the materials that go into the facades. The construction began in November 1933 and was completed in 1936, excluding the studies for the decorations of the main facade, which were never implemented. After the opening, the building immediately gained extensive visibility, in both positive and negative terms. Accusations of plagiarism – not a new issue for Terragni – were advanced in the first months of 1937, triggering a critical debate that was to last for decades.

23. In 1936, after the opening of the Casa del Fascio, Terragni began to work with dedication on the project for a kindergarten dedicated to Sant'Elia, to be built in a newly settled zone of Como. Terragni's general idea can be seen from the first pencil sketch of the plan: a building whose layout relies on the scheme of a courtyard closed on three sides and open on the fourth side towards a small garden. The internal spaces, a central room for recreation flanked by a dining room and offices, and four classrooms, have great flexibility because it is possible to combine the classrooms, producing a single hall for assemblies, or to extend the activities to the outdoor terrace formed by an awning supported by a concrete structure (left visible by the lateral shift of the volume with respect to the structure). The facility was completed in June 1937, after the initial project had been revised many times due to limited funding.

24. The publication of the *Manuale dell'architetto* by Mario Ridolfi dates back to 1946.

25. The first restoration of the Sant'Elia, made necessary by the conditions caused by lack of use and therefore lack of maintenance, was ordered in 1966 by the Ente Asili and carried out by its technical division. This intervention of renovation compromised the architectural image of the building with several operations that were not consistent with Terragni's design – such as the substitution of the original metal casements, cuts in the masonry, new additions, and the

demolition of the steps for access. About 20 years later (1984-86), the kindergarten, by then protected by the heritage authorities, was again restored, through the efforts of Emilio and Carlo Terragni, taking the building back to its original image.

26. Vittorio Gandolfi, a Rationalist architect, was born in Parma in 1919; the studied and worked in Milan, applying a language with ties to the Modern Movement and in particular to the work of Le Corbusier.

ILLUSTRATIONS

The choice and arrangement of sketches, drawings and images represent the materialization of the architectural narrative, which was only literary up to this point. The illustrations are not seen as necessary to the text, but attempt to constitute, through the use of a different form of expression, the visual vehicle of the same reality. Architecture is the result of an idea whose path passes through instinctive gestures, technical drawings, forms of three-dimensional representation, models: all highly personal and therefore different from one another.

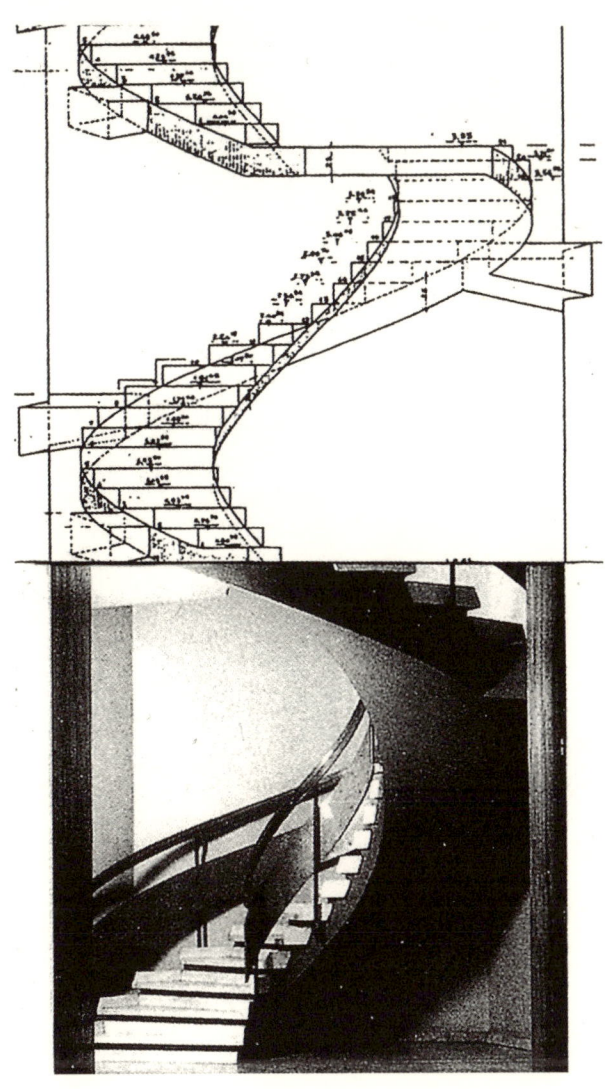

Franco Albini
INA office building
Parma, 1950-54

Studio Albini-Helg
Milan

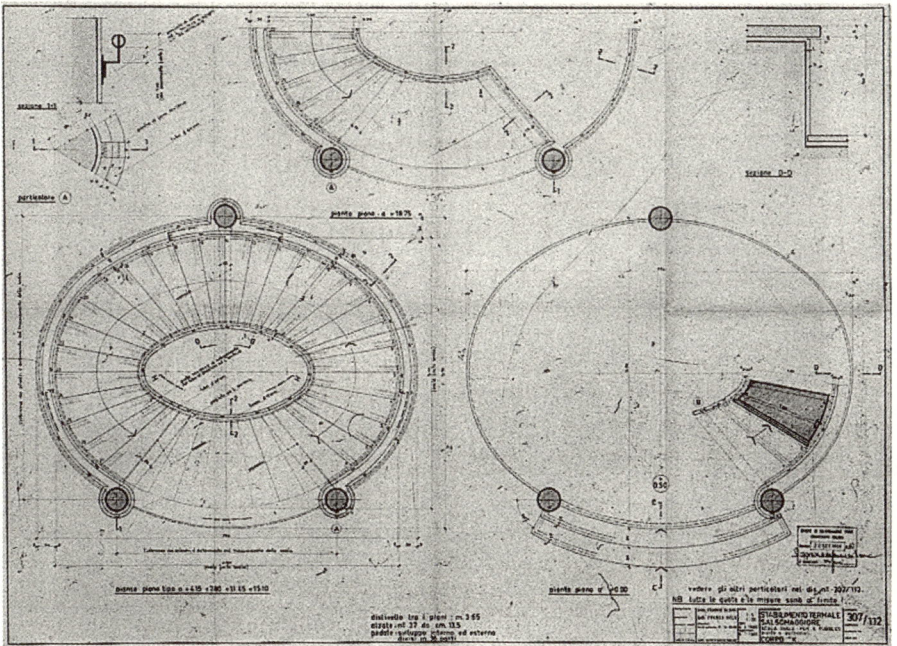

Franco Albini and Franca Helg
New "Luigi Zoja" Thermal baths
Salsomaggiore (Parma), 1967-70

Franco Albini
New municipal offices behind Palazzo Tursi
Genoa, 1952-62
(drawings by Aurelio Cortesi)

Franco Albini
New municipal offices behind Palazzo Tursi
Genova, 1952-62

Franco Albini (with R. Camus and G. Palanti)
Fabio Filzi complex
Milan, 1935-39

Franco Albini and Franca Helg
New "Luigi Zoja" Thermal baths
Salsomaggiore (Parma), 1967-70

Franco Albini and Franca Helg
La Rinascente department store
Rome, 1957-61

Franco Albini
Luisa chair
Produced by Poggi, 1950

Franco Albini
INA office building
Parma, 1950-54

BBPR
Torre Velasca
Milan, 1952-58

Oscar Niemeyer
Hospital Sul-América
Rio de Janeiro, 1952

BBPR
Torre Velasca
Milan, 1952-58

Pier Luigi Nervi
Hangar for Regia Aeronautica Militare
Orbetello (Grosseto), 1939-41

Mies van der Rohe
Seagram Building
New York, 1954-58

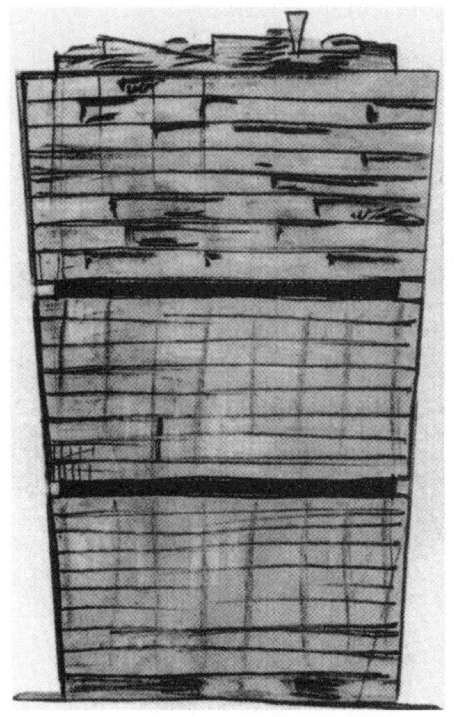 

BBPR
Torre Velasca
Milan, 1952-58

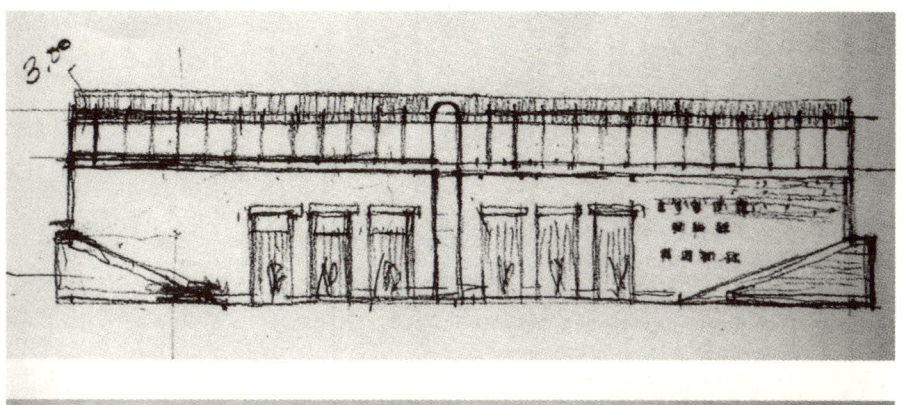

Ignazio Gardella
Study for the reorganization of Piazza Duomo
Milan, 1988

Ignazio Gardella
Cicogna apartment building at Le Zattere
Venice, 1953-58

Ignazio Gardella
Cicogna apartment building at Le Zattere
Venice, 1953-58

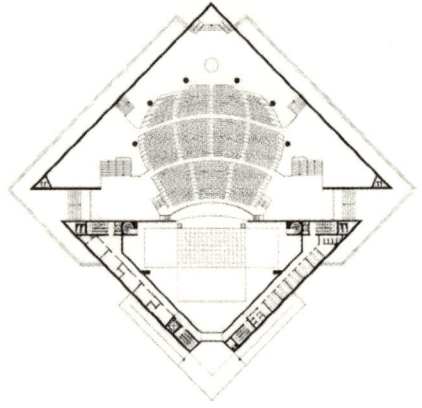

Ignazio Gardella
Competition project for the Teatro Civico
Vicenza, 1969

Ignazio Gardella and Jacopo Gardella
Project for expansion of Bocconi University
Milan, 1992

Ignazio Gardella
Department of Architecture
Genoa, 1975-90

Roberto Gabetti and Aimaro Isola
Bottega d'Erasmo
Turin, 1953-56

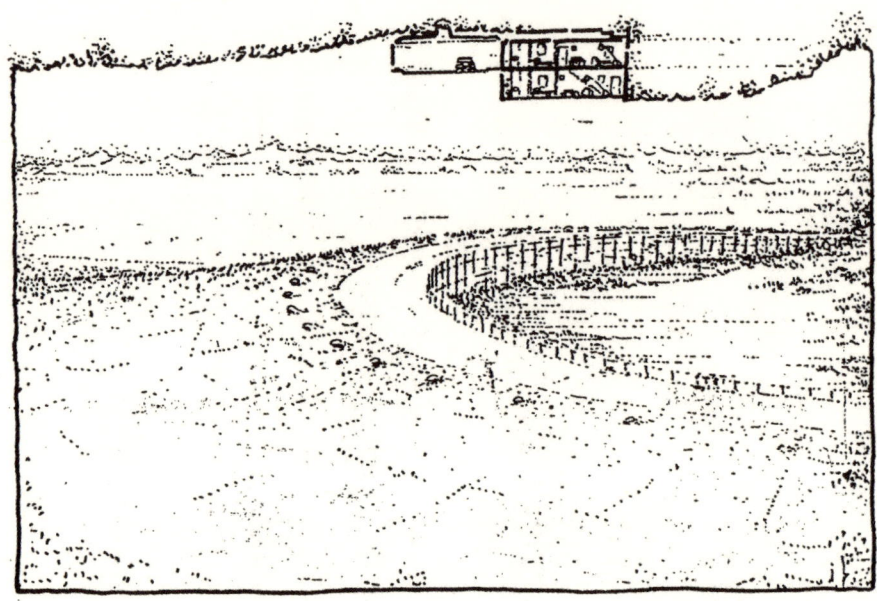

Roberto Gabetti and Aimaro Isola (with L. Re)
West Residential Unit
Ivrea (Turin), 1968-71

Roberto Gabetti and Aimaro Isola
Monument to the Resistance at Prarostino
Pinerolo (Turin), 1965-67

Roberto Gabetti and Aimaro Isola
Bottega d'Erasmo
Turin, 1953-56

Roberto Gabetti and Aimaro Isola (with G. Drocco)
Fifth Snam office building
San Donato Milanese (Milan), 1985-91

Roberto Gabetti and Aimaro Isola (with G. Drocco)
Residential complex
Sestrière (Turin), 1973-80

Paolo Portoghesi
Casa Baldi
Rome, 1959-61

Giovanni Michelucci
Project for a theater
Olbia, 1990

Paolo Portoghesi
Hot springs pavilion
Montecatini (Pistoia), 1987

Paolo Portoghesi
Hot springs pavilion
Montecatini (Pistoia), 1987

Paolo Portoghesi, Vittorio Gigliotti and Sami Mousawi
Mosque and Islamic Cultural Center
Rome, 1978-93

Paolo Portoghesi
IACP housing
Sesto San Giovanni (Milan), 1981, 1984-85

Aldo Rossi
Expansion of Linate International Airport
Milan, 1991

Aldo Rossi
Project for office building on Landsberger Allee
Berlin, 1991-92

Aldo Rossi
Contemporary art center in Clermont-Ferrand
Vassivière, France, 1988-91

Aldo Rossi
Renovation of Villa Alessi
Suna di Verbania (Novara), 1989

Aldo Rossi
Bonnefanten Museum
Maastricht (Holland), 1990-94

Aldo Rossi
Project for residential building on Schutzenstrasse
Berlin, 1991-92

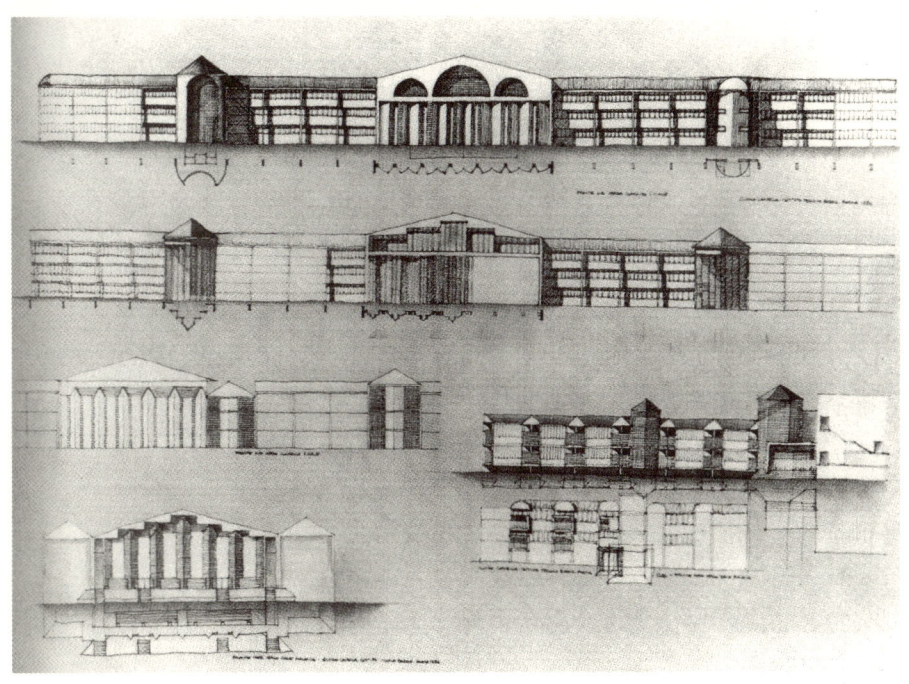

Guido Canella (with P. Bonaretti)
Istituto Tecnico G. Bodoni
Parma, 1985

Guido Canella (with M. Achilli and D. Brigidini)
Civic center with town hall, middle school and sports facility
Pieve Emanuele (Milan), 1971-78

Guido Canella (with M. Achilli, D. Brigidini and L. Lazzari)
Civic center
Segrate (Milan), 1963-66

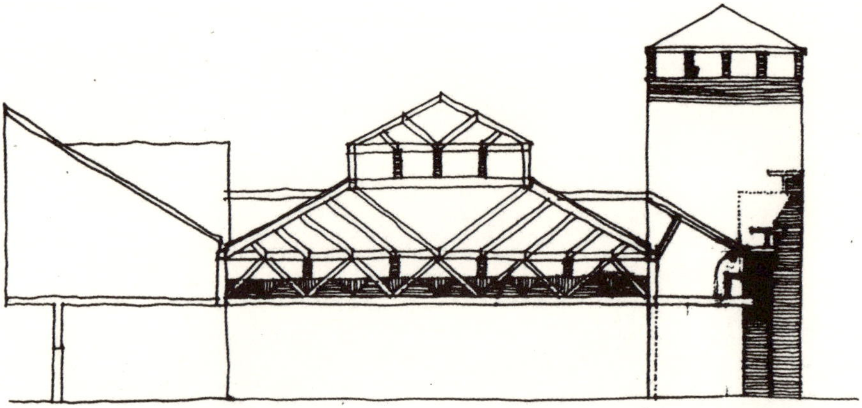

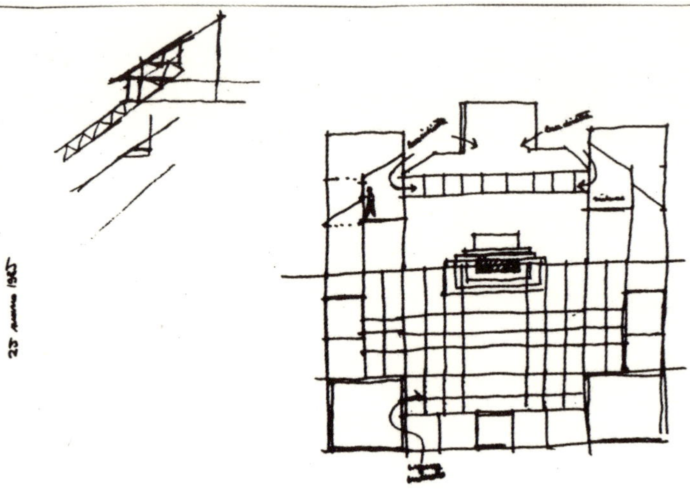

Guido Canella (with M. Achilli)
"Beato Riccardo Pampuri" church at Bettola-Zeloforamagno
Peschiera Borromeo (Milan), 1985-93

Guido Canella (with M. Achilli)
"Beato Riccardo Pampuri" church at Bettola-Zeloforamagno
Peschiera Borromeo (Milan), 1985-93

Guido Canella (with Eng. A. Valenti)
Single-family house at Meina
Novara, 1973-76

Vittoriano Viganò
Arteluce store on Via della Spiga
Milan, 1961-62

Vittoriano Viganò
"La Scala" house for André Bloc
Portese del Garda, 1956-58

Vittoriano Viganò
"La Scala" house for André Bloc
Portese del Garda, 1956-58

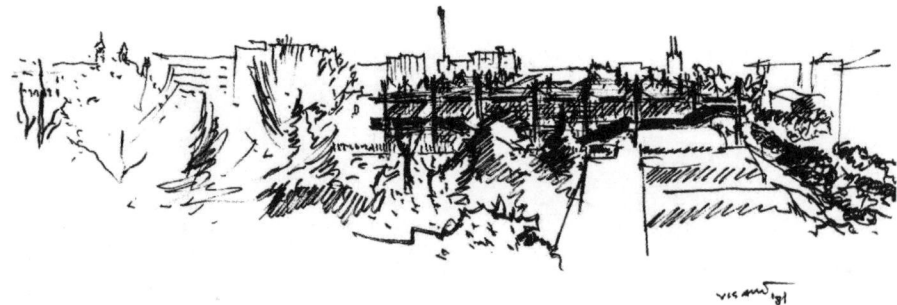

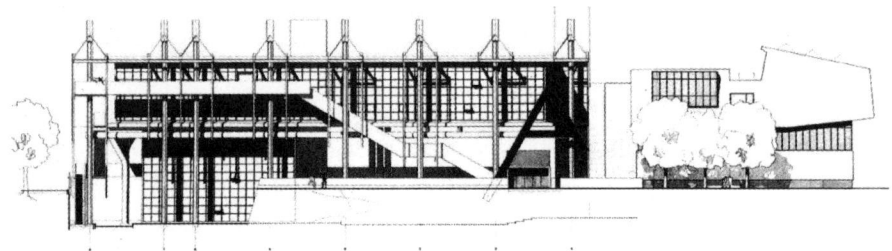

Vittoriano Viganò
Plan of expansion and renovation of the Department of Architecture of the
Politecnico di Milano, Via Ampère
Milan, 1985

Vittoriano Viganò
Mollificio Bresciano
San Felice del Benaco (Bergamo), 1968-81

Vittoriano Viganò
Istituto Marchiondi Spagliardi
Milan, 1953-57

Vico Magistretti
Tower on Piazzale Aquileia
Milan, 1961-63

Vico Magistretti
Arosio house
Arenzano (Genoa), 1956-57

Vico Magistretti
Cavagnariservice center for Cassa di Risparmio di Parma
Parma, 1981-85

Vico Magistretti
Barbettis chair
Produced by Poggi, 1980

Vico Magistretti
"Eclisse" bedside lamp
1965

Vico Magistretti
Cavagnariservice center for Cassa di Risparmio di Parma
Parma, 1981-85

Vittorio Gregotti, Lodovico Meneghetti and Giotto Stoppino
Housing for workers of the Bossi company
Cameri (Novara), 1956

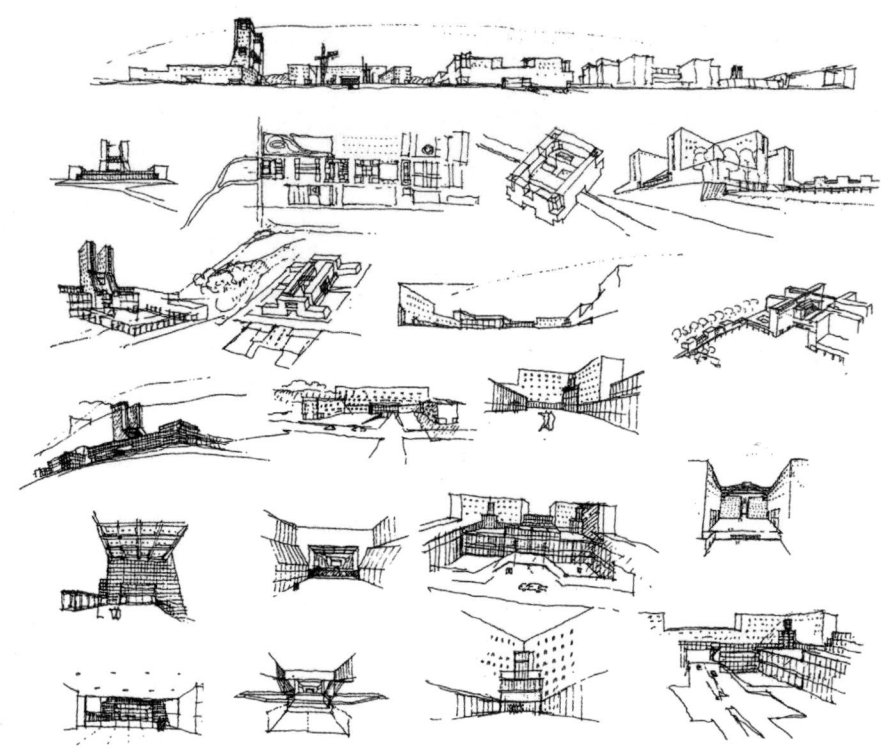

Gregotti Associati
International competition for the transformation of the Pirelli area at Bicocca
Milan, 1986-88

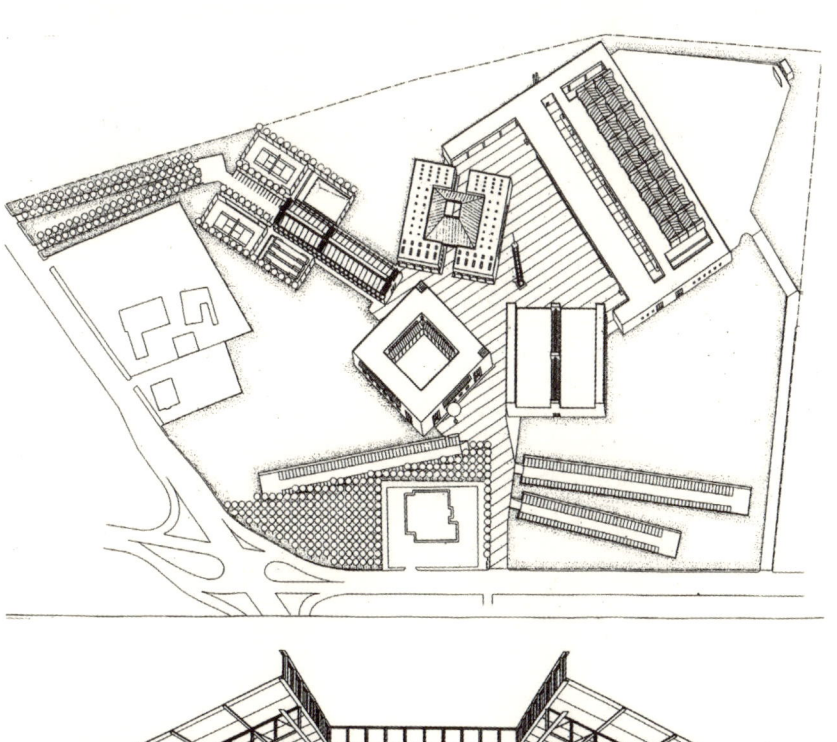

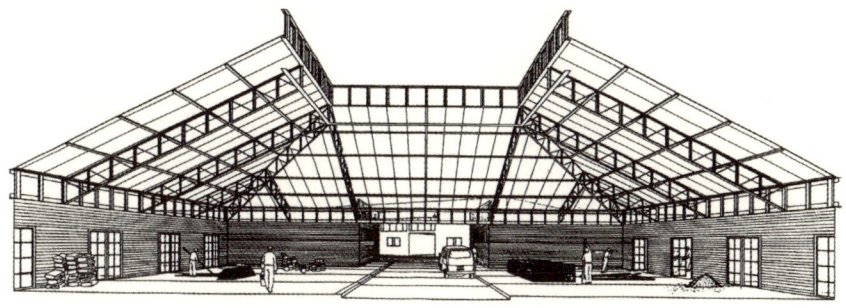

Gregotti Associati
New headquarters of Azienda Municipalizzata Pubblici Servizi
Parma, 1987-92

Gregotti Associati
Reordering of the Lutzowstrasse zone, IBA
Berlin, 1980-85

Gregotti Associati and Manuel Salgado
Belém Cultural Center
Lisbon, 1988-91

Vittorio Gregotti and Gino Pollini
New Sciences Departments of the Università degli Studi at Parco d'Orléans
Palermo, 1969

Giuseppe Terragni
Casa del Fascio
Como, 1932-36

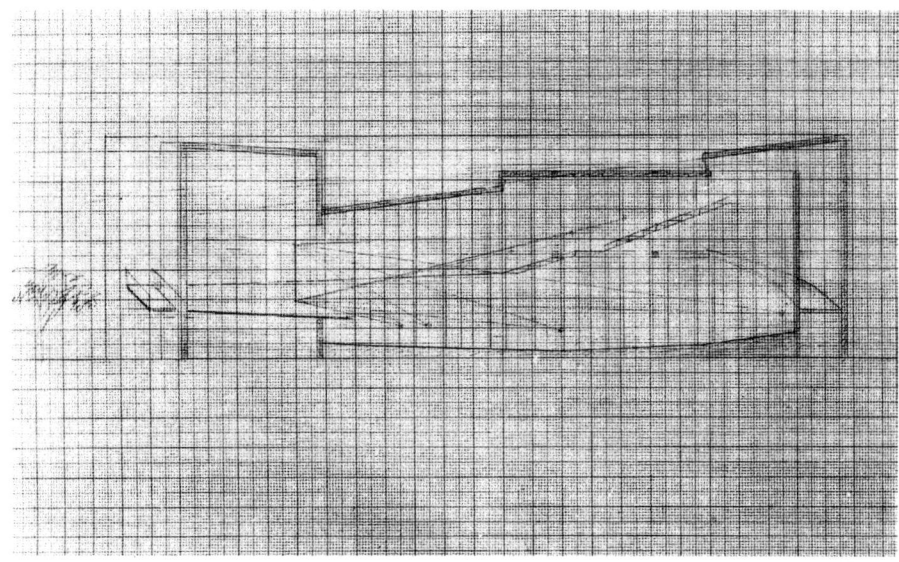

Giuseppe Terragni
Casa del Fascio in Rione Trasteverino
Rome, 1940

Giuseppe Terragni
Sant'Elia kindergarten
Como, 1936-37

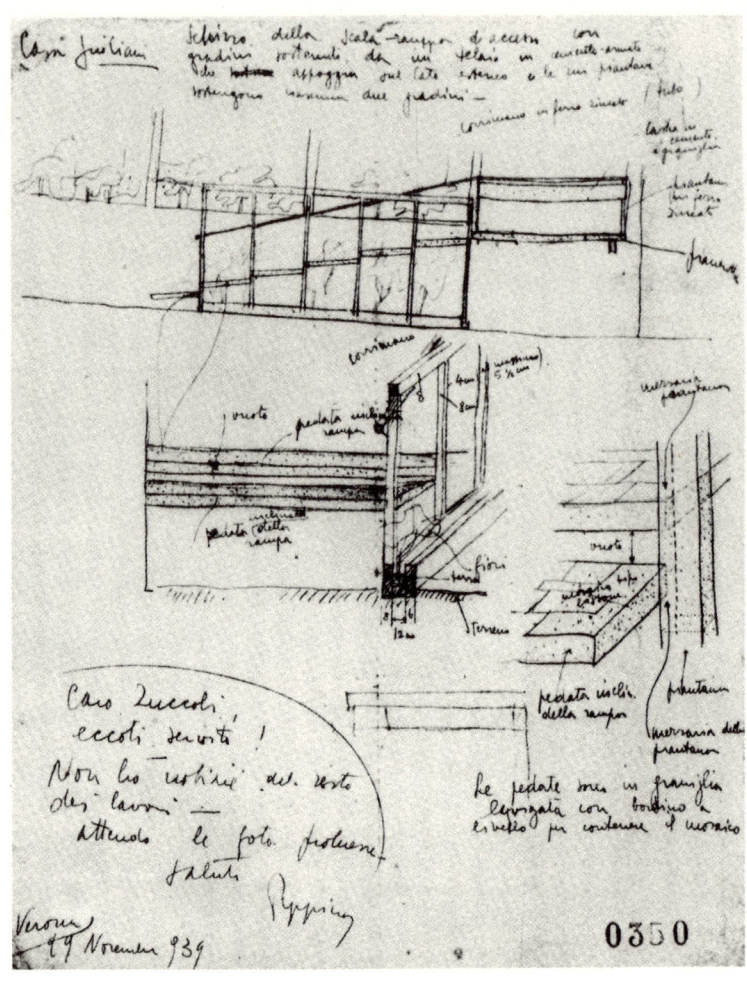

Giuseppe Terragni
Giuliani-Frigerio apartment building
Como, 1939-40

Giuseppe Terragni
Casa del Fascio
Como, 1932-36

Jacopo Zanguidi a/k/a Il Bertoja
Room of the Aetas Felicior
Palazzo Ducale, Parma, 1560-74

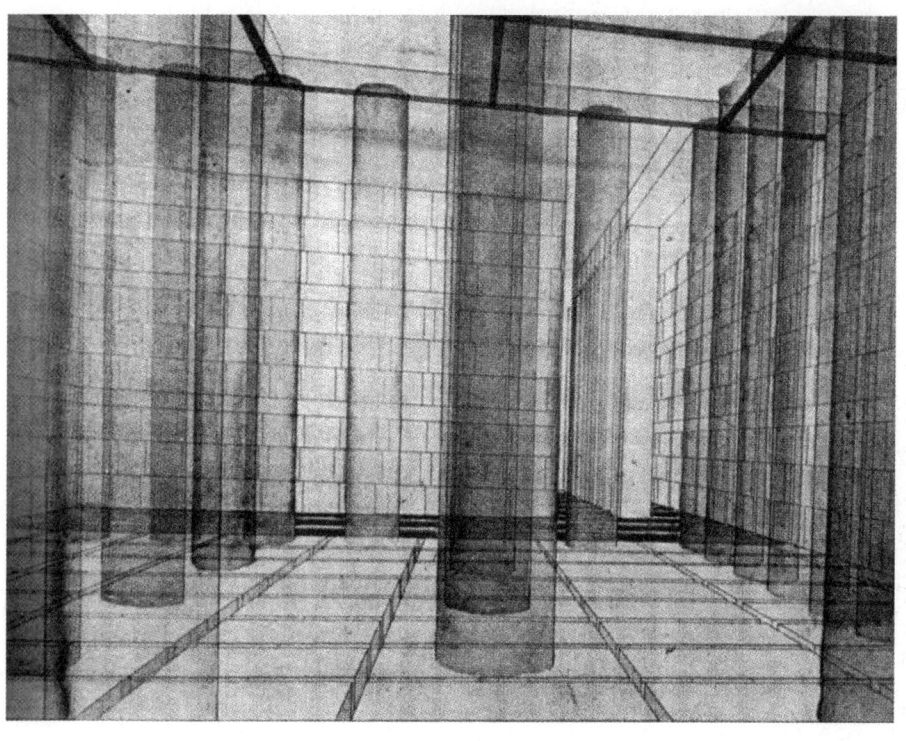

Giuseppe Terragni, Pietro Lingeri and Mario Sironi
Project for the "Danteum"
Rome, 1938

COMMENTARIES

Designing
in differences

A comparative reading of the *Dialogues* permits us to grasp ways of experiencing the moment of design that in their *differences* represent the compliance with types of logic that are not separable from the final architectural results. The bond is often emphasized, in fact, between imaginary and real worlds, *knowledge* and *construction*, a theme we find as a red thread in the cogitations of Socrates and his student Phaedrus in *Eupalinos, or the Architect*[1]. The position of the architect with respect to the method, and to everything that can be identified as the rational moment of design action, i.e. discarding values that cannot be traced back to norms, is connected to the tradition, in which the various components – and therefore technique – become more or less intentional phenomena of the project, case by case: in this sense the technical-structural aspects, along with the figurative ones, can be passively accepted or, to the contrary, an aware choice can be constructed.

The gap between project as *form* and project as *technique* has led to a gradual lowering of the quality of the constructed product, which can also be attributed to the marked segmentation of the various phases of design formulation and production of the artifact. Today's panorama reflects a clear ambiguity between the approach to form, mostly determined by choices of an intuitive nature, and the approach to technology, based primarily on encoded systematic procedures.

If the project is the synthesis of countless factors with the aim of resolving quantitative, spatial and morphological aspects, and if the choices have to be based on knowledge of the identity and nature of places rather than dictated by arbitrary considerations, we can assert that the remarks gathered here and the themes they address link back to precise design philosophies, truly lucid and conscious *attitudes*. The artist lives his own identity in relation to reality and to ideas about architecture, to the way of approaching problems of one sphere or the other. A greater leaning towards one of the two worlds reflects a diversity of interpretations on the part of the designers of the intellectual figure appointed to carry out the material modification of reality². In this sense the figures of Eupalinos and Tridon called into play by Valéry³ can be seen as paradigmatic, precisely in reference to *thinking* and *doing* in architecture. Not coincidentally, in dialogic form.

Eupalinos, architect, searches for the right method to carry out the tasks assigned to him through an exhaustive explanation, so much so that for any decision of a practical nature he also identifies a problem of a philosophical nature to be solved⁴. *Tridon*, shipwright, tends to apply technology in an experimental manner and to seek the construction method suitable for the specific case, whether from the tradition or in a totally new way, through an empirical relationship with matter and its laws⁵.

The figures of Eupalinos and Tridon in Valéry can be examined inside a logic in which explicit references to an overall and global vision of the project clearly emerge, oriented towards its materialization (from *idea* to *project* to *artifact*), in an interpretation of the architectural phenomenon not in an idealistic key, but through its conception, which aspires to be global⁶. In a metaphorical reading, the two characters introduced by Valéry could symbolize a schematic summary of the two cultural attitudes that often present themselves as opposites in the current debate: adhesion to the architectural project as "arché-type" (Eupalinos) or to the technologically evolved project (Tridon). For Eupalinos, *theoretician*, architecture possesses a high degree of autonomy and detachment from exclusive material problems, as cause and effect of issues also of a philosophical nature. The question of *how to do* something becomes secondary to *why it is done:* the two moments are consequential, intentionally separated and inserted in a ranking of value. For Tridon, *practitioner*, technical research constitutes a basis, a result to pursue in the specific design investigation: in this context, innovative technique may clash with the constructive tradition of architecture, which has to be called back into play and therefore revised.

The project is increasingly configured as the exploration of the *material component* of an *intellectual nature*, a set of ideas, of possibilities among possible solutions. To realize means to find stimuli of invention in nature to make architecture simultaneously rational and communicable, recovering a constantly new and engaging approach while conserving a conscious respect for the past. Hence the analogy between architecture and music offers clarification of certain very timely problematic issues. Valéry himself investigated the subtle correspondence existing between the two disciplines, which represent, in his view, the loftiest embodiments of art, faithful representations of the body and the soul: "the art by whose means imaginary forms are immobilized in the sun," in one case; "unreal and fugitive edification of sounds,"⁷ in the other. Man lives architecture, perceives it, feels like a part of it; likewise music penetrates into man, engaging him through the set of his sensory apparatus: "By means of two arts [the body] wraps itself up in two different ways, in their inner laws and wills, which are figured forth in one material or another, stone or air."[8]

In both architecture and music there is the coexistence of activities in which free compositional interpretation (the individual cultural background, hard to transmit in norms) and mathematical rigor (made of spaces, rests, measures, constraints with which to comply) fuse together. For many designers *to compose*, on a par with *to design*, implies formulating a sequence of mental operations of a subjective and an objective nature. To comply with an architectural genre, or with a musical genre, thus implies an expressive choice of language, with clear reflections on the method of composition, which goes beyond functional content. The twelve basic tones of the musical scale, the different duration assigned to each of them by the composer, the rests that are placed between them, constitute the apparently limited and circumscribed essence of any piece of music: it is from their particular succession, their "architecture," that the final result is achieved. Similarly, the design operation implies the use of a wide range of variables to be called into play. The essence of the individual elements does not leave substantial margins of modification: what can change are the type and way the variables are utilized, through their different combinations. Developing the metaphor, in architecture composers establish, through the different attitudes they adopt, a specific relationship with the composition itself, the *work of architecture*, and with the material implementers, the *technicians* and *makers*.

There is also a spontaneous impulse to align the "musical" metaphor with the "sculptural" metaphor. An architectural project that starts from considerations of a general character from which it gradually takes on more detailed form is comparable to the logical order that pertains to sculpture, in which the artist, already in the initial choice of the block to be sculpted, and therefore through a forceful work of synthesis, manifests an original idea that slowly and progressively takes on increasingly recognizable forms. Proportion, color, material and construction technique are already the intrinsic variables *at the outset* of the work. Franco Albini, an example of an *architect-musician*, composes through the assembly and sequencing of elements: the girder, the pillar, the cornice, like notes, rests and accents, are studied, assembled, broken down and reassembled, until the correct order has been found and they reach the desired state of equilibrium. Giuseppe Terragni, on the other hand, is instead an *architect-sculptor:* a slow, gradual way of giving body to architecture that starts from nebulous sketches to later reach precise choices, controlled down to the smallest details, in a "Michelangelesque" approach to the art of design.

It comes spontaneously to make a perhaps elementary schema of these extreme but not all-encompassing approaches to the process: one moves from the particular to the general, the other from the general to the particular. Hence characteristic modes of control of the design path do exist. As it is developed, the basic idea undergoes a series of trials, modifications, changes that are implemented through the encounter between the designer and the forms of expertise that have decision-making power in the construction, or through intermediate positions in which the designer is involved only in certain phases, or on specific topics, relying on other figures for some of the passages in the process.

In relation to the complexity of the context of operation, the objective of recognizability of the project proves to be of prime importance, a fixed point inside different methodological approaches and design paths. Every architect works in the direction of the safeguarding of the discernibility of the form or, more generally, of the poetic-artistic message, against a logic that is widespread in the production system that tends to interfere with the contents of works of architecture. The position of the individual figures express the need to constantly update personal methods of explanation of design content, through an approach to the architectural project capable of adapting to the changing conditions of the cultural and productive environment.

Design approaches like that of Franco Albini already incorporate to a great extent the determining factors of a technological and formal type with a very high level of prediction, to the point that the project becomes preventive control over all the actions of construction. In this way a sequential perspective is formulated leading to the concrete realization of forms and details the designer had already envisioned in the phase of ideation. This methodological approach of a "Gropiusian" type has recently undergone inevitable transformations: the entry on the scene of players and figures conveying other needs has been decisive in this sense, making it possible to assert that managing the rationality of the design process today from a basic hypothesis to the definitive design means "playing by ear"; as a result, it is necessary to also be capable of acting in a *corrective* manner on the project, to make a positive response to unexpected questions as they arise.

It is significant to observe how certain protagonists of architecture have accepted the invitation to investigate their work, their cultural roots, the origin of their background. The references to Milan as a center of debate in the postwar era, whose traces can still be perceived, are fuelled by citations of memories: Ernesto Nathan Rogers on the one hand, Franco Albini on the other, constitute two cornerstones in most of the thoughts, from which theory and practice have been reciprocally reinforced in an exemplary professional exercise. Two figures who have been able to express themselves best around tables of a different nature: the *meeting table*, the preferred site of the birth of projects (as in the famous gatherings of Rogers around the table of

Casabella); and the *drafting table* as in the work of Albini, site of the creative-design act and its projection towards the external places of production.

Albini's work reveals an extraordinary capacity for modification and adaptation, in terms of both forms and techniques, which remains constant across his entire evolution. Form and technique do not represent separate entities, but a perfect synthesis capable of exemplifying a balance created on the basis of a correct methodological set-up and a high degree of intervention in the various phases of the project. The interpretation of details demonstrates that the design process can be composed of many individual and identified elements, for the purpose of leading the architecture to a perfect unity: the variables in play are limited, while the possibilities of assembly are instead infinite. The Albini who follows new paths and engages in constant, in-depth research to draw new opportunities from the socio-economic context, without starting dogmatically from pre-set figurative conceptions, but reaching alternative conceptions precisely through research, is thus to be admired and emulated. Albini was able to aim the axis of his interest and his architectural research towards new horizons, while conserving a constant and ethically correct relationship with the technical dimension, as a "deployment" of those theoretical messages and alignments traced during that same period by Rogers[9].

Today the worksite is a dynamic reality, constantly changing, that cannot be governed through an absolute predetermination of all its parts: even the definitive drawings of architecture are subject to successive verification and revision throughout the construction process[10].

Updating Rogers' discourse, technique can be considered part of the "unburned dross" in the resources of the architect: a fundamental factor to recover in the architectural debate, with the aim of preventing design culture from enclosing itself exclusively in a "style." Only research that moves forward in a parallel way in the three fields of form-technique-production, in their historical *continuity* and not in opposition, can ensure a correct design synthesis.

The relationship between theory and practice is reflected in criticism and its tools of exegesis, also impacting the institutional transmission of knowledge in design teaching[11].

The *Dialogues* have diagonally crossed the various generations, making different reflections useful. That of the 1920s, unlike its successor, did not have someone like Rogers: it was lacking in that type of figure capable of summing up the values of the architectural narrative from the inside. Perhaps for this reason, it found itself under pressure, more than other generations, from the one to follow, which attempted, in any case, to re-emphasize the identity and above all the autonomy of architecture. An independence and a specificity regained from the past with the help of a marked regional orientation, recently translating into an architectural localism that has yet to be put into historical context.

The rethinking and inflection that address the world of architecture – unlike what happens for other "arts" that develop less precarious results – have brought about an absence not only of legitimation of a cultural product that previously existed, but also of recognizable and therefore transmissible tools. At present there exists a consequential relationship between today's ways of interpreting architecture and the lack of critical depth demonstrated by the institutions responsible for its making. The will to grasp the emerging factors of architecture, the various emblematic aspects, has been replaced by an effort aimed at instituting and positioning nomenclatures, establishing schools, nuclei of belonging, more or less lasting trends, at times weakened by the flow of the seasons, in a form extraneous to a useful and moral critical vision of the project.

To recover from the excessive separation from the real and the everyday implies a genuine mending of interdisciplinary relations on the part of education, stimulating this in the suitable modes, forms and tools. The concept of the *feasibility* of the work has to return to being the fulcrum of any understanding of design. The university, as the privileged place of learning, can constitute the main point of reference to provide a more complete effort of professional safeguarding and updating[12].

To see *theory* and *practice* as antithetical has proven to be a misleading strategy. They are in fact two spheres in a condition of synergy, with points of contact that demonstrate their interpenetration within the essential unity of *making*. This derives from the assumption of the substantial unity and inseparability of the entire process of formulation of the architectural work. Certain contingent obstacles such as the speeding up of the pace of production, the constant acceleration of technical progress, the loss of dialogue between the various protagonists of the construction process, must not cause an interruption – especially in the places set aside for the spread of knowledge – of the debate on the meaning of techniques in architecture, the relationships between the various languages and their related implementing instrumentation. To prevent this from happening, the debate on the primacy of architectural research or technological experimentation has to give way to a proposal of collaboration, so that the two moments can interact and converge.

On the one hand, we are seeing the recovery of a repertory of simple techniques, the most common and traditional, while on the other we can see the exhibition, often as an end in itself, of the "technological" factor. The technical component, like that of ideation, cannot express its potentialities of the formation of the architectural phenomenon in sterile isolation: *tech-*

nique demands constant research to be able to generate those synergies that are able to give rise to a complete integration in the architectural project. The *research* must develop from knowledge of techniques of execution, the phases to which they lead, the study of materials, their relationship with the natural and socio-economic context. Today education can re-establish the values in play, in a correct and methodologically transmissible way, based on the teaching supplied by history and its acknowledged *protagonists*[13].

"Being an architect – Rogers wrote[14] – is a vocation; teaching architecture is a vocation to the second power, because without a vital passion it is useless to try it. Those who teach by trade or even worse out of ambition and due to indirect personal interest (to have the word professor on their calling cards) betray their quality as *clercs* and chain themselves to the most dismal mystifications.

"To participate in an Italian school even requires a vocation to the third power, and those who enter there must accept all the obligations, including the sacrifices and humiliations suffered due to the lack of comprehension of the society inside and outside the school itself."

The progressive expansion and fragmentation of forms of expertise and professional roles involved in the formulation and control of the life cycle of the project, together with the increase in the degree of complexity of the project itself, bring about – with rare exceptions of great ability to tame the phenomenon – a growing separation between the *creative moment* and the *final result*. The very idea of the project has been transformed over time: with the arrival of modern rationality, the drawings have become exhaustive and complete, incorporating in advance all the forms of knowledge and the most subtle indications for implementation that were previously assigned, in part, to the various agents involved.

So what is needed is to interpret as well as possible the use of the available tools, in the awareness that the progressive heightening of the complexity of the contextual variable has led to a corresponding rise in the complexity of the project itself and its implementation procedures. Since the project represents one of the acts through which the society expresses and documents its capacity for transformation, the acceleration of evolutionary praxis and of the transformation of reality directly reflects on the tools and methods that are conventionally an integral part of design.

The *Dialogues,* as such, do not convey certainties, but dialectic positions, shedding light on two opposing design positions, with the inevitable simplifications: one that calls for the intervention in the spatial sphere having already put forward its main choices, both cultural and technological in nature, which even prior to the start of construction provide the image of the future product; and another that believes it is possible to "hint" at an idea through signs still to a great extent in an embryonic state, assigning the successive phases to other counterparts, with the task of bridging those levels of *intentional indecision*.

It is therefore useful to attempt to stimulate more organic relations between *design culture* and *industrial culture*, in an ideal continuity regarding the balanced relationships existing in the artisanal society, and at the same time to make an attempt at re-appropriation of the capacity of control over technologies and sciences, on both a cultural and a social level, to get beyond age-old dualities that still exist today: culture-practice, art-technique, linguistic experience-operative praxis, always refraining from favoring one side over the other[15].

This is a path that in tune with the practical message of Albini and the theoretical message of Rogers is able to track down the connections within the process of design-implementation, with the goal of surpassing the separation between form and technique in architecture, which increasingly leads to academicism and technicism[16].

After a period of disorientation in the interpretation of the architectural phenomenon, to again see the complexity of "differences," i.e. to make a revision of a theoretical character through the proactive investigation of the directions of research that have been outlined and by now consolidated, is a necessary operation to understand the next step to be taken.

The *cultural positions* regarding architectural design spotlighted by the *Dialogues* provide a mirror of definable lines of operation, apart from improbable classifications, of *consensus* or, oppositely, *dissent*. Belonging to the consensus or going against the current implies a cross-interpretation of references of a generational character, which set out the before and after of the articulated paths of architecture. In this scenario, a figure such as that of Ernesto Nathan Rogers has embodied the intellectual capable of postulating and activating the synthesis of the *disorientation*. The work of cultural elucidation he has expressed, and what can be grasped in the work of those who have spent time with him, have always remained a bit concealed, due to the quality of the message and the means of its expression, halfway between a historicized interpretation of place and an occasionally hazarded architectural design.

"Qualified architects – Rogers sustained[17] – have the task of taking possession of all technique and transforming it in contact with the culture. In this way they will demonstrate what many of them are already implicitly convinced of: not only the generic impossibility of separating means from ends, but also the obsolescence of certain means suggested for the most part by sentimental reasons. Even exceptional works not made to be repeated will have to contain, in their quality, the fertile seeds of quantification."

"How many billion blows of the chisel has Architecture cost since the beginning of the world?" This poetic query submitted in its provocative way for the perusal of the protagonists of the *Dialogue* confirms the fact that in line with the above-mentioned concept of feasibility, architecture in the years to come will have to come to grips with an availability and perhaps a quality of resources that will be different from those of the past. The construction of architectural artifacts, and the idea of the "architecture of the city" they imply, point to design research that will increasingly tend to come to grips with the contingent, with the real potential of the theme in the place where the architecture is inserted.

"The house has to please everyone, contrary to the work of art, which does not. The work of art is a private matter for the artist. The house is not."[18]

Terms like "conversation," "relationship," "debate," "connection" that return in the architectural dialogue offer tangible proof of the fact that the architect today has a privileged role as an interpreter of a reality of which technology is an essential, not alternative part.

A fundamental distinction is made here between technology and the figures involved in its use: the theoretical knowledge of a specific technical potentiality is one thing, while the real human "ability" to make it respond to a complex assumption, a plot traced by the "architectural" project, is quite another. It is the job of the designer, of the architect, through a complete absorption of the context, to grasp the possibilities of material translation of the immaterial content of the architecture.

The identity of places, in itself, contains many of the answers of a formal and technical nature that the architecture is seeking. The "joy of getting one's hands dirty in the contingency" has to become the mediation between poetry and matter. "To design," therefore, as "to interpret": to achieve the best understanding of the latent potential of both human and material resources. Only in this way can architecture – which is not just that of the Parthenon – regain its moral as well as its material value.

This ethical discourse stimulates the hope for greater respect towards architecture and its meaning: in a period in which the panorama of its roles increases by leaps and bounds, if "teaching architecture is a vocation to the second power" and "participating in an Italian school even requires a vocation to the third power," being an architect today becomes an "exponential" calling, a choice that has to go beyond motives of a practical nature. Moreover: the project sets out to interpret, as a synthesis between a lyrical moment and the ideal tools to make it manifest. "To design," just like "establishing a dialogue" with ourselves, implies deep reflection on the vision of present and future reality, in which we hope Architecture will play a leading role.

Notes

1. Paul Valéry, "Eupalinos, or The Architect," in *Dialogues*, New York, Pantheon, 1956, Vol. 4 of Collected Works of Paul Valéry, Bollingen Series XLV.

2. "In the years of my forced inactivity as a builder, I had the time to roam worksites and to see construction in progress, to observe every phase, every detail of this art [...]. Apparently banal experiences, but which lead you to no longer separate the work of he who designs from that of he who builds; to not set a diaphragm of category between man-architect and man-builder; and also, which I feel is of maximum importance, to not separate the architectural design from its constant reference to the vision of the constructed work. Therefore one of my drawings is never an abstraction, but a representation of the real." (G. Michelucci in M.C. Buscioni (ed.), *Michelucci. Il linguaggio dell'architettura*, Officina, Roma 1979).

3. Paul Valéry (1871-1945) can be considered one of the greatest thinkers, poets and essayists of the European 20th century. His text in "poetic prose" *Eupalinos, or The Architect* was published in 1921 for the editions of the "Nouvelle Revue Française" as the preface to an album of etchings titled *Architectures, Recueil publié sous la direction de Louis Süe et André Mare, Comprenant un dialogue de Paul Valéry, décoration intérieure, peinture, sculpture et gravure contribuant depuis mil neuf cent quatorze à former le style français*. One curious fact is that the request made to Valéry was for a text that due to matters of layout had to have the exact length of 115,800 letters, a very strict constraint that nevertheless, significantly did not prevent Valéry from expressing his convictions in a profound and intense way.

4. "PHAEDRUS: One day, dear Socrates, I spoke of this very thing with my friend Eupalinos. 'Phaedrus,' he was saying to me, 'the more I meditate on my art, the more I practice it: the more I think and act, the more I suffer and rejoice as an architect – and the more I feel my own being with an ever surer delight and clarity. I lose myself in long spells of expectation; I find myself again by the surprises I give myself; by means of the successive steps of my silence, I advance in my own edification; and I approach to such an exact correspondence between my aims and my powers, that I seem to myself to have made of the existence that was given me a sort of human handiwork. By dint of constructing,' he put it with a smile, 'I truly believe that I have constructed myself.'

SOCRATES: To construct oneself, to know oneself – are these two distinct acts or not?

PHAEDRUS: ... and he added: 'I have sought accuracy in my thoughts, so that, being clearly engendered by the consideration of things, they might be changed as of their own accord into the acts of my art. I have apportioned my attentions; I have arranged the problems in another order; I begin where I finished off formerly, so as to go a little further... I am niggardly of musings, I conceive as though I were executing. No more now, in the shapeless void of my soul, do I contemplate those imaginary edifices, which are to real edifices what chimeras and gorgons are to true animals. But what I think, is feasible, and what I do is related to the intelligible...'" (P. Valéry, *ibid.*).

5. Tridon, a decidedly bizarre character, halfway between wheeler-dealer and man of good sense with a complicated life behind him, is described by Phaedrus as a person capable of easily entering into situations, adapting to different trades, of great ability and elasticity to rapidly understand needs and relationships between people. In particular, in his lifetime he worked as a shipwright: thanks to his sharp intuition and empirical and material ability, he managed with great ease to introduce in his designs and constructions a series of variations on a theme, developing technological innovations connected with the complexity of the design issue of the *voyage of the vessel*, which is metaphorically complex because it is dynamic and marked by the unpredictability of events.

"His busy daemon urged him on to make the best ships whose keel ever cut wave. And whereas his rivals remained content to imitate the models then in use, and in copy after copy continued building the bark of Ulysses, if not the immemorial ark of Jason, he, Tridon the

Sidonian, ceasing not to fathom the unexplored regions of his art, breaking up the petrified combinations of ideas, and taking up things at their source..." (P. Valéry, *Ibid.*).

6. These are the words of Eupalinos, reported by Phaedrus: "Those among buildings that neither speak nor sing deserve only scorn; they are dead things, lower in the hierarchy than the heaps of rubble vomited by contractors' carts, which at least amuse the sagacious eye by the accidental order they borrow from their fall... As for the monuments that limit themselves to speech, if they speak clearly I esteem them. Here, say they, the tradesmen meet. Here the judges deliberate. Her captives groan. Here the lovers of debauchery..." (P. Valéry, *Ibid.*).

This is the description of Tridon: "He thought that a ship should, in some sort, be created by the knowledge of the sea, and should almost be fashioned by the very wave itself! ... But this knowledge consists, in truth, in replacing the sea, in our reasoning, by the actions that it exercises on a body – so that we have to discover the other actions which counterbalance those of the sea, and thus we have to deal only with an equilibrium of forces, both groups borrowed from nature, where they did not interact to any useful purpose. But our powers in this matter are limited to the disposing of forms and forces. Tridon used to tell me that he imagined his vessel hanging in one scale of a great balance, the other scale carrying a mass of water .... But I hardly know what he meant by that ... And then again, the restless sea does not remain satisfied with this equilibrium. All is complicated by movement. He sought therefore for the form a hull should have if the bottom was to remain more or less constant, whether the ship rolled from side to side – or danced in any other way about some center ... He would draw strange figures which for him made visible the secret properties of his float; but for my part I could see in them nothing in the least like a ship.

And at other times he would study the movement and the speed of craft; hoping and despairing in turn to imitate the perfection of the swiftest fishes. Those that swim easily on the surface, and play in the foam between their dives, interested him most of all. He would speak with the abundance of a poet of the tunnies and porpoises, amid whose leaps and gambols he had lived so long. He would sing their great bodies polished like weapons; their snouts that seem flattened by the mass of water that withstood their progress; their fins, as rigid and cutting as iron, but sensitive to their fishy thoughts, and steering towards their destinies as their whims dictate; and then their live mastery in the heart of storms! It was as though he himself felt their well-adapted forms conducting from head to tail, by the quickest way, the waters which lie in front of them, and which must be put behind them that they may advance ... It is an admirable thing, O Socrates, that on the one hand, if no obstacle impedes your progress, progress is quite impossible; all the efforts you make destroy one another, and you cannot push in one direction without pushing yourself away from the other with an equal force. But, on the other hand, once the necessary obstacle is present, it works against you; it drinks up your fatigues, parsimoniously metes out to you space in time. Here the delicate act of the artist intervenes in the choice of a form: for the form has to take from the obstacle what it requires in order to advance, but must only take what least checks the mover." (P. Valéry, *Ibid.*).

7. These too are the words of Valéry, who wrote them in 1891 in a short article titled *Paradoxe sur l'architecture* in which he hints at the theme of correspondence between architecture and music, which he would develop in greater depth in *Eupalinos*.

8. "SOCRATES: It ceases not to spur me on to expatiate upon the arts. I compare them, I distinguish them; I would hear the song of the columns and visualize in the pure sky the monument of a melody. This conceit very easily leads me to set on one side Music and Architecture; and over against them, the other arts. A painting, dear Phaedrus, covers a mere surface such as a panel or a wall: and thereupon it feigns objects and personages. Statuary likewise never adorns more than a portion of our view. But a temple, along with its precincts, or again the interior of this temple, forms for us a sort of complete greatness in which we live… We are, we move, we live inside the work of man! There is not a part of that triple extent that has not been studied out and reflected upon. In it we breathe in, as it were, the will and

preferences of someone, and attracted and subjugated by the proportions he has chosen, we cannot escape from him [...]. There are then two arts which enclose man in man; or, rather, which enclose the being in its work, and the soul in its acts and in the productions of its acts, as our former body was entirely enclosed in the creations of its eye, and surrounded with sight. By means of two arts it wraps itself up, in two different ways, in their inner laws and wills, which are figured forth in one material or another, stone or air.

PHAEDRUS: I well see that Music and Architecture have each of them this profound kinship with us.

SOCRATES: Both occupy the totality of one sense. We only escape from the one by inner severance; from the other only by movements. And each of them fills our knowledge and our space with artificial truths, and with objects essentially human.

PHAEDRUS: Therefore these two arts, being so directly related to us, must also have with one another a peculiarly simple relationship?

SOCRATES: Quite so; and you rightly say: 'Without intermediaries.' For the visible objects on which the other arts and poetry draw – flowers, trees, living things (and even the immortals) – when they are employed by the artist, do not cease to be what they are, nor to mix their nature and their own significance with the design of him who uses them to express his will. [...] Music and Architecture make us think of something quite other than themselves; they are in the midst of this world like the monuments of another world; or, if you will, like the examples, disseminated here and there, of a structure and duration that are not those of beings but those of forms and of laws. They seem dedicated to reminding us directly, one, of the formation of the universe, the other of its order and stability; they invoke the constructions of the mind, and its freedom, which is in search of this order and reconstitutes it in a thousand ways. They neglect then the particular appearances with which the world and the mind are ordinarily preoccupied: plants, beasts and men... I too have observed, at times, listening to music with attention equal to its complexity, that I almost no longer perceive the sounds of instruments as sensations of the ear. The symphony made me forget the sense of hearing. It transformed itself so promptly, so exactly, into animated truths and universal adventures, or even into abstract combinations, that I was no longer conscious of the sensible intermediary, sound. [...] To impose upon stone or communicate to the air intelligible forms; to borrow a minimum from natural objects, to imitate as little as possible: this is common to the two arts.

PHAEDRUS: Yes. They have these negative qualities in common.

SOCRATES: But, on the other hand, to produce essentially human objects; to make use of sensible means, which yet are not likenesses of sensible things nor duplicates of known beings; to give form and shape to laws, or deduce from laws themselves their form and shape: is this not equally characteristic of both arts?

PHAEDRUS: They can also be compared in this respect.

SOCRATES: We have tracked down the mystery with these few ideas. The analogy we were hunting for is perhaps connected with those half-concrete, half-abstract existences, which play so large a part in our two arts; they are singular existences, true creatures of man, partaking of sight and of touch – or else of hearing – but also of reason, number, and language." (P. Valéry, *Ibid.*).

9. "If, by some absurd hypothesis, it were possible to separate the elements of utility and beauty, which represent the inner, irreducible tension of the phenomenon, one could in isolation advance the observations of a technical-scientific type, and one could speak of a practical progress of architecture, at least for one of its characteristics; but it is clear that architecture, like any art, manifests itself with finished objects, perfect in their own right. This should make us capable of appreciating the figurative expressions of phenomena, notwithstanding the degree of technique that has given them structure. Technique is absorbed in the very essence of the phenomenon because its degree of development is inherent to the very essence of the

phenomenon, and this would be different in its totality if that were not the case. A work of architecture cannot be replaced by a successive work because each of them is an image of the historical period in which it is inserted. The consumption of taste is not deterioration of taste, but simply the evolution of a dialectic continuity, real and concrete each time, corresponding to the total evolution of experience. It follows that every technique is possible as long as it takes on a meaning and intrinsically collaborates to signify that meaning. This is true both for the way of making architecture and for the way of representing it in drawings." (E.N. Rogers, *Gli elementi del fenomeno architettonico*, ed. C. de Set, Guida Editori, Napoli 1981, p. 38).

10. "The relationship between drawing and reality could lend itself to a very interesting survey of cases, which I do not intend to enumerate herein; nevertheless, it is necessary to linger over some considerations that are directly pertinent to this discourse on the elements of the architectural phenomenon, because the process of drawing, or of other means of representation, is deeply inherent to the conclusive phenomenon: and not only for a philological or generally historical investigation, but also because to penetrate to the essence of a given object it is extremely interesting to know how it was made.

"There are sketches by Le Corbusier, that of the Chapelle de Ronchamp, for example, where with a few free signs of very small size he grants, to himself and others, the exact perception of the conclusive phenomenon.

I know that to arrive from the drawing to reality there have been renunciations and transformations, substantial at times, yet the eidetic meaning has remained in the completed construction, apart from its variations of means and scale. It is clear that here, rather than adapting to a previously sensed or symbolized form, Le Corbusier has dug into his own inner being to the point of being able to enact not a work of formal imitation of his own model, but one of identification with his own idea.

"And I know, because I witnessed it, just how deep was the torment of this artist who for years continued to alter certain structural means required for the physical consistency of his idea, nevertheless keeping faith with that idea throughout the process, precisely through the reduction of every empirical datum to the essential concept.

"The monument whose internal and external spaces, volume and concrete relations with existing environmental features we can now experience corresponds to the tangible and sensorial manifestation of the primitive inspiration, to the point that the first sketch perfectly foreshadows the commensurable physical representation of the constructed object.

"[...] Architectural history similarly provides us with many documents of arduously honed drawings, which translate into reality in a discrepant way, and while they do bear pathetic witness to the torment of the artist, they set its historical limits; these cases are not the proof, so to speak, of an impossibility "*coeundi*" but of an impossibility to predict the characteristics of the object generated, in the act of love, in a definitive, conclusive way" (E.N. Rogers, *Ibid.*, pp. 41-44).

11. "I do not want (nor can I) step back from the ultimate aim of my nature as an active architect, whose task is to base the experiences enacted into a single process, the action in criticism (also self-critique) and this, once more, in coherent programs, future projects; attempts, hopes, illusions, disappointments." (E.N. Rogers, "Il passo da fare," in *Casabella-Continuità* no. 251, 1961).

12. "Only the architecture school, teaching the elements of the architectural phenomenon in their essential reality, which is identification between principles and ways of doing, can represent the demiurge that produces the catalysis between the world of ideas and the effective world of constructed architecture. In this way, it will be possible to hope to help young people acquire the knowledge of the modern architect, versed in techniques and capable of translating them into figurative terms, not merely aesthetic but deeply representative of a society as a whole.

"[...] I have said that only the school can perform the task of the demiurge because I do not believe that the architect as an individual can operate under the illusion, as many have done, of being the demiurge himself: to teach young people the necessity of a common work is to accustom them to a modesty that is not humiliating, but effective for the exercise of the profession." (E.N. Rogers, *Gli elementi del fenomeno architettonico*, ed. C. de Seta, Guida Editori, Napoli 1981, pp. 56-57).

13. "The teaching of composition requires judgment that is not imposed from above but a matter of dialogue and, I might add, maieutic in nature. It is necessary to have exchanges with the world outside the school, taking from reality (contacts with production organisms, relations with professionals and with teachers also from outside the faculty)." (E.N. Rogers, "Professionisti o mestieranti nelle nostre Scuole di architettura," in *Casabella-Continuità* no. 234, 1959).

14. *Ibid*.

15. "We cannot avoid coming to terms with material due to the precarious control of technologies. In this way, at least two generations of Italian architects, without experience with construction, have been squandered. All that remains of them is the iridescence of images, the cries of their drawn allegories. If we reflect on this we cannot help but regret such a waste of talent, which had it been mixed with true knowledge of construction could have given us works our country could be proud of. Naturally the weakness in construction of the Italian architect is not the main cause of his by now obvious impotence, but it is certainly the first of the factors that have incapacitated him. Yet his historical studies constantly warn him that without theory there is no architecture, and that a theory can be sustained only by constructed works. So architecture, even as pure study, has to come to grips with the problem of its constructability, though it does not have that as a possible end" (A.R. Burelli, "Arse e Tèchne," in *Costruire in laterizio* no. 41, 1994).

16. "Academicism is always a latent danger in architecture schools, and not only when they encourage the use of traditional styles (a danger almost banished today), but also when they strive for modern taste, fossilizing it in the most forbidden formalism, at this point passively accepted even by the most backward clientele." (E.N. Rogers, "Professionisti o mestieranti nelle nostre Scuole di architettura?", *Ibid*.).

17. E.N. Rogers, "Il passo da fare," in *Casabella-Continuità*, no. 251, 1961.

18. A. Loos, *Spoken Into The Void*, MIT Press, Cambridge, 1982.

PORTRAITS

The biographical profiles of the protagonists emerge, in very short indications, from the physical and cultural environment in which their activity is conducted in everyday life: the studio, seen as the place of relations between ideas and the initial materialization of the project, an indicator of the architectural *Weltanschauung* of each. The portraits take their cue from details or episodes that surfaced during this work, and in certain cases thanks to the help of those who having lived in direct contact with the protagonists, have become spokespersons *from inside* their way of being.

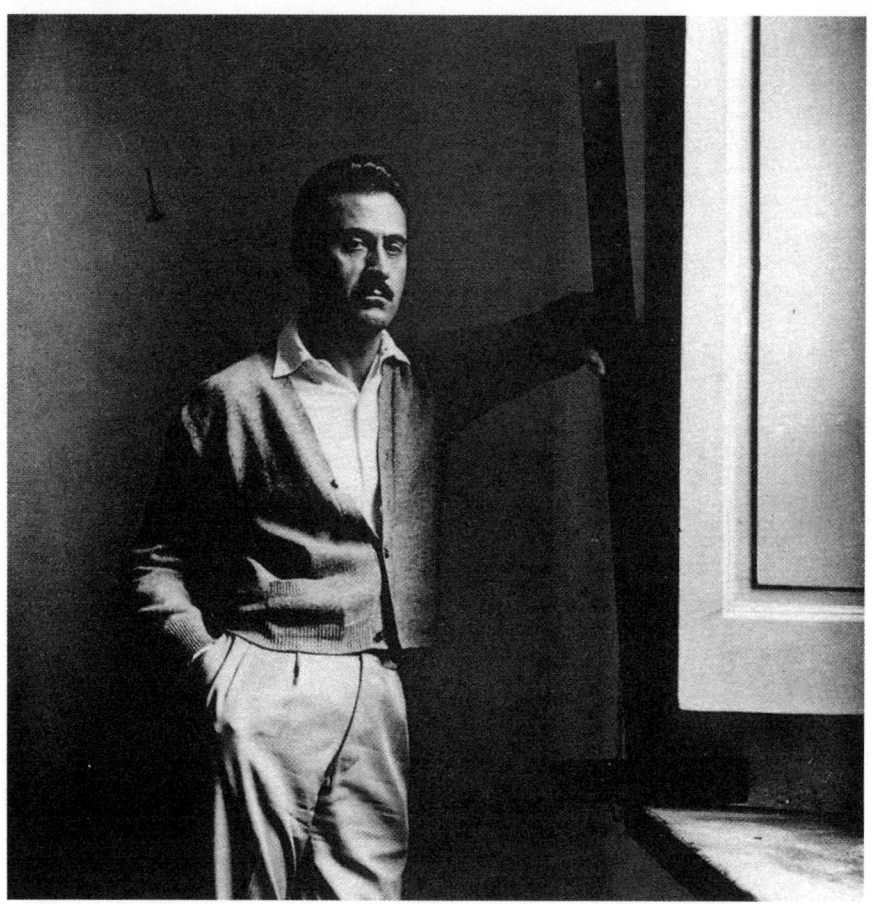

The studio on Via Panizza

The studio on Via Panizza

In the 1950s Albini's studio at Via Panizza was a reference point, though a secluded one, for Milanese design culture, also in relation to the studio of BBPR on Via dei Chiostri, the group that was the driving force of a larger gathering of forces.
The studio on Via Panizza – where Franca Helg was already a presence – was of modest size, on a dim Milanese courtyard outside Porta Magenta; it consisted of a porter's lodge and a large though rather damp room that contained everyone, separated by a few pieces of furniture. Then there were two other rooms. One for receiving visitors, a somewhat dusty space where I never saw anyone enter, fill of Albini's furniture: his marvelous tables, one of them covered with green felt, and the Margherita and Fiorenza armchairs; and another where Albini and Helg, face to face, worked while keeping the door open, vigilantly observing the behavior of the staff (I remember that to get a sheet of paper you had to pass in front of their room, kneel down, cut the paper, and return to your table: which implies that there was a small, subtle form of control over the way of working in the studio, and the management – of the paper, and of the studio itself).
In the two years during which I regularly spent time in the studio (but also later, when for one reason or another I was a constant presence), our group consisted of myself, Giuseppe Gambirasio – both recent graduates – a geometer and a secretary. I had been hired thanks to the intervention of Matilde Baffa, who was there to make the model of the villa of Roberto Olivetti at Ivrea; in the studio they needed someone with drafting skills to work on the drawings for the project in Havana.
Albini was always on the road, often abroad, for prestigious commissions, not only for works of architecture but also to participate in study groups and cycles of lectures. If he was in Milan he never arrived at the studio earlier than 9.00-9.30, when it had already been working up to speed for over one hour. The fundamental reference point for the rest of us was Franca Helg. She was a constant presence, coordinating and overseeing everyone's work. She would check on it, walking around the tables, questioning the staff: Albini did those things as well, but less frequently. Albini was certainly not an orderly person, and as often is the case for people with extraordinary talents, it was hard for him to have a perfect, rational management of the studio and his own activities. He was in any case a personality of great charm, and very elegant: I recall that he dressed in blue linen, with impeccable vents, and while walking amidst the draftsmen he would tug at his moustache, seeming to enjoy the Gothic linearity of his figure, tall, a fine silhouette thanks to his perfectly tailored garments.
Helg made a fundamental contribution to the organization of the studio: before her arrival (and mine), Albini relied on one important collaborator (whom I never met), Colombini, a very talented designer who later went to work for Kartell; as well as an efficient and legendary secretary, later the "wife of Colombini," Luisa (I never had the opportunity to meet her either, though her name was also the name of the famous armchair). Helg told us about Luisa, Colombini, Adriana, and the impossible costs of an architecture studio: all somewhere between myth and reality. (Aurelio Cortesi)

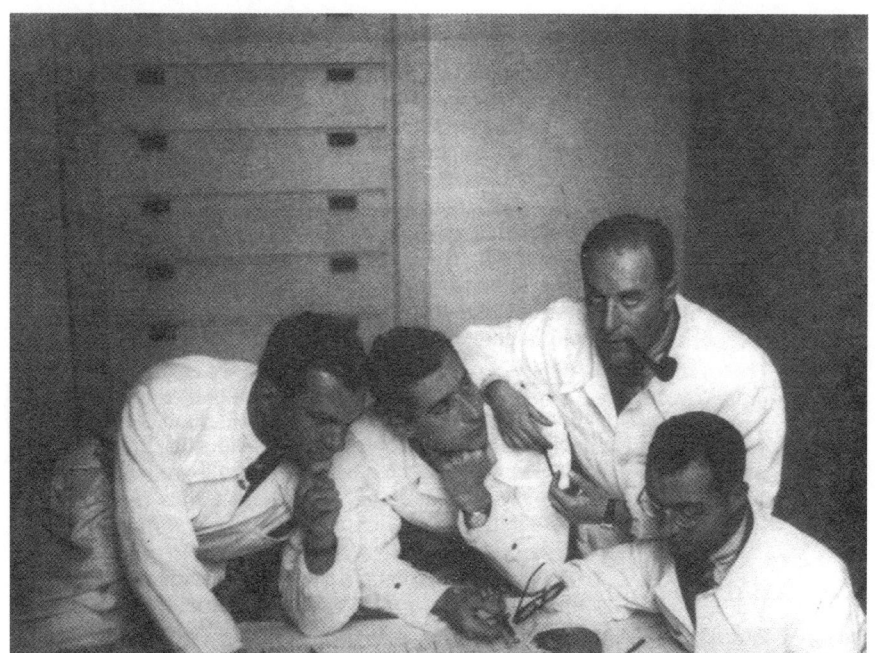

The table of BBPR

The table of BBPR

In the big rooms with very high ceilings, you can breathe in over half a century of architectural history: a wing of a 16th-century cloister in the center of Milan, where it doesn't seem as if you are in Milan at all, has been the site of the activity of the studio BBPR since 1939.

The spaces for drafting are large: a single room with a vaulted ceiling where the space is subdivided by tables, shelves, bookcases, chests of drawers, models. The meeting room is smaller: a tiny space facing the cloister, its walls covered by books, relics, memories, dominated by a table, it too of normal size, and not coincidentally square in shape.

A worksurface around which it is not hard to imagine the legendary "sessions" of the group, which had priority over any initiative of the studio, as a fundamental part of the design activity of BBPR since the university days and the debut in the world of construction. The group work, with its methodological reference to the Bauhaus school, is a principle that cannot be hampered by professional demands: a relationship based on deep affinity but above all on the cultural openness of four architects, protagonists of an intellectual circuit much larger than the small meeting room with its intimate, almost familiar atmosphere.

There is no need to search in books for the names of the remarkable personalities who have spent time in these spaces, who together with Ernesto, Lodovico, Enrico and Gian Luigi have produced fundamental chapters in the history of modern architecture: Gropius, Le Corbusier, Wright, Aalto, Niemeyer, Van de Velde, and many others who still take part in the life of the studio today, in the form of photographs, sketches, dedications, postcards, witnesses to an incessant flow of ideas that was vital for the liveliness of their interaction.

When the *Dialogue* with Lodovico Belgiojoso took place, only one item was missing in the entrance to the studio on Via dei Chiostri: during those days in 1994, the model of a tower built in Milan at the end of the 1950s was temporarily overseas for an exhibition at the Guggenheim Museum in New York. To prove that certain bonds survive, and not only on a faded postcard hanging on the wall of that small room, signed by "Frank L. W."

Ignazio Gardella: self-portrait

Ignazio Gardella: self-portrait

One has a pleasant sensation waiting for the arrival of the professor, observing Milan from the windows of his studio on the seventh floor of a modern building he designed in 1949.
The present headquarters is the latest in a series of different locations of Studio Gardella: "all intentionally small," he emphasizes proudly. For about ten years Ignazio, joined by his son Jacopo, who has the name of his grandfather and great-grandfather, has worked there, in a space that was first made as a residence, he likes to point out, and was then adapted as a place of work, though still with traces of its original purpose.
The old furnishings, especially several consoles in the Empire style, accentuate this private character: so it is not by chance that our coffee and his habitual herbal tea are served on what used to be the dining room, now used for meetings.
Through the windows Milan displays its past, present and – perhaps – its future. The cathedral and Torre Velasca, the Gothic Milan, seem to stand side by side to remind us of the most important moments of the career: the cathedral and its square, reorganized in a project by Gardella over half a century ago (in 1934, and then again in 1988); and the Torre Velasca, a reminder of one of his greatest friendships, that with the BBPR group.
If it is possible to judge an architect also by the cultural level of his clients, and thus of the figures who have spent time in his studio, Gardella is probably without peers. The *Professore* is still a daily presence at this place of work, sometimes for just a few hours: he arrives towards 10.00 in the morning, and stays there until lunch.
As he has always done, he walks amidst the drawing tables where his collaborators are developing projects, moving in a labyrinth of drawing cabinets that on their own can outline the chronological phases of an entire career: from certain pieces worthy of the finest antiquarian, to more modern cabinets containing the more recent projects, or the materials for competitions yet to be submitted.
The photography archive is a true "museum of architectural history": an open, dynamic museum, ready to welcome new works, new images.
The years of the most important architecture magazines are stored on the shelves of a wall that also hosts the computers and the more traditional drafting machines: past and present coexist in symbiosis, one supporting the other, in a slow, inevitable and in any case serene passage.
"I only work on the architectural aspects, today: I'm 90 years old," he tells us, almost as if to apologize.
The time is well past noon: Gardella, with his cigarette, bids everyone a good day. They all return his wishes with affection, looking forward to seeing him again, tomorrow.

Open letter to Roberto Gabetti and Aimaro Isola

Open letter to Roberto Gabetti and Aimaro Isola

The "stated rejection of theory or at least of the intentional systematization of their practice," in the words of Carlo Olmo commenting on the way of working of Roberto Gabetti and Aimaro Isola, is clearly perceptible in the sober elegance of their studio, located in a patrician building in the center of Turin, not far from the railway station. The opening of the studio in 1950 sealed the professional partnership of the two designers, who have lived on a daily basis since then in its spaces, practicing architecture with the same passion as on the very first day.
It is impressive to think that in those rooms with their simple, aristocratic atmosphere very different yet all very timely works of architecture have taken form: from a sophisticated antiquarian bookstore to a futuristic office building.
It is equally impressive for us to imagine that in those same rooms, perhaps at the same small antique desk that has been the point of departure for essays, articles and critical texts connected with 45 years of architectural history, our *Dialogue* was corrected and revised.
This impression becomes enthusiasm when in the midst of our everyday mail we see a white envelope, identical to the many such envelopes available on the market, but with the inimitable square stamp of the studio Gabetti & Isola imprinted on one corner.
Their letters dated 11 December 1994 and 1 March 1995, with which the architects transmitted the definitive results of their contribution to our publication, contain the entire secret of their love for this profession. To talk about architecture, to write about architecture are unique and inseparable operations, on a par with making architecture. The first letter begins like this: "Your text gave us a big job to do, the results of which we hope will be of interest. The writing you sent us was too dense to lend itself to corrections: so we had to start over again, from scratch."
To talk, to write, to design, *starting over from the beginning*; to always actively challenge oneself and one's own practice. Two encounters, two letters: a great lesson, for us. Thank you.

Rome, an architecture studio

Rome, an architecture studio

Paolo Portoghesi is a Roman architect not only by birth and by education, but also and above all as a man of culture: citizen-architect of the capital par excellence, citizen-architect of the world. The city where he studied, where he made his debut in this profession, where he has built and always lived, worked and taught, has made him into an emblematic example of the intellectual architect.
In about 35 years of his career, he has built things all over Italy, but above all he has played a direct part on the biggest worksites of "his" capital, demonstrating the fact that unfortunately, or perhaps luckily, building in Rome is not for everyone. But Portoghesi, precisely because he is a protagonist and not a spectator of the history of this city, embodies the Vitruvian and Renaissance idea of the "multiple man" who studies, draws, builds, writes and paints.
Above all an architect and builder, but also a man of letters, an architectural historian, he is one of the protagonists of the international debate, not only with projects and constructions, but also as an established critical presence: President of the Venice Biennale, professor at the Department of Architecture of the "La Sapienza" university of Rome, editor of many architecture magazines. These are roles he has always played with an approach of great mental openness thanks to his very vast and "universal" culture. His studio is a *salotto*, in the Roman sense of the term, the noblest sense. Portoghesi's attitude goes beyond the "craft," beyond the classifications of professional categories, and it is deeply rooted in the culture and history of Rome.
"Since I was a boy, the works of architecture of my city have become familiar counterparts, things to be questioned and with which to come to terms: tangible expressions of time lowered into space, through which it becomes possible to enter into contact with men who lived before us, and to understand continuity."
Portoghesi has made his city into a privileged observatory, a studio, not just for architecture, drawing on it for aesthetic models and cultural references, taking part firsthand in its history and its problems, contributing to the growth of an already immense historical legacy, without ever losing track of the intricate thread of continuity.

The "museum" of Aldo Rossi

The "museum" of Aldo Rossi

One breathes architecture in the studio of Aldo Rossi: the air is Milanese, Lombard, Italian and international, all at the same time. And every object has a story, secret or well-known: in the small rooms that face the single, deep corridor, you can sit on a "Parigi" armchair, discuss things around a "Consiglio" table, or make a telephone call leaning on a "Carteggio." Objects that thanks to industrial production are now available to many, but which inserted in the space where they were envisioned, enhanced by domestic and exotic memories and references, seem unique, almost as if they had emerged directly not from a catalogue but from one of those sketches of "Milanese interiors" that together with a multitude of other drawings enliven the walls in an orderly way.

The studio of Aldo Rossi in Milan contains about ten people, including collaborators, draftsmen, secretarial staff: it is here that most of the works are done, including those for foreign settings.

The architect, in order to ensure a constant, punctual presence in the places where he designs most often, moves between two other fixed locations: one in New York, with American employees, and one in Japan, again run by local people. Recently major commissions in Berlin have led to the opening of a studio in that German city, where the architects – after conducting the initial phases of the Berlin projects in Milan – have moved to Germany to closely monitor the progress of the works.

When it comes to the graphic rendering of the projects, the Milan studio often makes use of students and interns from foreign countries, especially from Swiss schools.

Apart from certain specific local habits, all the studios are managed and organized in the same way, and the work is conducted in similar methodological terms: Rossi and his collaborators have specific roles inside the individual projects, but at the same time the live in a reality marked by a certain flexibility of tasks, encouraging a sort of interchange of responsibilities where necessary.

Aldo Rossi's sketches, with their unmistakable style and vivid colors, deceptively like paintings, are actually architecture, buildings paradoxically framed and hung on the walls of a museum in a continuous state of becoming. They are drawings that reveal not just a refined touch, but also a capacity to envision what is to come, in which every stroke justifies itself in the various typological, volumetric, technological and material requirements.

Every sketch – already a project in its own right – contains a strong, driving idea from which to develop the entire project and the overall architectural image. But above all, the driving idea of the project always constitutes a plausible, never utopian episode, where the drawing encompasses an image that is ready to become reality.

Portrait of Guido Canella

Portrait of Guido Canella

During a recent lecture for his students in the course of Composition he teaches at the Politecnico di Milano, Guido Canella, on the topic of German Expressionism, focused on the culture of the society, the business world and clientele of the 1920s in Germany, the controversies and torments of the New Objectivity, at the dawn of the culture of mass production. He also indicated some cherished reading matter, and his listeners were struck by the very mysterious figure of Zapparoni. Reading back now, this pulls us into a very particular analogy.
In fact, like Canella, Zapparoni, the fantastic builder of automata in *The Glass Bees*, a late novel by Ernst Jünger from 1957, had a beautiful library in his studio, with the books in perfect order, but from which one seemed to be touched by an almost tragic beauty, full of mysterious texts (alchemy, primitive technology) offering the knowledge required for the invention and production of very sophisticated and apparently magical automata, capable of performing very complex tasks, of which the "glass bees" were only one very mysterious example.
In like manner, Canella's library offers knowledge on themes that run parallel to the work of design, a knowledge given form through writings, publications and magazines, formulating a critical, ethical and aesthetic panorama composed of specific depictions on typological themes and contexts, on different cities.
In fact, the work of critical research that leads to the preparation of a magazine, or of teachings at the university, is formalized in a marvelous collection in which nature (of works of architecture and contexts in the world) and artifice (of organization, written observation, of the historical and critical essay) are reunited, as in a secret garden. The actual design work is thus conducted in different spaces.
The layout of the house of Zapparoni separated the private study and library, where he welcomed only a very few people, from the large factory where the inventors carried out their work of research and production. The house, built in a monastery, faced the gardens of the historic complex, fenced off and secret to contain marvelous and mysterious applications of his projects, artificial bees, natural flowers, set into function and interaction with the mechanisms of nature. Separately, the factory had at its center the most secret laboratories, where the automata of Zapparoni and his prototypes were designed, assembled, reassembled, perfected by many highly skilled inventors were summoned to take part in a wealth of common labors, though not without situations of conflict.
But what made Zapparoni rightfully famous were the great needs his automata were able to realize. Making abstract forms concrete through the functions these machines physically performed, he went beyond the pure response to the technical demands that produce an economic value, with the veiled thought of a questioning of the also ethical and civil value that benefits collective behaviors. Zapparoni, aware of this doubt, gave form – as do great architects – to new human behaviors called forth in new spaces produced by marvelous machines. (Luca Monica)

Studio Viganò: a home for architecture

Studio Viganò: a home for architecture

The spaces in which Vittoriano Viganò makes architecture are places very dear to him, which have always been in the family. His father Vico, a painter, lived and worked in them, gradually handing them over to his son: at the outset, in the first years of Vittoriano's career, there was a period of parallel use of the spaces, which later became entirely his creative and professional workplace. From house to studio, then, but without completely losing the domestic atmosphere of the original function: it has remained in a widespread sense of welcome and familiarity one feels upon entering or spending time there. A *home for architecture* where moments of work and relaxation complete each other, and are indispensable for each other.

The very high frescoed ceilings are rhythmically paced by a pattern of wooden joists that reveal the structure. Past the entrance, several armchairs form a corner, a place of waiting and at the same time of connection between the three main rooms: the vast archive, also used for secretarial and administrative operations of the firm; the drafting room, with tables and drafting machines side by side, in which the presence of a chair in painted brass and beech stands out, designed by the architect many years ago and now produced in a number of specimens by Fratelli Pozzi of Seregno; and the study, more private and personal, with desks, antiques, shelves packed with books, where Viganò spends most of his day.

In a corner, in front of the main desk, stands a folding chair from a movie theater in air force blue, almost as a reminder that the architect, today more than ever, is called upon to be simultaneously the actor and spectator of a reality in which he is a privileged manipulator.

On the white walls, in forceful contrast with the black matte surfaces of the doors, paintings are hung in delicate balance, classical subjects, abstract compositions, along with period photographs of portions of Milan, newspaper clippings, and a sketch dated 1994 of the Department of Architecture. Among the many autobiographical fragments, the Diploma of the Accademia di San Luca, received in 1991.

In these apparently unadorned spaces stools, seats, antique and modern armchairs coexist - though they are different from one another - in a sort of tacit agreement, based on the awareness of sharing a common purpose.

On the tables, scattered in a sort of orderly disorder, many markers of the same type indicate the preferred spots for drawing and writing. They form a chromatic trail of his passage; the colors, obviously, are two in number: black and red.

Vico Magistretti and the "non-existent" studio

Vico Magistretti and the "non-existent" studio

It would be superficial to think that in an architecture studio the importance of the name and the size of the space are directly proportional. The case of Vico Magistretti offers concrete proof, in fact, that this is not the case.
The studio he inherited from his father, who was also an architect, seems even smaller if we think about the great quantity of buildings, and above all of objects, that were invented there. Objects most of which are present and take part in the life of the studio, not just on display but also as functional items, since they are all rightfully in use. The three main spaces are more than sufficient for those who work there: an entrance, a meeting room and – connected to both – the drafting room where time seems to have stood still, oblivious to the formal and technological evolution to which the objects bear witness.
A *laboratory of ideas*, on Via del Conservatorio, which Magistretti himself displays with full awareness and satisfaction for the choices he has made. "My studio is very small; in practice, there is just one person, the geometer Montella, who has worked with me for over 30 years. In England they have even written articles about my 'non-existent' studio."
This arrangement corresponds to a modern and sophisticated way of thinking about architecture; in the age of specialization the designer has to sell above all the idea, relying on an external organization that does not become a burden in the management of the firm.
 "Years ago I met Alvar Aalto in Finland, also at the helm of a very small studio, two persons in all: on that occasion he told me something that impressed me greatly, namely that for an architect it is vital to have time to think, something that becomes impossible if the studio is transformed into a small or medium-sized business. I try to do the same thing, and thus far I have been successful; in over 30 years, Montella has never had to work nights or on weekends, and neither have I."

The workshop on Via Bandello

The workshop on Via Bandello

The fact that in the same studio heterogeneous projects have been developed, like the overall planning of a residential complex or the installation of an exhibition, a planning variant for a big city or the design of a handle, the definitive project for a stadium or the layout of a magazine, is cause for admiration in a period of increasing professional specialization: few architects or groups of architects bear witness today, in Europe, to such faith in the methodological continuity of one of the most significant ideal principles of modern architecture, pithily expressed in the famous expression of Hermann Muthesius, "from the spoon to the city." No less surprising is the fact that such an output is produced by a studio organized not like a modern "managerial" structure, but like an old crafts "workshop." This ideal model of the "*bottega*" can be glimpsed in the spatial organization of the studio on Via Matteo Bandello, a true "settlement principle" of Gregotti Associati since the year of its founding: a single large room with a very high ceiling, partially cut in half by a metal loft, in which the characteristics of visual openness and transparency contribute to the circulation of ideas and people, across various fields of activity.

[...] Those who enter the "*bottega*" of Via Bandello today thus discover a very dense and progressively saturated space, which nevertheless carefully conserves the particular "artisanal" atmosphere of group work. The rhythms are more intense, the development times are shorter, the interdisciplinary exchanges have perhaps been reduced or have become more formal, but one can still sense, inside the walls of this former terracotta factory, the presence of an immutable spirit of adventure and research, concentration and creative tension.

Only the presence of this kind of *shared tension* can explain, perhaps, how Gregotti Associati has been able to develop such a differentiated range of projects with a highly variegated and mutable team. Though undoubtedly of great impact, the charismatic presence of Vittorio Gregotti as the clear leader of the group cannot suffice, on its own, to explain the enigma of how the work is organized inside an indubitably anomalous professional structure, balanced between the family scale of a crafts "workshop" and the managerial dimension of a large corporation. (Pierre-Alain Croset, in the anthology *Gregotti Associati 1973-1988*, Electa, Milan 1990).

The photograph shows a part of the Como Rationalist Group on a visit to Rome for the Mostra dell'Impero in 1937. We can recognize, from the left, Gianni Mantero, Giuseppe Terragni, Ico Parisi (who took the photograph) and, second from right, Attilio Terragni.

The everyday life and studio of Giuseppe Terragni

The everyday life and studio of Giuseppe Terragni

In the correspondence with friends and the oral testimony of those who worked and in any case lived with him, we find the indications of what we might define as a "particular day," in the sense of his external relations and working activities.
Encounters could take place at any moment of the day, both for particular events or for enjoyment, in a condition of normality.
The condition of work and "dedication" to his particular "design laboratory" was quite a different matter. In fact, with the exception of the moments of definitive preparation of projects, done with his direct collaborators, the workshop went into action in the late afternoon, and the work did not cease until late at night.
Those were therefore the moments of creative peace, those that set down on white sheets, on graph paper, the matrices and images of his projects.
This patient work was then conveyed, late the next morning or in the early afternoon, on drafting tables or in discussions, also outside the studio in Milan, for example with Pietro Lingeri and Mario Sironi, Luigi Zuccoli, Cesare Cattaneo, Gianni Mantero and all the others who to differing extents collaborated with him on his most famous works.
Terragni's unique, particular relationship with the opposite sex also permitted a sort of everyday autonomy, so particular as to at times leave his friends and collaborators perplexed and embarrassed, in their patient "expectation." (Enrico Mantero)

APPENDICES

Selected bibliography

The protagonists of the *Dialogues* are among the most significant figures on the Italian architecture scene from the 1950s to the present, both for their production and for their participation in the critical-theoretical debate of that period. A bibliography that sets out to be exhaustive regarding the personalities and topics of this text would require a space that would go beyond the specific objectives of this research.
In this perspective, the bibliography represents a critical selection of texts of reference for a preliminary orientation and for study in greater depth of the stories, trends, figures, episodes, critical contributions and iconographies of Italian architecture from after World War II until the present. Certain thematic areas of reference have also been identified, which may be useful for exploration of issues and scenarios closely connected to the *Dialogues*. The texts indicated can be considered valid not only for their content, but also for a specific bibliographic investigation of the individual themes.
To update this third edition in Italian and the first edition in English, the work of bibliographic research and selection has advanced as far as December 2018.

The composition of the selected bibliography reported in this volume was elaborated in collaboration with Cecilia Rostagni.

For the position of Italian contemporary architecture inside the wider international panorama and for investigation of the history of modern architecture and the cultural debate in Milan:
- R. De Fusco, *L'idea di architettura. Storia della critica da Viollet-le-Duc a Persico*, Edizioni Comunità, Milano 1964.
- AA. VV., *Teoria della progettazione architettonica*, Edizioni Dedalo, Bari 1968.
- L. Quaroni, *Progettare un edificio*, Mazzotta, Milano 1977.
- B. Zevi, *The modern language of architecture*, University of Washington Press, Washington 1978.
- M. Grandi, A. Pracchi, *Milano. Guida all'architettura moderna*, Zanichelli, Bologna 1980.
- V. Gregotti, *New Directions in Italian Architecture*, George Braziller, New York 1981.
- M. Tafuri, F. Dal Co, *Modern architecture I/II*, Rizzoli, New York 1986.
- M. Tafuri, *The sphere and the labyrinth. Avant-gardes and architecture from Piranesi to the 1970's*, translated by P. d'Acierno and R. Connolly, Cambridge, Mass.; MIT Press, London 1987.
- D. P. Doordan, *Building modern Italy. Italian architecture 1914-1936,* Princeton University Press, New York 1988.
- G. Grassi, *Architecture dead language*, Rizzoli, New York 1988.
- G. Ciucci, *Gli architetti e il fascismo: architettura e città, 1922-1944,* Einaudi, Torino 1989.
- M. Tafuri, *History of Italian architecture 1944-1985,* MIT Press, Cambridge, Mass., London, 1989.
- C. Dardi (ed.), *The Scale of space. Contemporary Italian architects*, CLEAR, Roma 1991.
- R. A. Etlin, *Modernism in Italian architecture 1890-1940,* MIT Press, Cambridge, Mass. 1991.
- A. Belluzzi, C. Conforti, *Architettura italiana 1944-1994*, Laterza, Bari 1994.
- P. Zermani, *Identità dell'architettura,* Officina, Roma 1995.
- F. Irace, G. Basilico, P. Rosselli, *Milano moderna. Architettura e città nell'epoca della ricostruzione*, Motta, Milano 1996.
- F. Dal Co (ed.), *Storia dell'architettura italiana. Il secondo Novecento*, Electa, Milano 1997.
- R. Gabetti, *Imparare l'architettura,* Bollati Boringhieri, Torino 1998.
- E. Faroldi, *Esperienze costruite. Temi e aforismi di architettura,* Libria, Melfi 1999.
- V. Magnago Lampugnani (ed.), *The architecture of the contemporary city,* YKK Architectural Products, Tokyo 1999.
- P. Portoghesi, R. Scarano (ed.), *Il progetto di architettura: idee, scuole, tendenze all'alba del nuovo millennio,* Newton & Compton, Roma 1999.
- A. Mangiarotti, *Il progetto di architettura. Dall'euristico all'esecutivo,* Clup Milano 2000.
- G. Gramigna, S. Mazza, *Milano. Un secolo di architettura milanese dal Cordusio alla Bicocca,* Hoepli, Milano 2001.

- W. J. Curtis, *Modern architecture since 1900,* Phaidon, London, 2002.
- G. Ciucci, G. Muratore (ed.), *Storia dell'architettura italiana. Il primo Novecento,* Electa, Milano 2004.
- W.J. Curtis, *Modern Architecture since 1900,* Phaidon, Londra 2006.
- K. Frampton, *Modern architecture: a critical history.* Thames & Hudson Ltd, London, 2007.
- G. Nardi, *Tecnologie dell'architettura. Teorie e storia,* Maggioli, Rimini 2008.
- L. Benevolo, *Storia dell'architettura moderna,* Vol 1-2, Laterza, Bari 2010.
- F. Bucci, M. Mulazzani, *Luigi Moretti Opere e scritti,* Electa, Milano 2011.
- P. Nicoloso, *Mussolini architetto,* Einaudi, Torino 2011.
- R. Moneo, *L'altra modernità: considerazioni sul futuro dell'architettura,* Christian Marinotti, Milano 2012.
- D. Ghirardo, *Italy. Modern architectures in History,* Reaktion, London, 2013.
- P. Scrivano, *Building transatlantic Italy. Architectural dialogues with postwar America,* Ashgate, Farham 2013.
- K. Frampton, *A genaealogy of modern architecture. Comparative critical analysis of built form,* Lars Muller, Zurich 2015.
- F. Andreola, M. Biraghi, G. Lo Ricco (ed.), *Milano. L'architettura dal 1945 a oggi,* Hoepli, Milano 2018.
- P. Ciorra, J.-L. Cohen (ed.), *Zevi's Architects. History and counter-history of Italian architecture 1944-2000,* Quodlibet, Macerata 2018.

Regarding the practice of the individual architects who are the protagonists of this book we feel it is worth indicating references (especially the most important monographs) in which to find elements of research and specific areas of in-depth investigation.

Franco Albini
- S. Leet, *Franco Albini. Architecture and Design 1934-1977,* Princeton Architectural Press, New York 1990.
- A. Piva, V. Prina, *Franco Albini 1905-1977,* Electa, Milano 1998.
- F. Bucci, A. Rossari (ed.), *I musei e gli allestimenti di Franco Albini,* Electa, Milano 2005.
- F. Bucci, F. Irace (ed.), *Zero Gravity. Franco Albini: costruire la modernità,* La Triennale e Mondadori Electa, Milano 2006.
- G. Bosoni, F. Bucci, *Il design e gli interni di Franco Albini,* Electa, Milano 2009.
- F. Bucci, *Franco Albini, La Scuola di Milano/The School of Milan,* Electa, Milan 2009.

BBPR
- E. Bonfanti, M. Porta, *Città, museo e architettura. Il gruppo BBPR nella cultura architettonica italiana 1932-1970,* Vallecchi, Firenze 1973 (ristampa 2009).
- AA.VV., *BBPR a Milano,* a cura di A. Piva, Electa, Milano 1982.
- L. Fiori, M. Prizzon (ed.), *BBPR. La Torre Velasca,* Abitare Segesta, Milano 1982.
- E. N. Rogers, *Esperienza dell'architettura,* Einaudi, Torino, 1958.
- E. N. Rogers, *Il senso della storia,* con un saggio di L. Semerani, Unicopli, Milano 1999.
- E. N. Rogers, *Lettere di Ernesto a Ernesto e viceversa,* a cura di L. Molinari, Archinto, Milano 2000.
- E. N. Rogers, *Editoriali di architettura,* Zandonai, Rovereto 2009.
- C. Baglione (ed.), *Ernesto Nathan Rogers (1909- 1969),* Franco Angeli, Milano 2012.
- E. Bordogna, *La Torre Velasca dei BBPR a Milano: simbolo e monumento dell'architettura italiana del dopoguerra,* Clean, Napoli 2017.

Ignazio Gardella
- F. Nonis, S. Boidi (ed.), *Ignazio Gardella,* catalogue of the exhibition held at the Harvard University, Graduate School of Design, Gund Hall Gallery, Cambridge, Massachusetts, April 22 - May 9, 1986, Harvard University Graduate School of Design, Cambridge, Mass., 1986.
- AA.VV., *Ignazio Gardella. Progetti e architetture 1933-1990,* catalogo della mostra a cura di F. Buzzi Ceriani, Marsilio, Venezia 1992.
- A. Monestiroli, *L'architettura secondo Gardella,* Laterza, Roma Bari 1997.
- M.C. Loi (ed.), *Ignazio Gardella. Architetture,* Electa, Milano 1998.
- M. Casamonti (ed.), *Ignazio Gardella architetto 1905-1999. Costruire la*

modernità, catalogo della mostra, Electa, Milano 2006.
- A. Monestiroli, *Ignazio Gardella,* Electa, Milano 2009.

Roberto Gabetti & Aimaro Isola
- C. Olmo, *Gabetti e Isola. Architetture,* Allemandi, Torino 1993.
- B. Guerra, M. Morresi, *Gabetti e Isola. Opere di architettura,* Electa, Milano 1996.
- R. Gabetti, *Case & Chiese,* a cura di S. Giriodi, Umberto Allemandi Editore, Torino 1998.
- S. Giriodi (ed.), *Roberto Gabetti. Scritti scelti sul sapere architettonico,* Umberto Allemandi Editore, Torino 1998.
- C. Piva (ed.), *Gabetti & Isola. Conversazioni sull'architettura. Il mestiere,* Clean, Napoli 2001.
- S. Pace, *Architetture per la liturgia: opere di Gabetti e Isola,* Skira, Milano 2005.
- M. Petrangeli, *Architettura come paesaggio. Gabetti e Isola. Isolarchitetti,* Allemandi, Torino 2005.
- G. Canella, P. Mellano, *Roberto Gabetti 1925-2000,* Franco Angeli, Milano 2017.

Paolo Portoghesi
- C. Norberg-Schulz, *Architetture di Paolo Portoghesi e Vittorio Gigliotti,* Officina Edizioni, Roma 1982.
- P. Portoghesi, *Postmodern. The architecture of the postindustrial society,* Rizzoli, New York 1983.
- G. Priori (ed.), *Paolo Portoghesi: progetti e disegni 1949-1979,* Zanichelli, Bologna 1985.
- M. Pisani, *Paolo Portoghesi. Opere e progetti,* Electa, Milano 1992.
- P. Portoghesi, *Nature ad architecture,* Skira, Milan 2000.
- R. Scarano, P. Portoghesi, *L'architettura del sole,* Gangemi, Roma 2004.
- P. Bernitsa, M. Ercadi (ed.), *Paolo Portoghesi,* Skira, Milano 2006.
- F. Gottardo, *Paolo Portoghesi architect,* Gangemi, Roma 2011.
- P. Bernitsa, *Paolo Portoghesi. The architecture of listening,* Gangemi, Rome 2013.

Aldo Rossi
- R. Bonicalzi (ed.), *Aldo Rossi. Scritti scelti sull'architettura e la città 1956-1972,* CittàStudi, Milano 1975.
- A. Rossi, *A scientific autobiography,* (postscript by V.Scully ; trans. by L. Venuti), MIT Press, Cambridge Mass., 1981 (1st it. ed. *Autobiografia scientifica,* 1981).
- A. Rossi, *The architecture of the city,* MIT Press, Cambridge, Mass., 1982 (1st it. ed. *L'architettura della città,* 1966).
- AA.VV., *Aldo Rossi. Architect,* Academy Editions, Londra, 1994.
- A. Ferlenga, *Aldo Rossi. Opera completa (1993-1996),* Electa, Milano 1996.
- F. Dal Co (ed.), *Aldo Rossi. I quaderni azzurri (1968-1992),* Electa, Milano 1999.
- A. Ferlenga (ed.), *Aldo Rossi. Tutte le opere,* Electa, Milano 1999.
- P. Portoghesi (et al.) (eds.), *Aldo Rossi: the sketchbooks 1990-1997,* Thames and Hudson, London 2000.
- G. Celant (ed.), *Aldo Rossi. Teatri,* Skira, Milano 2012.
- A. Monestiroli, *The World of Aldo Rossi* (it. ed. *Il mondo di Aldo Rossi,* 2015*),* LetteraVentidue, Siracusa 2018.
- D. S. Lopes, *Melancholy and Architecture. On Aldo Rossi,* Park books, Zurich 2015.
- B. Lampariello, *Aldo Rossi e le forme del razionalismo esaltato: dai progetti scolastici alla città analoga, 1950-1973,* Quodlibet, Macerata 2017.
- M. Biraghi, G. Braghieri, M. Landsberger (ed.), *Aldo Rossi. Il gran teatro dell'architettura,* Silvana Editoriale, Cinisello Balsamo 2018.
- D. Y. F. Ghirardo, *Aldo Rossi and the spirit of architecture,* Yale University Press, New Haven-London 2019.

Guido Canella
- K. Suzuki, *Guido Canella,* Zanichelli, Bologna 1983.
- E. Bordogna, *Guido Canella. Opere e progetti,* Electa, Milano 2001.
- I. Boniello, G. Canella (ed.), *A proposito della scuola di Milano,* Hoepli, Milano 2010.
- E. Bordogna con E. Prandi e E. Manganaro (a cura di), *Guido Canella. Architetti italiani del Novecento,* Marinotti, Milano 2010.

- L. Monica (ed.), *Guido Canella. Un ruolo per l'architettura*, Clean, Napoli 2011.
- E. Bordogna, G. Canella, E. Manganaro (a cura di), *Guido Canella 1931-2009*, Franco Angeli, Milano 2014.

Vittoriano Viganò
- AA.VV., *A come architettura. Vittoriano Viganò*, Electa, Milano 1992.
- AA.VV., *Vittoriano Viganò. Una ricerca e un segno in architettura*, Electa, Milano 1994.
- V. Viganò, *L'esperienza del progetto*, Officina di Architettura, Dispense del Cavaliere azzurro 6, Facoltà di Architettura del Politecnico di Milano, marzo 1995.
- E. Cao, A. Piva (ed.), *Vittoriano Viganò. A come asimmetria*, Gangemi, Roma 2008.
- F. Graf e L. Tedeschi (ed.), *L'Istituto Marchiondi Spagliardi di Vittoriano Viganò*, Academy Press, Mendrisio 2009.

Vico Magistretti
- V. Pasca, *Vico Magistretti. L'eleganza della ragione*, Idea Books, Milano 1991.
- V. Pasca, *Vico Magistretti: elegance and innovation in postwar italian design*, Thames and Hudson, London 1991.
- F. Irace, V. Pasca, *Vico Magistretti. Architetto e designer*, Electa, Milano 1999.
- V. Magistretti, *Vico Magistretti: il design dagli anni cinquanta a oggi*, Genova, Palazzo Ducale, 2 febbraio-2 marzo 2003, Fondazione Schiffini, Genova 2003.
- P. Proverbio, *Vico Magistretti*, Hachette, Milano 2011.

Vittorio Gregotti
- M. Tafuri, *Vittorio Gregotti. Building and projects*, Rizzoli, New York, 1982.
- AA.VV., *Gregotti Associati: 1973-1988*, Electa, Milano 1990.
- J. Rykwert, *Vittorio Gregotti & Associates*, Rizzoli, New York, 1996.
- V. Gregotti, *Inside architecture*, (trans. by P. Wong and F. Zaccheo), MIT Press, Cambridge, Mass., London, 1996.
- V. Gregotti, *Architettura, tecnica, finalità*, Laterza, Roma 2002.
- V. Gregotti, *L'architettura del realismo critico*, Laterza, Roma 2004.
- V. Gregotti, *Autobiografia del 20 secolo*, Skira, Milano 2005.
- V. Gregotti, *L'architettura nell'epoca dell'incessante*, Laterza, Roma 2006.
- V. Gregotti, *Contro la fine dell'architettura*, Einaudi, Torino 2008.
- V. Gregotti, *Architecture means and ends*, (trans. by L. G. Cochrane), University of Chicago Press, Chicago, London 2010
- V. Gregotti, *Tre forme di architettura mancata*, Einaudi, Torino 2010.
- V. Gregotti, *Architettura e postmetropoli*, Einaudi, Torino 2011.
- V. Gregotti, *L'architettura di Cèzanne*, Skira, Milano 2011.
- V. Gregotti, *Incertezze e simulazioni: architettura tra moderno e contemporaneo*, Skira, Milano 2012.
- V. Gregotti, *Il sublime al tempo del contemporaneo*, Einaudi, Torino 2013.
- V. Gregotti, *Il possibile necessario*, Bompiani, Milano 2014.
- G. Morpurgo, *Gregotti & Associates. The architecture of urban landscape*, Rizzoli, New York, London 2014.
- V. Gregotti, *Quando il moderno non era utile*, Archinto, Milano 2018.

Giuseppe Terragni
- T. Schumacher, *Surface and symbol: Giuseppe Terragni and the architecture of Italian rationalism.* Princeton Architectural Press, New York, 1991.
- T. Schumacher, *The Danteum: architecture, poetics, and politics under Italian fascism*, Princeton Architectural Press, New York 1993.
- G. Ciucci (ed.), *Giuseppe Terragni: opera completa*, Electa, Milano 1996.
- S. Poretti, *La casa del fascio di Como*, Carocci, Roma 1998.
- G. Rocchi, *Le Corbusier, Terragni, Michelucci*, Alinea, Firenze 2000.
- E. Mantero, *Architettura. Diario collettivo*, a cura di F. Bucci, Unicopli, Milano 2002.
- P. Eisenman, *Giuseppe Terragni: transformations, decompositions, critiques*, Monacelli Press, New York 2003.
- A. Terragni, D. Libeskind, P. Rosselli (ed.), *The Terragni atlas: built architecture*, Skira, Milan 2004.
- J. Schnapp (ed.), *In cima. Giuseppe Terragni per Margherita Sarfatti. Architetture della memoria nel '900*, Marsilio, Venezia 2004.
- A. Coppa, *Giuseppe Terragni*, Cataloghi, 24 Ore Cultura, Milano 2013.

Sources of illustrations

- Archivio delle Terme di Salsomaggiore
- Archivio dell'Ufficio Tecnico del Comune di Salsomaggiore Terme
- Archivio Istituto Nazionale Assicurazioni, Parma
- Gregotti Associati, Venezia
- Studio Albini-Helg-Piva, Milano
- Studio Canella, Milano
- Studio Cortesi, Parma
- Studio Faroldi, Parma
- Studio Gabetti e Isola, Torino
- Studio Gardella, Milano
- Studio Magistretti, Milano
- Studio Maniero, Cernobbio (Como)
- Studio Nodo, Como
- Studio Portoghesi, Roma
- Studio Rossi, Milano
- Studio Viganò, Milano

Photography credits

Gabriele Basilico / 243, 271
Federico Brunetti / 221
Barbara Burg e Oliver Schuh / 257
Marco Buzzoni e Mauro Davoli / 259
Pietro Canella / 262
Mario Carrieri / 275
Studio Casali / 231, 238, 239, 267
Elisabetta Catalano / 318
Renzo Chiesa / 314
Carla De Benedetti / 266
Pino Dell'Aquila / 316
Giuseppe Maestri / 272
Paolo Monti / 231
Ico Parisi / 330
Irving Penn / 310
Paolo Portoghesi / 252, 253, 254
Uwe Rau / 328
Daniele Regis / 246, 247, 248
Fabrizio Ruffo / 322
Ezra Stoller / 235
Stefano Topuntoli / 255, 258, 263, 265
David Underwood / 232
Maria Pilar Vettori / 283
Lucienne Viganò / 324
Arne Weychardt / 320

The photographs taken by persons unknown and the images not provided by the sources indicated herein have been reproduced from the following publications:
- Catalogo Poggi / 229, 276
- T.L. Schumacher, *Il Danteum di Terragni - 1938*, Officina, Roma 1980 / 290
- Le Corbusier, *Verso una architettura*, a cura di P. Cerri e P. Nicolin, Longanesi, Milano, 1984 / 10
- E. Cellini, C. D'Amato, *Gabetti e Isola, Progetti e architetture 1950-85*, Electa, Milano 1985 / 244
- "Casabella", n. 524, 1986 / 280
- AA.VV. *Gregotti Associati 1973-1988*, Electa, Milano 1990 / 279, 282, 284
- G. Ciucci, F. Dal Co, *Architettura italiana del '900*, Electa, Milano 1990 / 234, 291
- S. Leet, *Franco Albini. Architecture and Design 1934-77*, Princeton Architectural Press, New York 1990 / 222, 225, 226, 228, 230
- *Giovanni Michelucci a Sant'Agostino. Disegni per il Teatro di Olbia*, Sagep, Genova 1991 / 250
- V. Pasca (a cura di), *Vico Magistretti. L'eleganza della ragione*, Idea Books, Milano 1991 / 273, 277, 326
- P. Zermani, *Gabetti e Isola*, Zanichelli, Bologna, 1993 / 245
- S. Maffioletti, *BBPR*, Zanichelli, Bologna 1994 / 233, 236, 312

Index of names

Aalto, Alvar Hugo Henrik / 315, 329
Abercrombie, Patrick / 143, 153
Achilli, Michele / 154, 155, 262, 263, 264, 265
Alberti, Leon Battista / 132
Albini, Franco / 17, 26-54, 61-63, 67, 75, 77, 79, 86-88, 93, 105, 123, 134, 151, 159, 160, 166, 195, 196, 201-203, 208, 210, 211, 213, 221-230, 297, 298, 299, 302, 313
Albini, Marco / 53, 54,
Albricci, Gianni / 53, 86
Alessi / 135, 139, 258
Alfieri, Bruno / 68
Amati, Carlo / 153
Amman, P. / 75
Annoni, Ambrogio / 141, 153
Argan, Giulio Carlo / 30, 31, 51, 79, 87, 162
Artesani, Cecilio / 155
Asnago, Mario / 202, 213
Asplund, Erik Gunnar / 131
Aulenti, Gae / 44
Aymonino, Carlo / 105, 137
Azzola, Spartaco / 199
Baffa Rivolta, Matilde / 54, 311
Balsari Berrone, Elena / 87
Banfi, Gian Luigi / 61, 66, 206
Banham, Reyner / 142, 153, 168
Barabino, Carlo / 84
Barbieri, Umberto / 138
Barrera, Angelo / 107
Batista y Zaldìvar, Fulgencio / 32
Baudelaire, Charles / 133
BBPR / 17, 30, 41, 45, 52, 54, 59, 61-68, 79, 86, 151, 169, 197, 201, 202, 206, 213, 231, 233, 236, 313-317, 315
Belgiojoso, Lodovico Barbiano di / 10, 53, 56, 60-68, 77, 80, 86, 206, 315
Bergman, Ingrid / 32
Berlage, Hendrik Petrus / 131
Binelli, Giorgio / 155
Bloc, André / 169, 268, 269
Boito, Camillo / 144, 204, 214, 215
Bonaretti, Pellegrino / 154, 261
Bonfiglioli, Arrigo / 67
Borges Acevedo, Jorge Luis / 100
Borromini, Francesco / 118, 125, 127
Bottoni, Piero / 52, 86, 204, 208, 213-215
Braghieri, Gianni / 137, 138
Brandolisio, Marco / 139
Brigidini, Daniele / 154, 155, 262, 263
Broglio, Mario / 48

Brunelleschi, Filippo / 163
Buonarroti, Michelangelo / 118, 157, 203, 205, 213
Burelli, Augusto Romano / 308
Caccia Dominioni, Luigi / 105
Cagnardi, Augusto / 199
Calvino, Italo / 208
Camus, Renato / 47-49, 86, 87, 213, 226
Canella, Guido / 17, 44, 63, 137, 140-155, 160, 164, 168, 261-266, 324, 325
Canina, Luigi / 74
Caronia, Giuseppe / 197
Cassi Ramelli, Antonio / 144
Cassina, Cesare / 175, 181
Castiglioni, Achille / 42, 45, 161, 168
Castiglioni, Luisa / 52
Castro, Fidel / 34
Cattaneo, Cesare / 75, 138, 213, 214, 333
Cecchi, Raffaello / 199
Cellini, Benvenuto / 157
Cellini, Francesco / 106
Cerri, Pierluigi / 199
Cerutti, Ezio / 52, 86
Chessa, Paolo / 161, 168
Chiolini, Paolo / 134, 139
Ciocca, Gianmarco / 138
Cioran, Emile M. / 103
Clausetti, Paolo / 49, 87
Colombini, Luigi / 48, 313
Colombini, Luisa / 313
Cortesi, Aurelio / 26-48, 50-54, 224, 313
Costa, Lucio / 68
Cosulich, Piero / 68
Cozzaglio, Gabriele / 154
Crespi, Luciano / 154
Croset, Pier-Alain / 331
D'Amato, Claudio / 106
Danusso, Arturo / 59, 60, 65, 67
Da Pozzo, Giovanni / 138, 139
Dassi (ditta) / 47
Da Vinci, Leonardo / 207
De Carlo, Giancarlo / 52, 161, 168
De Ferrari, Giorgio / 107
De Luigi, Mario / 73
De Miranda, Fabrizio / 154
De Seta, Cesare / 32, 49, 52, 54, 308
d'Espouy, Raymond / 47
Dodi, Luigi / 129, 137, 214
Drocco, Guido / 105-107, 247, 248
Drugman, Fredi / 54
Duchamp, Marcel / 174
Durand, Jean-Nicolas-Luis / 144
Eupalino / 119, 295, 296, 304, 305

Fabre, Xavier / 139
Fagiolo, Marcello / 31, 51
Fanfani, Amintore / 142
Faroldi, Emilio / 91
Fassino, Remo / 106
Federici, Fortunato / 118, 126
Fera, Saverio / 139
Figini, Luigi / 75, 168, 214
Filarete, Antonio Averlino (detto il) / 36, 202
Finzi, Bruno / 134, 139
Fiorese, Giorgio / 155
Forti, Giordano / 144, 154
Foster, Norman / 180, 183
Frette, Guido / 214
Fuselli, Eugenio / 52
Gabetti, Roberto / 17, 63, 99, 100, 105-108, 119, 243-248, 318, 319
Gadamer, Hans Georg / 103
Galli, Aldo / 48, 213
Gambirasio, Giuseppe / 313
Gandolfi, Vittorio / 211, 216
Garatti, Vittorino / 34
Garda, Loris / 105
Gardella, Ignazio / 17, 29-31, 34, 35, 41, 44, 49, 51-54, 61, 62, 70, 73, 86-88, 134, 137, 161, 237-242, 316, 317
Gardella, Jacopo / 86, 241, 317
Gigliotti, Vittorio / 126, 253
Giolli, Raffaello / 84, 86, 87
Giovanardi, Bruno / 154
Giussani, Gabriele / 214
Gottardi, Roberto / 34
Grassi, Giorgio / 44, 197
Gregotti, Vittorio / 17, 41, 44, 68, 184, 193, 197-199, 279-284, 331
Grevenstein van, Alexander I / 130
Griffini, Enrico / 137, 143, 153
Gropius, Walter / 39, 141, 214, 315
Guarnieri, Libero / 153
Guttuso, Renato / 202
Helg, Franca / 31, 37, 38, 40, 41, 43, 46-54, 222, 223, 227, 228, 313
Hoffmann, Joseph / 123
Isola, Aimaro / 17, 63, 90-108, 119, 243-248, 318, 319
Johnson, Philip / 87, 135
Jünger, Ernst / 325
Kahn, Louis / 119
Kafka, Franz / 31, 51
Kocher, Marc / 138, 139
Lancia, Emilio / 27, 47
Larco, Sebastiano / 214
Laurana, Luciano / 118

Lazzari, Laura / 154, 263
Le Corbusier / 42, 47, 68, 143, 153, 157, 165, 166, 169, 203, 204, 212, 214-216, 307, 315
Lévinas, Emmanuel / 103
Libera, Adalberto / 210, 214
Lingeri, Pietro / 213-215, 291, 333
Loos, Adolf / 131, 211, 308
Magistretti, Vico / 17, 42-44, 161, 168, 170-182, 273-278, 328, 329
Maillart, Robert / 165, 169
Maldonado, Tòmas / 68
Manfredini, Enea / 34, 50, 52
Mantero, Enrico / 200, 213, 214, 333
Mantero, Giovanni / 215
Manzoni, Alessandro / 149
Marangoni, Guido / 67
Marcenaro, Caterina / 49
Marchesotti, Franco / 138
Martini, Luigi / 87
Masotti, Giuseppina / 134, 138
Matsui, Hiromichi / 199
Mazzoleni, Giuseppe / 49, 86, 87
Mel'nikov, Konstantin / 150, 155
Mendini, Alessandro / 68
Meneghetti, Lodovico / 197, 198, 279
Michelucci, Giovanni / 29, 30, 45, 122, 127, 250, 304
Mies van der Rohe, Ludwig / 47, 131, 132, 138, 151, 166, 169, 195, 235
Minoletti, Giulio / 49, 86, 87
Mollino, Carlo / 105
Moncalvo, Enrico / 106
Monica, Luca / 325
Montella, Franco / 329
Morandi, Riccardo / 117, 126, 165, 169
Moretti, Gaetano / 47, 153
Moretti, Luigi / 168
Morini, Franco / 75, 86
Mucchi, Gabriele / 49, 52, 86, 87, 208, 215
Mousawi, Sami / 126, 253
Muthesius, Hermann / 131, 331
Muzio, Giovanni / 139, 144, 154, 207, 210, 215
Nervi, Pier Luigi / 113, 153, 162, 163, 165, 168, 208, 215, 234
Neufert, Ernst / 215
Nicolin, Pierluigi / 199
Niemeyer, Oscar / 23, 64, 68, 232, 315
Nizzoli, Marcello / 53
Noebel, Walter Arno / 199
Odradek / 31, 51
Olivetti, Roberto / 34, 313

Olivetti / 31, 38, 51, 52, 87, 98, 106, 181
Olivieri, Giuseppe Mario / 52
Olmo, Carlo / 319
Okpanum, Innocent / 154
Oud, Jacobus Johannes Pieter / 142
Pagano, Giuseppe / 47-49, 67, 86, 161
Palanti, Giancarlo / 47-49, 52, 67, 75, 86, 87, 213, 226
Palladio, Andrea / 132
Parma (ditta) / 40
Paolo Uccello (Paolo di Dono) / 163
Parisi, Ico / 332
Pasolini, Pier Paolo / 45
Persico, Edoardo / 27, 47, 48, 54, 67, 77, 86, 162
Peressutti, Enrico / 53, 61, 64-67, 206
Perret, Auguste / 105, 165
Phaedrus, 295, 304-306
Piano, Renzo / 123, 177, 179
Picasso, Pablo / 158
Piccinato, Luigi / 153
Piermarini, Giuseppe / 36
Piovene, Guido / 48
Pirovano, Giuseppe / 48, 50, 54
Piva, Antonio / 52, 53
Plato / 9, 75
Poggi (ditta) / 40, 41, 42, 229, 276
Poggi, Roberto / 53
Pollini, Gino / 75, 161, 168, 186, 197, 214, 284
Ponti, Gio / 27, 47, 144, 154, 201, 202, 207, 208, 210, 211, 215
Porro, Ricardo / 34
Portaluppi, Piero / 47, 129, 137, 141, 144, 153, 154, 202, 213
Portoghesi, Paolo / 17, 32, 52, 84, 87, 105, 110, 124-127, 153, 162, 249, 251-254, 321
Pozzi (ditta) / 325
Proust, Marcel / 133
Pucci, Mario / 52, 86, 214, 215
Purini, Franco / 198
Putelli, Aldo / 52, 86
Radice, Mario / 213
Raineri, Giorgio / 106
Raineri, Giuseppe / 106
Rava, Carlo Enrico / 214
Re, Luciano / 105, 106
Reinhart, Fabio / 88, 137
Reginaldi, Michele / 199
Rho, Manlio / 213
Ridolfi, Mario / 45, 87, 102, 114, 123, 125, 143, 144, 151, 153, 155, 201, 202, 206, 210, 215

Rivetti, Marco / 131
Rogers, Ernesto Nathan / 14, 20, 30, 42, 45, 46, 49, 53, 61, 63-68, 75, 77, 79, 86, 105, 129, 132-134, 137, 141, 142, 144, 149, 152, 153, 159, 172, 181, 197, 202, 206, 214, 298, 299, 301, 302, 307, 308
Romano, Giovanni / 48, 49, 77, 86, 87
Romanò / 37
Rosselli, Alberto / 42
Rossellini, Roberto / 32
Rossi, Aldo / 17, 44, 63, 85, 88, 105, 128-139, 162, 197, 198, 255-260, 322, 323
Ruskin, John / 133, 152
Salgado, Manuel / 198, 283
Salomon, Peter / 199
Samaritani, Aldo / 58
Samonà, Giuseppe / 30, 31, 50, 51, 61, 86, 88, 142, 153
Sampo-Olivetti (negozio) / 31
Sangallo, Antonio da (il Giovane) / 118
Scarpa, Carlo / 61, 88, 151, 166
Scheurer, Massimo / 138
Schiaffonati, Fabrizio / 154
Schinkel, Karl Friedrich / 138
Schumacher, Fritz / 142
Semerani, Luciano / 68
Sibilla, Angelo / 88
Sironi, Mario / 291, 333
Socrate / 295, 304, 305, 306
S.O.M. (Skidmore, Owings and Merril) / 32
Sommaruga, Giuseppe / 204, 207, 214, 215
Stacchini, Ulisse / 155
Stoppino, Giotto / 197, 198, 279
Tafuri, Manfredo / 133
Taut, Bruno / 142
Tentori, Francesco / 30, 31, 51, 143
Terragni, Attilio / 213, 332
Terragni, Carlo / 216
Terragni, Emilio / 216
Terragni, Giuseppe / 17, 54, 75, 161-163, 168, 200-216, 285-289, 291, 297, 332, 331
Tevarotto, Mario / 52, 86
Tridone / 296, 304, 305
Turri (ditta) / 47
Ungers, Oswald Mathias / 194
Uslenghi, Renato / 207, 214, 215
Uva, Luigi / 138
Valenti, A. / 155, 266
Valéry, Paul / 79, 119, 296, 304-306
Valle, Mario / 88
Van de Velde, Henry / 315
Varaldo, Giuseppe / 101, 106, 108
Vasari, Giorgio / 133

Velasca (torre) / 57-68, 151-153, 181, 197, 202, 208, 231, 233, 236, 317
Vender, Claudio / 202, 213
Vietti, Luigi / 213
Viganò, Bruno / 199
Viganò, Vico / 327
Viganò, Vittoriano / 17, 42, 44, 45, 156-169, 199, 267-272, 326, 327
Vignola, (Jacopo Barozzi) / 74
Visconti, Luchino / 202, 213
Vitruvius, Pollio / 119, 204
Vivaldi, Antonio / 79, 80
Wachsmann, Konrad / 123
Weber, Max / 76
Wright, Frank Lloyd / 315
Zanguidi, Jacopo / 290
Zambelli (villa) / 37, 53
Zanuso, Marco / 42, 45, 137, 161, 168
Zappa, Mario / 52
Zevi, Bruno / 61, 125, 153, 162, 213
Zorzi, Silvano / 165, 169
Zuccoli, Luigi / 213, 214, 333